RECOMMENDATIONS

Jay Straub is both my friend and a friend to Jesus. He loves to share the good news of Jesus Christ with others. As I have gotten to know Jay, the divine intervention that saved his life multiple times, the trials that he has experienced, and the insights into the things of God that he has gained through all of this have produced true gold. I highly recommend you sit down, read, and absorb this example of God's grace, mercy, power, and deliverance.

—JOEL RICHARDSON, NYT Bestselling author, teacher, and filmmaker

There have been several people in my life who have literally changed me. Jay Straub is one of them. He began his career as a pilot at the age of eighteen, a young man's dream. When he was a young captain, that dream was cut short by a horrifying ground accident over which he had no control. He has prevailed, thanks to his absolute faith in the mercy and grace of God and in the assurance that all things work together for ultimate good to those who love Him. Today, after surviving very significant head injuries, Jay continues as an inspiration to us all. A true survivor, a man's man, with a sweet spirit that defines him. It will be time well spent to take in Jay's story of God's intervention and how He has used it to bring hope to others!

—CAPTAIN C. D. EWELL, chief pilot and vice president flight,
American Airlines, rtd.

"Getting ready to begin our trip, I had no reason to think that later in the day I would be in the same emergency room as John F. Kennedy on that fateful day exactly 26 years earlier. Our flight to DFW was uneventful. Jay and I had walked down the jet bridge stairs to the ramp where a crew van was going to shuttle us to our next flight to Nashville. That's when Jay looked up at the top of the stairs, saw Linda's (flight attendant) bags setting there and said, 'I'm going to go get her bags for her.' I remember thinking, that's typical Jay. A moment later I heard a loud noise and turned my head just in time to see a vision that is still etched in my memory. Unfortunately, that image was of Jay landing headfirst onto the concrete ramp. At that point, time seemed to stand still. I remember asking myself, 'Did that really just happen?' I ran to him, and there was so much blood that I couldn't tell where it was coming from. I just knew that I had to elevate his head, or he would drown on his own blood. Then all I could do was pray for a miracle. God answered mine and many others' prayers. Enjoy reading his miraculous story of God's divine intervention in Jay's life."

—ANS WISHING, American Airlines Pilot, and friend

Jay Straub is a testimony to God's faithfulness, grace, and forgiveness. Jay, like us all, has suffered from both his own failings and those of others. And just like Jay, we can only find peace when we pray, "Father, forgive us our trespasses as we forgive those who trespass against us." Jay's life is filled with amazing turns, and he has certainly suffered his share, but his life message is a tribute to God's redemption and restoration when we forgive others as He has forgiven us.

—CURTIS HAIL, missionary

Captain Straub's account of his first year after sustaining a devastating head injury and the multiple setbacks he encountered on the road to recovery should bring hope to other patients and families who find themselves on a similar journey. His courage and his determination were an inspiration to everyone involved in his care.

—DR. BRUCE MICKEY, MD, Neurosurgeon

It was a true honor being one of the neurosurgery trauma nurses caring for Captain Straub following his traumatic brain injury. His account of the tribulations that he experienced allowed me to better understand what my patient's experience during recovery. I found his words insightful and inspirational.

—MICHAEL LEVY, MSN

I met Jay through our church and a small group we called an Eteam (for encouragement). We ended up spending nearly two decades studying the Word, having topical discussions, and eating breakfast every Friday morning. We also shared a love of aviation and enjoyed being captains at American Airlines. I was home when I heard of Jay's accident, so immediately I and fellow friend and Eteam member Captain Dave Slack hurried to the hospital. Somehow, we were graciously allowed to see Jay, though it was only about six hours after the fall. Having spent twenty years in the military, I had witnessed many injuries but had never personally seen anyone survive with injuries as severe as what I witnessed that evening. The rising pressure in Jay's battered skull was forcing his eyes nearly out of the sockets, and his face appeared black with the bruising. What followed in the months and years after the accident clearly demonstrated the power of his relationship with Jesus. Finally, back on his feet after learning to walk and eat again over countless months, Jay felt led to use his love of aviation in ministry. He purchased an aircraft. Knowing he would never regain his pilot's license due to his trauma, he gathered some of us, his pilot buddies, to fly his airplane with him and, in that way, help him provide charitable transportation for cancer victims in remote locations, hurricane relief supplies, and mission work. You will find this book hopeful, encouraging, and inspirational.

—CAPTAIN DAVID NELSON, American Airlines, rtd.

They Call Me Miracle Man

A Life of Success, Tragedy, Betrayals, and Hope

JAY STRAUB

Author Note: This book is a personal and professional memoir. I have tried to tell my story with respect for my colleagues, friends, and relatives while addressing issues of public concern and the experiences that may occur in any family. I have tried to make the account as accurate as possible in all respects. Names and other details for the individuals identified by the following names have been fictionalized: [*Brent-Cindy-Arlene-*. Melissa Any resemblances between these fictionalized names and any real people are strictly coincidental.

Trademarks. This book makes descriptive reference to trademarks that may be owned by others. All terms mentioned in this book that are known to be trademarks or service marks have been appropriately capitalized. Use of the term in this book should not be regarded as affecting the validity of any trademark or service mark and additionally should not be viewed as an intention of trademark infringement. The use of such trademarks within this book is not an assertion of ownership of such trademarks by the author or the publisher and is not indented to represent or imply the existence of an association between the author or publisher and the lawful owners of such trademarks.

*To my sweet and lovely wife, Letha Straub,
who has shown me true love and a heartfelt desire
to live out our lives as husband and wife
in the way God designed it.*

CONTENTS

FOREWORD

The crowd sat on the edge of their seats, and most of them held their faces in disbelief. Jay Straub was in the middle of sharing his story of the accident that changed his life. Looking at the pictures of him before and after left them without words. When the tall Texan had finished his tragedy that turned into a triumph, he was swarmed by men and women who said they had never seen anything so shocking in their lives. I sat there speechless myself. The group knew heartbreak and difficulty. We were in the Gaza Strip. This group thought they'd seen it all.

Straub got his first flying job when he was just eighteen, and as a teen he had his whole life mapped out. He was on the fast track, and soon he had the ideal job as an American Airlines pilot. It was what he prayed for, trained for, and dreamed of. But after thirteen years, his dream turned into a nightmare. He never could have anticipated the life that God had prepared him for. Nobody could have. But Jay became the ideal tool in the hand of God to help people through pain and suffering in a region that is synonymous with them, the Middle East.

Jay is inspiring, and so is his story. Others would've given up, but not Jay. He had the firm belief that no matter how bad things got, God was still there and was going to somehow use the ups and downs of his journey to change people's lives. Boy, was he ever right.

I've invited Jay to speak in several countries with people suffering because of war, political strife, and refugee displacement, and each time he has risen to the occasion to bring comfort and healing with his story. Jay has helped thousands of people around the world.

As one preacher told me when I was a young minister, "There's a broken heart in every pew."

I have seen this to be true. But not everyone can bring the love of God that encourages others to not give up but rather to trust God for more even when it seems He is absent. Jay has mastered this lesson. In fact, God has given him the spiritual capacity to endure through pain and injustice.

There is a need in the world to identify with people's suffering. They need a voice whether they are persecuted Christians, homeless refugees, under the threat of war, or wracked with disease; too many feel forgotten and that nobody cares. God cares, and He appointed Jay personally to deliver this crucial message. I've been honored to hear Jay share the good news many times and to see the results.

Paul in Romans 8:28 said, "For God causes all things to work together for the good of those who love Him." For most Christians, this is a well-known verse. But Jay has lived this verse and seen the truth of it day after day. It has become his foundation.

Hang on to your hat; you're about to ride on a roller coaster that has been Jay's life. But along the way, you'll see God and His incredible love and power for His children in action like never before. I highly recommend this book. In Christ, we are more than conquerors!

Tom Doyle
President of Uncharted Ministries
The author of *Dreams and Visions-Is Jesus Awakening the Muslim World?*
Standing in the Fire-Courageous Christians Living in Frightening Times

PREFACE

Monday, November 22, 1999, I woke up early in the layover hotel in Tulsa, Oklahoma. I was forty-one years old and the captain of an American Airlines Boeing 727. Except that God intervened, this would have been the last day of my life.

I wonder what if I had been told as I looked in the mirror that morning: the world as you know it will never be the same; the career you love and your identity as Captain Jay Straub is gone. You will have to fight to live, and you will never look the same as you do now. Your sense of smell and taste will be mostly gone, and your hearing will not be like it was when you awoke. Your sense of life will be snatched from you, and your marriage will completely wither away.

This would have been unthinkable, and more than my heart, mind, or soul could have borne.

I am humbled and honored that this book has found its way into your hands. As I open my heart and share my story, the bitter and the sweet, the highs and the lows, the unimaginable and the miracle of it all, my prayer is that my story will open your heart and bring a breath of fresh air to give you hope in the middle of your own storm of life.

May Jesus Christ meet your needs both physically and spiritually on your journey in this life.

ACKNOWLEDGEMENTS

To my dear cousin Curtis Hail, more brother and friend than cousin, who gave me wise counsel in my early years, spread the word of my need for prayer around the world, and got me involved with his ministry to help in sharing the good news.

To Dr. Eugene George, Dr. Bruce Mickey, Dr. Mary Carlile, Dr. Kimberly Mezera, Michael Levy MSN, The DFW Airport Ambulance Crew-E.M.T.'S, and all the other dozens of doctors and nurses who did everything possible to sustain my life and help bless me with another nineteen years so far.

To Michael Mabrey for being a true and lifelong friend, who put me on a road to have a dream and have it fulfilled.

To Bill Hines for giving me wise counsel and being a great friend who has blessed me with wonderful fellowship and teaching for over twenty years.

To former American Airlines Vice President of Flight Captain Cecil Ewell, First Officer Ans Wishing, Captain Dave Slack, former American Airlines Vice President of Flight-Captain John Hale, Captain Billy Parker, Captain Larry Foster, Captain Zane Lemon, Captain Norm Patterson, Captain Dennis Eckenrod, Captain Randy Popiel and many whom I can't name who spoke on my behalf when I was unable to speak and were true wingmen.

To all those in the DFW Flight Office and the DFW Ramp Tower who showed me their kindness and compassion as I came from hospitals and rehab back to a somewhat normal life.

To Tom and JoAnn Doyle for seeing a value in sharing my story of God's mercy and grace in my life with our brothers and sisters in the Middle East and for blessing me with their friendship.

To Captain Phil and Jan Atkinson, Captain Carter and Mary Lynn Jordan, Captain Bob and Carmella Gole, Captain Denny and Sandy Parker, Captain Rob and Teresa (deceased) Shepperd, Captain Dale (deceased) and Teresa Biery, Captain Lou and Cheryl Cardon, Captain Dennis and Dee Kurts, Captain Doug Weyer, First Officer Ray and Jeanna Wood, Captain John and Rachel Bowling, and Captain Tim Sikorsky for being there, lifting me up, and giving me their love and support in more than one trying event.

To Captain John Bowen, John Elliot, Rich Speakman, Jamie Jordan, Ron Cornelius, Bob Kulick, Steven Cox, Joe Flanigan, Captain Bobby Wenzel, and Chad Hennings for being willing to hear my testimony, my thoughts on certain subjects and blessing me with their fellowship and being true wingmen.

To Ray and Gloria Harper, Chris and Kim Newman, Mike and Mikie Doyle, and everyone at Covenant Fellowship Church for their love, kindness, and support when I attended there.

To Captain Dave Nelson, Captain Dave Slack, First Officer Blair Johnson, Lionel Garcia, Dr. Hal Stewart, Danny Loe, Mike Kirkpatrick, Vince Zeller, Ken Kendall, Terry Lawrence, Ken Hamilton, and Mike Liles for their prayers, fellowship, and including me in their Men's Group.

To Greg Hanson for sticking it out with me for the last sixteen years at the Tuesday Morning Men's Bible Study and to Mike Scherer and Charles Stolfus for continuing to come and teach us.

To Gerry Hammontree and Fran Chupp, for getting me involved in the latest Men's Bible Study and to Scott Wilson, Danny Volgamore, Doug Nurss, Doug Hughes, David Phillips, Rich Lipke, Brian Stanton, Andre Marrou, Klaus Dannenburg, Jim Gardiner, John Kirk, Gregor Smith, and Terry Scholze for blessing me with hosting this study for the better part of the last five years.

MY EARLY KICKS ON ROUTE 66

I

Looking back, I see life began in Amarillo, Texas. I was an only child, and my parents had waited until they were in their thirties to marry and had been married ten years before I came on the scene. Mom was forty; Dad was forty-five.

We lived in a two-bedroom house on Hillside Road, which at that time was barely a two-lane paved road. Now it's a four-lane major thoroughfare. Three or four lots to the east of us, my grandmother and great-grandmother on Mom's side lived. About a block to the west of us lived mom's brother, Uncle Clinton, Aunt Carolyn, and my cousins, Pamela and Curtis.

My grandmother, whom I called Nana, and my grandfather, who passed away over ten years prior to my birth, had owned a grocery store/gas station in walking distance to their home. It was determined by the Powers That Be that the business Nana had owned and operated was sitting right in the middle of where the new Canyon Expressway (I27) needed to be. So, it was gone a year prior to my coming on the scene, but I have heard a lot of good stories.

One of the first things I recall is my early adventure at the age of three. I really loved Nana and Grandma and loved to spend time with them. I also loved Nana's cooking. Our home was on a very large lot and had a chain link fence all the way around the property with two gates. One of them was out front at the driveway, and the other was at the back of the property. Those gates were always kept closed and locked so I could go outside and play.

I recall looking at Nana's house through that chain link fence and longing to go visit her, but that was not possible with these gates that kept me hemmed in. *Wait a minute*, I thought. As I looked things over, there was about an eight-inch space between that back gate and the ground. If I worked really hard at it,

I might be able to take a deep breath, worm my way under that thing, and run to Nana's house.

Sure enough, it worked. I made it under and took off running. I went up to Nana's back porch and knocked on her door. When she opened it and saw her three-year-old grandson staring up at her, she probably went into shock.

She let me in, picked me up, kissed me, and asked how I got there. I wasn't going to give up my secret, though. Then she sat me down and immediately called Mom to tell her I was there. And since it was early in the morning, she proceeded to fix me some scrambled eggs, bacon, and toast with jelly. Wow! I had hit pay dirt with this. I could sneak out, get a great breakfast, and get to spend some time with Nana and Grandma.

I was successful at this adventure several times. I even recall a couple of times when Mom spotted me walking that way and came running after me. As soon as I saw her, though, I took off running, beat her there, and got to my destination. Every time I did that I was sternly lectured on my disobedience.

I'm not quite sure how I dodged the switch or the belt on this. I guess they couldn't bring themselves to that when I just wanted to go see Nana and Grandma. Anyway, Mom finally sat me down and told me that she just had to know how in the world I was managing to get out. She promised me that it was just our secret and that no one else would know.

I had already been well instructed on how wrong it was to tell a lie, so I trusted Mom that it was our secret. I'm sure you already know what I discovered the next day when I went out to make my venture to Nana's. There it was: a piece of plywood attached to the back gate that went from the bottom of the gate to ground level. I pushed, pushed, and pushed some more. There was no budging it. Well, humph! I really did love spending time with Nana and Grandma and didn't like this development at all.

II

The next thing that comes to mind in those years was a real struggle I had with allergies and asthma. From the age of two, I remember lying in bed at night under what was called the "croup tent." Mom and Dad would put a card table over my bed with a sheet over it. Sitting barely under the tent was the vaporizer with Vicks liquid poured in where the steam came out. To top it off, they would rub my chest with Vicks and put a cotton cloth and my pajamas over it. I was constantly sneezing and having a barking cough, asthma, and bronchitis.

After dealing with this for two years, my parents were told to take me to Oklahoma City to see a doctor who specialized in allergies. The allergy doctor there informed us that I was allergic to almost "everything under the sun" relating to food and plants. I was allergic to elm trees, which surrounded our house on Hillside, and Bermuda grass, which covered our yard. It went all the way to regular house dust, which led him to recommend that we move.

All of the food allergies had me down to really nothing but meat and vegetables. I faced being stuck with that and taking allergy shots once a week for several years, until I was able to retest some things to see if they were still causing me problems.

At that time my cousin Curtis lived just down the street from us. We were more like brothers than cousins. When I would spot Aunt Carolyn pulling into the drive at Nana's house, I would run in and tell Mom, "Curtis is down at Nana's; please let me go play with him."

I would get to go down to play, and we would do all the wonderful boy stunts. Curtis would chase me around Nana's house until I was about to drop.

We would play hide 'n seek, and the grand finale would almost always be the rock fight. If you're not familiar with that, it's similar to a "Shoot Out at the OK Corral." We would throw rocks at each other about the size of a quarter to a half dollar, and there was plenty of that type of ammunition on Nana's rock driveway. Now as Curtis was four years older than I and with my asthma kicking in as soon as I started running, I'm sure you can figure out who would win these battles, but I loved it and couldn't wait for the next battle.

Another of our escapades etched on my mind was actually down at Curtis's house. It was close to Independence Day, and we were out playing with firecrackers, bottle rockets, and sparklers. Curtis had all his little green army men and little military jeeps and trucks. We were setting off the firecrackers and having a battle-to-end-all-battles with this stuff. I was crawling around on the ground and was scratching around in some of the shrubs. You won't believe it. I discovered an Easter egg that nobody had found months back during the Easter egg hunt.

I grabbed it and went running to Curtis and said, "Look what I found."

I'm sure your mind is already contemplating the end result of this. That's right; we had to put a firecracker under this thing and blow it up. You're probably also cringing at the end result of that. We had no idea what a boiled egg three months old and that had sat out in the hot sun was going to produce when it was blown to smithereens.

Oh, my gosh! The smell was horrendous. When Aunt Carolyn caught a whiff of that, our day was done.

Shortly after that was when we moved as the doctor had recommended, and the Hails moved as well, way out in the country on Tascosa Road. That was really sad for me. It felt like I had lost a brother. We would still get to see each other occasionally, but nothing was as it had been.

As required, we went back to Oklahoma City to have the allergy tests re-done and see how things were proceeding. You know how there are certain things that you never forget? On our journey back from Oklahoma City to Amarillo, we pulled into a gas station in Clinton, Oklahoma. That was back when it was a full-service station.

The attendant came out to gas up our car, and in a very distressed tone of voice said, "What a sad day for our nation."

Since there was no radio in our car, Dad asked what he was talking about.

The attendant asked, "Oh, you haven't heard? President Kennedy was just assassinated in Dallas."

Oh my. My mom burst into tears and cried all the way to Amarillo, and Dad couldn't talk. That will always be etched in my mind.

Asthma was a burden for most of my childhood. It was pretty miserable. The strange thing was that exercise of any kind would trigger it. It was so embarrassing growing up. In physical education when the coach would have us run laps, after about a hundred yards the asthma would kick in, and I couldn't breathe. I would come in last every time. What a pain it was when a coach would force us to run a lap for some disciplinary purpose and then say that whoever is last can run another. Needless to say, athletics was not going to be of much interest to me.

III

In this same time frame Mom decided I needed to start school. At the age of five years and four months, you would think kindergarten, right? Not exactly; she heard about a two-room private school, the Little Red Schoolhouse. It had a kindergarten and first grade. She wanted me to go into first grade. The teacher, Ms. Gann, was hesitant to put me in first grade at that age, but Mom was persistent.

So, Ms. Gann said she could give me some tests to see if I had the aptitude to do that. After the tests were done, she said I could, so that's what happened.

The next year when I went into public school it caused a problem. When Mom went to Ridgecrest Elementary, which was right out the back gate of our home on Hancock Street, to register me, they said that I wasn't old enough to go into second grade.

The principal went back and forth with Mom and finally came up with a silly idea. He wanted me to do half the year in first grade and the second half in second grade. Fortunately, Mom wouldn't stand for that, but the principal wouldn't budge either.

Mom and Dad still owned the house that we had lived in on Hillside. It was completely debt free, and they owned four lots on the west side of the house. So, she went to the principal of the elementary school in the district where that house and land was. She explained the problem with the principal at the other school. This principal was willing to let me go right into the second grade; however, we didn't live in that district.

Mom asked, "What if we start the process to move to that district immediately?"

The principal said he would agree to that.

Mom went home and told Dad we were going to build a new home on the third lot down from the old house to get as far from the elm trees as possible and with no Bermuda grass.

Well, as I'm sure you can imagine, things were a little testy at home over this sudden development. That's what we did, though.

Just prior to this move, however, a major—and I do mean major—event in my life took place when I was seven or eight years old. Dad was a devout Catholic who went to church every Sunday, but that's all I knew. He really never discussed God or the church. Mom was a Baptist who never went to church but watched it on television every Sunday.

After I had watched First Baptist Amarillo with her for many months, I was convinced. I came to the realization that I was a sinner, needed forgiveness, and that faith in Jesus Christ was the only thing that could give me that. I saw on television how baptism was an important thing in coming to faith and started to beg my mom to take me to that church so I could be baptized. She told me that she would have to talk with Dad about that.

Well, the next Sunday morning, Dad woke me up early and said, "It's time to get up; we're going to church."

He had bought me a suit, dress shoes, white shirt, and clip-on tie.

Off we went to St. Hyacinth's Catholic Church. That wasn't what I was expecting. I wanted to go to First Baptist and have Pastor Moore baptize me. Mom and Dad told me I had been baptized shortly after I was born by a priest. I didn't understand any of it. After listening to Pastor Moore on television, I wondered why we couldn't go to First Baptist to do that.

Of course, I learned later that when a Roman Catholic marries someone who is not a Roman Catholic, they have to vow that all their children will be raised in the Roman Catholic Church. So, that was it. I was going to spend my early years at church with Dad. The true blessing of it all, however, is that from watching Pastor Moore I was born again. I knew without a doubt that I was a sinner and that I needed forgiveness. I also knew that Jesus Christ paid the price to give me that forgiveness and that I needed to follow Him to receive that.

IV

During these years just before and when I was in elementary school, I experienced quite the variety of life experiences from health, to family, to school. I found a number of things in school I liked and disliked. I really liked to read, and my favorite classes were history, geography, and science.

I enjoyed music as well and still can't believe that in the fifth grade, I managed to get dressed up in a little German outfit and play *"Muss I Denn"* on my dad's Hohner push button accordion while the choir sang it. (That's the only song I ever learned on that thing, by the way.)

Another fond memory from this time in my life was Dad and his *walk behind* Sears garden tractor. He had plowed those entire four lots on the west side of our original house and grown enough black-eyed peas to feed an army with that thing. As a matter of fact, people would constantly stop and ask if they could go harvest some.

In wrapping up those childhood memories, I can remember sitting out on the front porch with Dad a great deal as he hand-watered his grass and flowers. As we sat there, I would just watch the B-52 bombers and F-4 fighters fly by out in the distance, doing their approaches at the former Amarillo Air Force Base. I watched them for hours, totally intrigued by it all, just seeing those behemoths so big they looked like they were barely moving. I wondered how it all worked and how they actually flew those things. Back then, it never crossed my mind that I might one day be sitting out in the pointy end of something similar.

Jay and dad in the pea patch

THE NEED FOR SPEED
VIA PROP AND TWO WHEELS

|

The next year I transitioned from elementary school to junior high school. The first day at Bonham Junior High was quite the shocker. Every year prior to that, Mom had taken me up to school for registration and given them my name and all of the other information. This year, the school system went on computers, and they had all the data.

They didn't need a parent to give them my name or any of that. The first day in homeroom the teacher started calling the roll. She rattled off name after name and everyone replied, "Here."

Then she called out, "Herman."

Nobody replied. She called it again, still no reply, and I'm kind of seeing some humor in it. In my six previous years of school I hadn't had a classmate named Herman.

The teacher finally says, "Herman Straub."

I looked up, bewildered, and said, "That's my Dad."

She said, "Well, it says here that's you, Herman Straub Jr."

Gulp! With the knot in my throat now, I raised my hand and said, "Here, I guess?"

You can imagine the immense amount of laughter in the room as well as the questions I asked when I got in the car that afternoon. Having never been called anything but "Jay" by anyone and never being told I was named after my dad really was a surprise. Fortunately, almost everyone continued to call me Jay.

Much to my mom's disapproval, I managed to get a minibike for Christmas that year. We wound up having to return the first two bikes immediately due to mechanical defects, and surprisingly I managed to get a Honda 70, which for me was an absolute dream come true.

That was pretty much the remainder of the seventh grade for me: go to school, come home and ride, do my homework, go to bed, and repeat the process the next day. Other than being glued to the TV in April keeping up with the worry over Apollo 13, that summer was all Honda, except for church and the occasional book.

II

The next year, eighth grade, we had a new student at Bonham. I was out riding my Honda, and when I came up close to the school in one of the vacant fields we rode in, I looked, and he was standing at the curb waiting for his mom to pick him up.

Since I recognized him, I waved, and he came across the street to talk. It was Michael Mabrey. He immediately told me he had a candy-apple red Honda 70 as well. I thought surely that he lived somewhere fairly close, and I asked why I hadn't seen him riding.

I was really surprised when he explained his family was living out at the old Amarillo Air Force Base. He went on to share that his dad was in charge of operations at Texas State Technical Institute, which was located out there. I was curious how and why he went to school at Bonham and lived way out there.

He explained that his dad had just taken this position and they had just moved to Amarillo from Derby, Kansas. They were building a new home in Puckett Place, which was in the Bonham school district. Michael's mom showed up, and we said goodbye.

After our conversation, I liked Michael and felt like I had made a new friend. The Lord had truly blessed me with that friendship, though then I didn't know how great a blessing it was.

Michael and I started to talk to each other quite often, and soon Michael asked me to come out to TSTI on a weekend with my Honda. He said there were a lot of great places to ride. I told him I would ask my parents.

I was really glad that my parents were willing to let me do that, and I still can't believe how we were able to pull the back seat out of Dad's old '51 Chevy, fold down the handlebars on my Honda, and put that thing in the back of Dad's car. That was a great day riding around out there with Michael, and I loved getting to meet his mom.

III

Michael and I had become very good friends and talked every chance we got. One day he showed up at school, not very long after our riding adventure, and said, "This weekend I'm going to take a flying lesson."

My eyes about popped out of my head. "You're gonna do what?"

He repeated it, and I just stood there in shock trying to make heads or tails of what I just heard. I understood that Michael's dad was a former colonel in the Air Force and flew everything from P-51s to F-4s, but I couldn't see how at the age of thirteen that put him in an airplane learning to fly.

At the end of the day Michael said he would check with his dad and see if I could go with them. How cool would that be? That night he called and told me it would be fine for me to go. I had already asked my mom and dad, and they had told me it would be fine if Michael's dad approved. I was way excited but had no clue what a life-changing event this was going to be.

That Saturday I joined Michael and his dad on the journey out to Tradewind Airport, the smaller airport in Amarillo where most of the general aviation aircraft operated. We drove up to Amarillo Flying Service, the Cessna dealer and a flight school and charter operation. We went in, and Kimble Neel came up, introduced himself, and asked how he could help us.

Michael's dad told Kimble that he was interested in their flight school and a lesson for his son. Kimble proceeded to give Mr. Mabrey all the information on the price of the lessons. He took us out to show us the Cessna 150s that would be used for the training. After that, we went back to Michael's new home in Puckett Place. We were both way excited and had lots of things to talk about.

I was so enthralled with it all and couldn't quit thinking about it. I went home and begged my parents to let me take some flying lessons with Michael. What a surprise though! You would think if anyone would be on board with the son's taking flying lessons, it would be the father, and the mother would be dead set against it. In my case, Dad didn't like the idea, and Mom was very supportive.

Mom won out, and I got to take my $5 coupon for the introductory flight, get in an airplane for the first time in my life, and actually fly and touch the controls. You have a twelve-year-old here, remember. I was a year to a year-and-a-half younger than my classmates and going up with Kimble Neel in a Cessna

150 and actually doing some turns and banks, climb, descent, and wings level flying. I was hooked.

When I got home, I couldn't stop talking about it. Mom was quite interested, but Dad was still a bit out of the loop on this. I took a lesson for about a half-hour of flight time every week. Most of the time, Michael and I would go together and each have a lesson the same day.

After five months of lessons and my accruing 9.5 hours of flight instruction, Kimble sat us down and told us that we really couldn't accomplish much with this until we were of a legal age, according to the Federal Aviation Regulations, to get a student pilot certificate.

At the time, that was sure disappointing, but very admirable that Kimble, a young man, probably twenty years old or close to it, was looking out for our best interest. When I think about it now, it blows my mind that an hour of flight instruction back then was $21 per hour. Yes, you heard that right, $21. It was $15 per hour for the aircraft and $6 per hour for the flight instructor. Nowadays, it's approximately $120 per hour for the aircraft and $40 for the flight instructor. My private license cost a little over $800, and now it costs from $6,500 to $12,000 according to what I saw online.

IV

With putting the flying lessons on hold, my spare time went back to the Honda. After eighth grade came to a close for summer, Curtis had gotten his driver's license and would come by fairly often to take me with him in his new Dodge Charger to see the motorcycle races out at the Amarillo Speedway. I always looked forward to that.

We would also go to many of the indoor flat track races inside the Amarillo Civic Center. The smell of the fumes of that Castrol-two stroke oil is still ingrained in my nostrils from those events.

Curtis and I would always root for one of the riders, Sam Line, the brother of Curtis's girlfriend, Amy. Of all the races, my favorite was going to watch Sam race "the mile" on his BSA 650.

I loved watching them accelerate to over 100 miles per hour down the straightaway, get to the turn, "throw it sideways," crank the throttle more, and see the "rooster tail" of dirt that the rear tire would be throwing in the face of the rider behind them.

I did a lot of racing with friends in the neighborhood but never did the real deal. I'm sure it's quite fortunate for me that my parents would never let me get into true racing.

V

Right at the very end of summer I had developed a real—you remember the term in *Top Gun*— "need for speed." I was really wanting a true motorcycle that could be at the very least a little faster, and I needed a job to pay for it. My friend Don Stevens' parents were good friends of the manager of one of the convenience stores close to my home, Mrs. Jones.

Don was working there part-time and helped me get hired by Mrs. Jones. So, off I went after school to earn my $1.25 per hour to put toward a new Honda SL100, candy-apple red, of course. Dad let me go ahead and get it, but I had to pay my share of it. He paid half of the $500, and I paid the other half.

With summer gone, I experienced a true blessing at the beginning of my freshman year at Bonham. The asthma pretty much went away. I could run and not be hit with an inability to breathe. I can't tell you how fantastic that was. I was so thankful to the Lord.

After all those years of coming in last when we had to run laps, now I could do better than some people. The allergy problem was still there to bring on frequent sinus infections, but I was so very thankful to have the asthma gone.

There was also a not-so-good event at the beginning of that year. One day a bunch of us—the guys who lived close together and had motorcycles—were racing. We were making a turn, and Craig, a friend and fellow freshman at Bonham, was inside me on the turn, and his front wheel was about even with my foot pegs.

I have no idea how, but his bike got entangled with mine, and he went down. I continued the race, and when we crossed the finish line, I looked back. Craig was still down. We all hustled back to him, and he was still lying on the ground tossing and turning with severe pain in his foot. When he finally tried to get up, he couldn't, so we took off to go get his dad and tell him what happened. In fact, you could see Craig's house from where we were.

Craig's dad got there and loaded him in the family car to take him to the hospital, and we got his motorcycle back to their house. The next day was really bad news. From what I recall, as he went down Craig's foot got caught in something. All of the metatarsal bones in that foot were separated at the joint, and the surgeon had to drill through the bones that made up his toes and put pins in them to keep them in place in order to heal.

Craig was going to be on crutches for a long time. Here we were, at the beginning of football season, and Craig was the quarterback on our team. I felt totally miserable over that.

VI

A few months after that I had my own ordeal. It was nothing near as critical as Craig's, but it could have been much worse. Frequently, my bike had been sliding out from under me in turns and the like but nothing serious. We were doing our usual racing. Coming down a straightaway, I was really trying to get around the guy in front of me. The problem at this point was that the trail had narrowed down to just the width of one bike.

No problem, I thought. *I'm going to go around him, trail or no trail.* I opened it up and veered off to the left into the weeds. I was doing close to 40 mph and was about to veer back to the right, in front of the guy I had just passed. All of a sudden, my bike went from 40 to 0 mph in a split-second. I went flying over the handlebars and tumbled three or four of those gymnastic tumbles before it ended with me lying face down and lightheaded.

As I tried to get up, I felt a really sharp pain in my left shoulder. It was really hurting. I got up and went back to the bike to see what in the world had happened. When I found the spot where I had come to a complete stop, there was a two-inch in diameter pipe sticking up out of the ground for about two feet. It had been perfectly camouflaged by the weeds. I had to have nailed that thing dead-on.

When I got home, I didn't say anything, but I was really starting to hurt, so after a few hours I told Mom what had happened and that it was really hurting. She said, "Well, maybe that'll teach you a lesson."

I couldn't believe it. Granted, when I got my first mini-bike, she was strongly against it, and I had come home bleeding plenty of times and needing some bandages. I had a few scars, but nothing ever serious enough to even go to a doctor for. Now when I truly needed to, she wasn't taking me.

Dad wasn't there to take me. His job as foreman at the Helium Plant in

Amarillo had incurred some major changes. The plant was in the process of eventually being shut down permanently. Losing his position in Amarillo, he had to transfer up to the plant in Keyes, Oklahoma. He had bought a thirty-five-foot travel trailer and parked it up there. He would go up there, do his week of shift work, and come home for his two days off.

When he got home, I didn't say anything, but it didn't take him long to figure out something was up. I could hardly move my left arm due to the pain. He let it go a little while and then asked me why I wasn't moving my left arm. I told him what had happened, and he asked me what the doctor had said. I told him what Mom had said and that she refused to take me to see a doctor.

His eyes got big and he asked, "What the hell?"

He set out to find Mom, but then he turned back around and just said, "Get in the car, Jay. We're going to the hospital."

They x-rayed me in the emergency room and told us it was a cracked collar bone that was very close to a complete break, and they gave me a brace to wear and told me it would just take time to heal. While that full-faced helmet I had was great in a lot of ways, that collar bone would probably have been fine had I been wearing a standard helmet. Gee!

Things were mighty quiet when we got home from the hospital. Sad to say, it was like that a lot as I grew up, and it was the most intense after a family feud at Nana's passing. Mom didn't really have any respect for my dad, and she would insult him and his family quite often.

When it happened, some cuss words would fly out of Dad's mouth, and he would escape to the garage to work on something. If it were good weather, he would go outside to groom the yard some more. I still miss his beautiful Kentucky bluegrass yard that he kept immaculate.

One of those insult sessions is ingrained in my mind. As usual, Dad turned and went outside, but I sensed some real pain. I waited a few minutes and quietly opened the door to go into the garage. He wasn't in the garage, and the garage door was up. I could hear the water coming out of the spray nozzle, just around the corner on the side of the house.

I couldn't see him, but I knew he was sitting in his folding chair hand watering the grass. I quietly walked over and peeked around the corner. There was my strong Dad, who worked so hard for us and for Mom's mother when she was alive, sitting there, water hose in hand with tears just streaming down his face. I so wanted to run and wrap my arms around him and hug him, but I was afraid it might embarrass him. I certainly wish now that I had.

VII

Throughout that freshman year, I continued to ride my Honda a lot, but I was also spending even more time reading. History was my favorite class, and I spent a lot of time reading books related to history. I also spent a good deal of time reading God's Word, the Bible. I had actually been doing that some for several years already, but I got into it much deeper that year. That was what gave me peace in a lot of what I just shared.

There are some other great memories from that year. Curtis came over a lot. I can't count the number of sessions he and I had playing hockey on the floor of our front bedroom, down on our knees. I sure wish we had had a table to put that on where we could stand up and do it, but we had a great time down on our knees manipulating those little hockey players and moving the puck. We also made many a run to Ellwood Park or Amarillo College to play tennis. Curtis taught me the game, and I even beat him occasionally.

Another fond memory was going to see a movie with Dad, just me and him. As a matter of fact, I think that's the only movie he ever went to his entire lifetime after I was born. He may have gone to some prior to that, but none after. Anyway, he took me to see *On Any Sunday*. What a treat that was, getting to see a documentary on motorcycle sport directed by Bruce Brown. That was my favorite movie for a long time. Getting to see the pros do it, Mert Lawill, Malcom Smith, and, yes, Steve McQueen, along with all the others and everything that went into the sport was a real treat.

VIII

My years at Bonham Junior High were wrapping up and what better way than the final game of "war ball." I loved that game. Coach Hamilton only let us do this a couple of times a year. He'd line up about six volleyballs down the half court line in the gym and divide the class into two teams, with one team at each end of the gym. Then he would blow a whistle, and each team would charge to the center court line and try to grab one of the balls. Each team member would have to stay on their side of the center court line. If you got one of the balls, you would immediately throw it as hard as possible at an opposing team member to hit them, inflict pain, and send them to the bench.

Now if the opposing team member caught your ball and held on to it, then you would go to the bench. If you hit an opposing player in the head, you would go to the bench for that as well. If you had a ball in your hands and someone else threw at you, you could deflect their ball with the ball in your hands. If their ball knocked the one you had out of your hands though, you would have to go to the bench. This would go on until there was only one player per team left, and they would throw at each other until one of the players aced the other.

Many times, one of the two would catch the others throw, and the guy who threw would lose. Much to my surprise, I actually won one of the games that year. The trick was to hit the other player down close to the ankles, which would make it hard for him to catch it. That's what I did. I let loose aiming at the ankles. He tried to jump in hopes that the ball would go under his feet.

To my surprise, he didn't jump straight up. Somehow, he went up at an angle and the wrong angle at that. The angle he was at, and the velocity of the ball I threw, made his legs even less perpendicular to the floor. He came crashing down to the floor on his side. Ouch! Ah, the thrill of victory and the agony of defeat.

Jay's first birthday

A receipt of Jay's flying lesson in 6638G, the plane he did his first solo flight in

REBELS & RACISM—SANDIES & SOLOS

|

The next leg of my journey of life was at Tascosa High School, where we were known as the Tascosa Rebels. That was based on our school mascot, General Johnny Reb. It was just like when I started at Bonham Junior High. I was met with the same challenges in changing schools, but unfortunately, I was dealt a blow that no one could have foreseen to help prepare me for. Sadly, it's the main thing that comes to mind from that year.

I was still not old enough to drive, so Mom or Dad had to take me to school and back. It was a normal day at school, and at the conclusion of it I came out of the building and headed for the usual spot where they picked me up. Unfortunately, we had some significant snowfall that day, and wouldn't you know, I was wearing shoes with a slick leather sole.

The snow was at least six inches deep, so a number of students had blazed a trail about two feet wide out to the sidewalk and curb where Dad was parked. The problem was that trail was hard-packed snow slicker than glass with those leather-soled shoes I was wearing. When I got to the car, it dawned on me that I had forgotten to bring a book that I needed to do homework that night.

I put what I had in the car and told Dad I had to go back. I turned and started walking, very slowly, back down the slick trail. About halfway back to the building, I heard a bunch of laughter and chatter coming from a good distance to the right and back behind me.

The next thing you know, another student wearing tennis shoes pounced about two feet in front of me, with his arms crossed, blocking my way on the path. It was one of the Black students who happened to be in my homeroom. I had never talked with him, but I had actually said hello and smiled at him multiple times, which was always met with a scowl. In spite of that, I had continued to be kind and friendly.

As he stood there with his arms crossed, I said, "Excuse me." With no response, I said it again and still no response. I obviously didn't like it, but I decided to play his game. So, I stepped over into the deep snow and went around him. That wasn't good enough for him. He was immediately in front of me again, arms crossed. I decided I had enough snow in my shoes, so I gently did what I could, to squeeze by him without stepping into the deep stuff again.

As I proceeded on, I heard him cursing me from behind. The next thing I heard was a derogatory name for White people, which I was clueless to, followed by a swift, hard kick that caught both of my legs just above the ankles. Thanks to the packed slick snow, my feet flew up in the air bringing me down hard to the sidewalk.

I rolled over and got on my knees with my hands down in hope of getting back on my feet. As I raised my head to look up, it was quickly apparent that was not the thing to do. It had positioned me face to foot. The next thing I heard was another derogatory name, and his foot was planted right in my mouth, knocking me over again backwards.

This had all happened very quickly, but by the time I got to my feet, Dad was there and got between us. Dad told him, "Get the hell out of here!" which he did. At that point, the laughing and jeering down the way had morphed into cursing and screaming. That was quite humiliating, but I was glad Dad was there to intervene.

I had busted lips but no broken nose or teeth. Thank the Lord. I turned around and headed back to get the book I needed. I hurried as quickly as I could, being concerned for Dad with the number of teenage males and even females who were screaming and cursing just a few hundred feet back from his car.

When I got back to the car, I thanked Dad and told him I was sorry he had to come to the rescue. He was shocked and said I had nothing to be sorry about. He went on to ask if I had done anything to provoke that. I told him that I had done absolutely nothing and went on to tell him what I already shared with you about my experience with this fellow. At that point I could almost see steam coming out of Dad's ears.

When we got home, and Mom saw my swollen and busted lips, she was so distraught that it made the remainder of the day even more difficult. As I sit here and think back on all of this, it certainly shows how protective my parents had been of me as an only child. Here I was, a sophomore in high school, and I was really unaware in some areas.

It's a bit humorous as I reminisce on it now. I remember the shocked look on Dad's face quite well when I asked him why the guy kept calling me donkey, as he attacked me. Gee whiz, I wasn't even aware of the racial slur he was hurling at me. I didn't know "honkey," so Dad had to inform me of what had actually been said.

As the evening went on, I was thinking that I should go the next day and inform the principal what had happened to have this guy disciplined. The more I thought about it, though, I came to the conclusion that I could very easily wind up being the one disciplined. Other than Dad or perhaps my friend Don, who rode with us and saw it, who would back me up and defend me?

If this guy spewed some bald-faced lies in an attempt to justify what he had done, you could bet that his cohorts who were screaming and cursing would be there to defend my attacker. So that's where it was left.

I have prayed many times over the years that this man and those who were cheering him on that day have overcome the hatred that drove them to do that. And most important of all, forgive them just as I have been forgiven by our Lord.

II

A fond memory of that year was a little hobby that I got into. When I went to have my photo for the school annual done, the photographer, John Miller, of Autry's Studio, also had a little hobby shop attached to the business that sold radio-controlled airplane kits and accessories. There was a club who flew these things out at Southeast Park in Amarillo. They even had a little asphalt runway out there for takeoffs and landings.

I got my first kit and proceeded to construct and assemble it. I glued the balsa wood pieces for the fuselage and then the same with the wing. I finished out the wing with an orange heat shrink plastic wrap. The wrap does the same job as the metal material you see on the outside of the wing of a real aircraft. Then I also put heat shrink wrap on the fuselage and horizontal and vertical stabilizers. Next on the list was to install the main and nose landing gear, the engine, and the control rods for the rudder, elevator, and engine throttle.

Now it was time to go to the field and fly this thing. After church that Sunday, Dad and I headed to Southeast Park. We got there, and John was there flying his RCs. We pulled my plane out, attached the wing to the fuselage, put the fuel in the gas tank, and we were ready. John came over, and we got the engine started. He then taxied it down to the end of the runway, opened the throttle, and seconds later it was airborne. He flew it around a bit to check everything out.

John had adjusted the trim setting on the elevator through the radio transmitter to the full nose low position, but if he released the control stick to neutral, it would still go nose up and climb. He told me he needed to land, so we could adjust the control rod to put the elevator in a position where it would stay level when you release the control stick. John landed; we made the adjustment and went airborne again. He flew it around a bit more and was happy with it.

At that point, John handed me the transmitter. I took it and over controlled a bit at first but got fairly acquainted with how it handled. One thing I didn't like right away was the fact that it just had a rudder and didn't have ailerons. Ailerons are the control surfaces on the trailing edge of the wing that move up and down to make the aircraft bank. The rudder is the moving control surface on the back of the vertical stabilizer that basically makes the nose of the aircraft point to the left or right.

Controlling the aircraft is pretty easy when it is going away from you. If you want to turn left, you push the stick to the left. If the airplane is coming toward you, everything is the opposite. If you want it to go to your left, you have to push the stick to your right. That was a bit hard to adapt to.

After about ten minutes of my flying, trying to learn and become proficient, John stated that the fuel was probably getting low, so we needed to land. He talked me through it, and I was having quite a challenge. I was having trouble making the turns with just the rudder, and I was too high as I got closer. Being too high and not lined up with the runway doesn't work. OK, it's time to execute the go-around. I went back to full throttle, climbed, and proceeded to make the rectangular traffic pattern to come back and do it again.

This time I got a little closer to being lined up with the runway but wound up setting it down in the field quite a distance out. At least it didn't hit nose first; after it touched down, though, the nose gear got caught by a tall clump of vegetation, and the immediate deceleration flipped it over on its back. I went running, to pick it up and see what I had done to it. Thank goodness, nothing got broken.

John flew his aircraft a while and then came back to assist me again. This time I did the takeoff, which was fairly easy, but the approach and landing were giving me a tough time again. That day went pretty well, but John had to come to the rescue a couple of times.

The next week I did much better and actually got a couple of landings on the runway instead of in the grass. I was out there every Sunday afternoon for several months and got pretty proficient with it. I had seen a number of the guys crash some planes over those months and was dreading the inevitable. I knew my time was coming; and sure enough, I was just about to bring it in and land, but it ran out of gas.

That happened almost every day to someone. You just do a controlled glide to get it down safely. Unfortunately for me, I was too low and too far out. I got a little too slow; it stalled and dropped, doing some considerable damage. With a lot of work, it could have been repaired, but I was ready for one that had the ailerons that would make tighter turns and allow me to do some more aerobatic maneuvers such as the aileron roll.

The next RC model was a bit larger than the old one, and it actually had a name that I thought didn't match it, Das Ugly Stik. Dad and I got it built in about a month, and I had a great time flying it. It had a Gold Top O.S. Max .60 engine. I had a few minor mishaps with it that year, which required some minor repairs, but it really was a good one.

III

My sophomore year at Tascosa High School ended. I would no longer be a Rebel, and Johnny Reb would no longer be my school mascot. Around three years prior to this, the original Amarillo High School had caught fire and burned to the ground. They rebuilt it out at the southwest side of town fairly close to my home, and it was going to open at the beginning of the next school year.

The next year as a junior, I would be a Sandie at Amarillo High School, the home of the Golden Sandstorm. Everything was brand new, and what a treat it was having air conditioning in August, September, and May, which was lacking at Tascosa. My favorite class was Texas history, and I was taking my third year of Spanish. It's really a shame that I can't remember more of that after taking it for three years. That year was also a lot of the same activities and work that I mentioned.

Fairly early in the year, Michael Mabrey and I learned about a new Explorer

Scout group focused on aviation. The leader was a gentleman, Mr. Porterfield, who worked for Braniff International Airlines at the Amarillo International Airport. He and his wife were a real blessing in the time they spent with us, showing us some potential careers in aviation.

We met at the Amarillo Airport, and one of the first memorable events was when they took us out to meet the crew of the Braniff flight that had just arrived. The captain talked to us and took us down to the aircraft that they had just brought in from Dallas Love Field. Michael and I couldn't wait to get in the cockpit and see all the switches, gauges, and instruments. Someone took a picture of us up there, and I don't think we had a clue what was going on, but the next day our picture showed up in the Amarillo Globe Times.

Who in the world would have thought that twenty years later, I would be a captain on that very type of aircraft, the Boeing 727? If someone had suggested that could happen, I would have probably said, "I wish," and just laughed it off. At this point in life, I had actually been reading the Bible a considerable amount but was still pretty clueless as to the possibility of God's blessings if we put our focus on Jesus.

I really enjoyed that group, and I made an acquaintance who would be very helpful to me in the future. The most memorable part of it was the adventure for our group that Mr. Porterfield came up with. He planned out a trip for our group to fly to Dallas and see some of Braniff's facilities. That was a great adventure. We got to see the training center for their pilots and flight attendants along with the aircraft maintenance hangar at Love Field. The highlight for me was seeing the simulators and everything where the pilots trained.

IV

There was some incredibly eye-opening stuff toward the end of the year at my previous school, Tascosa. There was a major eruption, and it all brought back a very bad memory for me of that snowy day when I got kicked in the face. At the time, I didn't have a clue as to what was behind it; neither did any of my former classmates at Tascosa, based on what I read many years later on the anniversary of the event.

It turned out to be over the school mascot, the Southern emphasis, the Confederate flag, and the Dixie fight song that was done at games. To us, the White students, it had zero significance to race. There are always a few bad apples in any group of people, but I personally didn't encounter a single White student that year with a racist bone in their body.

As a matter of fact, my class that year was happy to elect Ed Dowd, one of the Black students, as president of our class. At the end of the day, though, it pretty much boiled down to one thing. These students were being forced by the Federal Government to ride a bus to a school that had a mascot they saw as someone who went to war to keep them in slavery.

In all of that, I learned that we need to always be willing to listen and care for our fellow man's concerns, and it appears that is what took place when this came to a head. In keeping, we need to not hold people accountable for the sins of their fathers. On my end, that couldn't even have been in the equation since my family didn't get here until around 1900.

Jesus summed it up when He was asked for the greatest commandment. He said, "Love the Lord your God with all your heart, with all your soul and with all your mind. Second, love your neighbor as yourself." If we would just meditate on that and how He said we are to conduct ourselves in all areas of our lives, what a change and joy that would be!

V

The best part for me toward the end of that junior year was turning sixteen, finally getting my driver's license, getting my car, and taking flying lessons again. At the end of April, I made a beeline out to Amarillo Flying Service. What a joy it was to see Kimble, tell him I was sixteen, and I was ready to proceed.

He informed me that I needed to get my student pilot certificate from an aviation medical examiner (AME). He gave me a list of AMEs; I picked one and scheduled an appointment. He was basically a retired doctor who still did aviation medical exams out of his home in Puckett Place, which was the subdivision adjacent to my school, Amarillo High.

I showed up for the appointment, and he gave me the student pilot certificate application to fill out. Part of the application included the student pilot certificate itself, which the AME would fill out and issue to the student pilot at the completion of the exam. The doctor gave me explicit instruction on how to fill out the application. He was emphatic, giving the indication that he would not be happy if he had to discard the application and start with a new one because of my making an error in filling it out.

Goodness, that put me on edge right off. I guess the fact that the application included a numbered Federal Aviation Administration (FAA) Student Pilot-Medical Certificate meant he probably had to account for every one of those to the FAA and wouldn't like having to document what happened to one that was discarded.

I proceeded to fill out the application, which was very thorough in getting all of my personal information. The tedious part was the section that we all love to fill out when we go to a new doctor, the part that asks our medical history and has the mile-long laundry list of potential ailments that we have experienced. I went through the list and checked no on everything but two of the items.

I was thinking everything was good, no problem, right? Wrong! The doctor came back in, sat down, and examined the application. He looked up rather quickly and with a stern voice and facial expression asked, "You have hay fever and asthma?"

I said, "I have hay fever occasionally, but I have not had any asthma in three years or more."

He told me how serious asthma was and that he could not grant me the student pilot certificate without a letter from my doctor that I had not experienced asthma or been treated for it, just as I stated, in the last three years.

I got an appointment with my doctor and gave him the letter from the AME. We talked, and he told me that it was fortunate that my asthma had gone away. He had a letter typed up for me, I went back to the AME, and gave him the letter.

He did the rest of the exam for me to receive the third-class medical certificate. He tested my vision and hearing, listened to my heart, checked my blood pressure, and checked my urine sample. He also told me that if I were experiencing any hay fever that I could not take any medications for it that were not approved by the FAA and that if my head were completely stopped up, I should not fly.

He went on to tell me to study the *Airman's Information Manual* closely pertaining to the rules for flight and medical issues. That was a serious revelation pertaining to medical issues and flight safety. It would become quite pertinent in the future.

VI

One month later, May 26, 1974, we were practicing take offs and landings. Kimble had told me this one would be a full stop, so I assumed the lesson was done and we would taxi back to the hangar. I cleared the runway, and as I taxied, he told me to stop and set the parking brake. I did as I was instructed.

He undid his seatbelt, popped his door open, and as he jumped out, he told me to do three take offs and landings and he would see me back in the office. He waved and took off walking. Oh, my God. My heart was in my throat. It was pounding like I had never experienced, and my eyes were probably bugged out about twice their normal amount. Kimble never looked back.

I sat and watched him walk away, and I finally got the courage to release the brake and advance the throttle enough to proceed to taxi the aircraft. As I proceeded back to the end of the runway, I was thinking, *This can't be for real. I have only had about three hours of instruction since the lessons back in 1971.*

I was so nervous!

I got to the end of the runway and turned the Cessna 150 into the wind to do the run-up and to check the magnetos and carburetor heat. I then did the 360-degree turn to check for other aircraft in the traffic pattern, grabbed the mic, and announced, "Tradewind traffic, Cessna 6638G is taking the active for takeoff, Runway 17." I pulled out on the runway, applied the power, kept it down the center line, and went airborne.

I flew the runway heading and held the best rate-of-climb airspeed, which was 70-75 mph to an altitude of 400 feet above ground level (AGL), and at that point I made a non-standard right turn to do the crosswind leg of the traffic pattern. As I continued to climb to the traffic pattern altitude, which was a non-standard 1,000-feet AGL. I made the right turn to fly the downwind leg.

When I came perpendicular to the end of the runway, I engaged the carburetor heat and pulled the throttle to idle, and shortly after that I made the right turn for the base leg of the pattern. The next thing was the turn to final and land.

After touchdown, I immediately applied the power, disengaged the carburetor heat, took off, and did it all over again for a total of three times. I taxied in, parked the plane, opened the door, and got out; my legs felt like rubber. I had drenched my shirt with perspiration. When I walked in the office, Kimble and everyone came and shook my hand, congratulating me on a job well done.

Wow! What a thrill! Kimble signed my logbook; I jumped in my car and couldn't wait to get home and tell Mom and Dad. I flew into the driveway and went running into the house. When I told them what had just happened, they were as stunned as I had been. They gave me a hug and congratulated me. What a way to end my junior year in high school.

VII

Over the summer I made a lot of trips to the airport, becoming a bit of an "airport bum." I loved to go out and just watch the airplanes take off and land and sit in some of them and think about flying them. Whenever I had some money to spare, I would take a lesson. I also studied up and took my private pilot written test. I had to go out to the flight service station, which was located at the main airport, Amarillo International, to take that. It had sixty questions going into everything from Federal Aviation Regulations, to weight and balance, to weather, and to aerodynamics.

As I was about to get in my car to go home, I glanced over and saw a TWA Boeing 727 taxiing out for takeoff. I had to run over to get a better position to watch. It was incredible. As far away as that thing was when it passed by where I was standing, it was like I could feel the ground shake below my feet from the thrust those three engines were creating, and I had to hold my ears. It was so loud. Wow, what a dream, to be up there advancing the throttles on that thing knowing the power that was at the tips of your fingers.

Around the middle of summer, I did my first cross-country flight with Pat Oles as my instructor. I remember so well how exciting it was. I had to learn all about the sectional chart, how to plot the course, check the weather, figure the fuel requirement for the trip, and everything else that it entailed. I was thrilled with every part of it and couldn't wait to do it. We were going from Amarillo to Childress, Texas, from there to Plainview, Texas, and then back to Amarillo.

I had to lay out the sectional and draw the line from the departure airport to the destination airport. Then I took the plotter and laid it where the line crossed over a longitudinal line on the chart to determine the true course. At that point, I used the E6B computer to figure out what the wind correction angle would be, based on the winds aloft report at my cruise altitude, which I got from the FSS. That would give me my true heading.

Then I had to look on the chart to find the magnetic variation component along my route of flight. I would add or subtract that to arrive at my magnetic heading. The next step was to add or subtract the compass deviation, displayed under the magnetic compass in the aircraft, to arrive at the compass heading that I would hold on the flight. After that, I would check the weather, file the flight plan with the FSS, jump in the plane with Mr. Oles, and get 'er done.

A little over a week later, Kimble examined my flight plan, checked all of my work, signed me off, and sent me to do my very first solo cross-country flight. I went from Amarillo to Dalhart, Texas, to Tucumcari, New Mexico, then back to Amarillo. I have to admit, I was a bit nervous on that trip. There weren't many landmarks to see along that route to make sure I was on course.

VIII

Back at school, Michael and I would usually run to McDonalds for lunch, and talk about flying and who knows what else. Actually, I do remember one thing that I talked about extensively. I had read a book that I found at Hasting's Books and Records, *The Late Great Planet Earth,* by Hal Lindsey.

The book delved into the subject of biblical eschatology, which pertains to the last days prior to the second coming of Jesus Christ. God used that book to prompt me to keep watch for our Lord's return as we have been commanded to as Christians by Him in scripture. I have been studying God's word and keeping an eye out ever since. I don't think Michael found much interest in it, but I couldn't resist talking about it.

On those trips to McDonalds we were always waited on by a young girl who caught my attention. Her name was "Cindy," and after several months of seeing her there every day, I finally got the courage to ask her out. We started dating quite regularly, and I really enjoyed spending time with her. I learned that she was two years older than I was, and she and her family had just moved to Amarillo, from Clovis, New Mexico. I found her to be a strong Christian, and I truly appreciated that.

IX

A major issue at the end of the year was the fact that I didn't have a clue what I would do the next year about my education. Cindy gave me a good deal of help and guidance in that. We picked up the catalog of classes and potential associate degree programs at Amarillo College, home of the Badgers.

As we looked through it, I discovered that they had an associate degree program in aviation management. We thought that should have some good potential since I enjoyed flying and aviation so much. Cindy's help really put me in a place that would be a major benefit to my upcoming career, which I didn't have a clue about at the time. I thank her immensely for that.

Graduation day came and was really a joy. Because Dad had not had the opportunity to graduate from high school, he was very happy and proud of me, as was Mom. Cindy was very happy for me as well. As I sat there in the coliseum, I thought about all that had transpired over those twelve years.

Those years ran from the Little Red School House, where Mom sent me to first grade at barely the age of five, to graduation at Amarillo High School twelve years later, at the age of seventeen years and two months. I thought of all those hours that Michael and I had spent on the phone helping each other do our algebra homework, riding motorcycles, flying, and becoming best friends. Our friendship had become a close bond, and I knew in my heart that regardless of our senior year's end, he would be my forever friend.

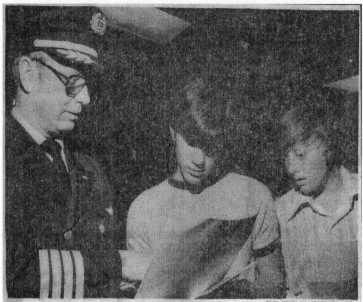

—Staff Photo by JOHN EBLING

Braniff Official Briefs Scouts

MAR 2 1 1973

Capt. W. O. Heivel, executive adviser of Braniff International in Dallas, explains operation of an Explorer Scout Troop in the aviation field. Participating in the orientation session Tuesday for Amarillo area teens interested in the Troop were Michael Mabry of 3909 Justin, center, and Jay Straub of 4836 Hillside.

Jay and Michael checking out the 727-flight deck at an Aviation Explorer Scout meeting

BUSHLAND, BADGERS, AND BEECHCRAFT

I

During that summer I had done next to zero in the flight arena. Around the end of July, I went out just to do a few take-offs and landings. When I completed that and walked back in the office, Kimble said I needed to do another solo cross country. So, the next time he signed me off to go from Amarillo to Gage, Oklahoma, to Elkhart, Kansas, and back to Amarillo.

Everything went well on the Amarillo-to-Gage leg. I landed, got my logbook signed, and took off for Elkhart. I held the magnetic heading I had computed, and all of the landmarks on the sectional chart seemed to be right where they should be. But as the destination city should have been coming into view right in the flight path as it was on the chart, it didn't.

I headed for the town that appeared to be closest to where it should be, and when I got there, I could see that the airport wasn't in the right area in relation to the town. Fortunately, the town grain elevator had the town name on it, so I found it on the chart, and easily found my way to my true destination.

That was embarrassing but at least I got there, a little bit late, but unscathed. I got my logbook signed, and the leg from Elkhart to Amarillo was a piece of cake with no problem.

A week or two later, I made one more solo cross country to get the required cross-country hours to obtain my private pilot certificate. I flew to Lubbock, Texas, just down and back. In the next two weeks, Kimble handed me over to Mario, another flight instructor, to give me the final lessons prior to the check ride.

After I completed that, Kimble flew with me for the final progress check, and then Mario found me competent to take the Private Pilot practical test under Part 61 of the Federal Aviation Regulations.

At the end of August 1975, Kenneth Brown gave me the test and passed me. Wow, what a thrill. Seventeen years old, and I had my private pilot certificate. I could now rent a plane and take a passenger with me. A day or two after receiving my license, my first passenger was my mom. She wasn't that comfortable, so it was a short flight, but at least she did it.

Over the years I had gone all over Tradewind Airport looking at all the different types of aircraft. All my time had been in Cessna Aircraft, and I wanted to get checked out in some other types.

So, I immediately went to the other flight school to get checked out in a Rockwell Commander 112A, which was an aircraft with retractable landing gear. The next day I rented it, and Cindy and I flew to Clovis, New Mexico, where she had lived for several years before they moved to Amarillo.

II

Now it was time to head back to school, this time: college. I showed up at AC ready to buckle down and give it my best. I was going to be taking English, Aviation Electronics, Speech, and a number of others for a full load of classes.

Along with school, I was still working at the Agriculture Experiment Station in Bushland, part-time and in a different department where the allergy issues weren't as likely. However, I was running around with a radioactive probe that I had to drop down into pipes in multiple fields around the station.

The probe had a lead shield around it that was quite heavy, and it had an electric cable attached to the probe. I attached the cable to a monitor that gave readings that I had to record as the probe went deeper and deeper into the ground. I had to wear a badge that monitored my radiation exposure.

The first day of class I ran into "Brent," whom I had met in the Aviation Explorer Post a couple of years prior. What an enlightening and beneficial meeting that was.

I was rather stunned to learn that he was already earning a living at flying, and he was not doing flight instruction. I had pondered getting the flight instructor certificate, but I was pretty certain that teaching was not my strong suit. In talking to him, he was pretty convincing that I didn't have to go that route.

Brent was a year or two older than I, and at the age of eighteen he had earned his commercial license. He said he would be glad to take me along on some of his trips and let me fly to log some time. That was truly a blessing.

Along with the flying career he had going, he had started skydiving. I, however, was of the view, "There's no way I'm going to jump out of a perfectly good airplane."

Fortunately, Brent got me introduced to the guys in the Amarillo Skydivers and helped me with another avenue for building flight hours. On the weekends I would go out to Buffalo Airport, just south of Amarillo, and load the guys into the Cessna 172.

I would climb up to an altitude of around 10,000 ft. MSL, which was about 6,500 ft. above the ground for them to jump out. Once that was done, I would do a rapid descent to save money on the per-hour aircraft rental cost.

Within a month Mom got her courage up and decided she would like to fly to Lubbock, so I took her, Michael, and Cindy in the Rockwell Commander. Dad came on board and asked for a demonstration of my skills a few days later.

Things were going so fast. Brent convinced me I needed to get my multi-engine rating so I could go with him and log some time. Since he was not a flight instructor, I couldn't log the time that I actually flew unless I were multi-engine rated.

III

One month later, after about ten hours of instruction in a Piper Seneca, Bob Meredith gave me the check ride and passed me, and I had the multi-engine rating on my license. I was now a private pilot, airplane, single and multi-engine-land. Back then there were only three types of licenses, private, commercial, and airline transport. The different categories were airplane, rotorcraft, glider, and so on. The classes were single-engine land, single-engine sea, multi-engine land, and multi-engine sea.

While all of this was taking place, I was taking a full load at school and trying to spend as much time as possible with Cindy, whom I had proposed to. She was a very kind-hearted and sweet girl who was very supportive of me and enjoyed spending her spare time with me, as I did with her.

Most of all, her faith meant a lot to me. Our plan was to get married when I finished the program at AC, and my hope was by then to be where Brent was, making a living at flying.

I made an A in English, which, I was told, wasn't all that easy at AC, since one of the professors wrote the textbook. I did well in speech, which still shocks me since I always dreaded speaking in front of the entire class. I think the fact that I had my pilot's license and made a lot of my speeches based on aviation-related things helped.

In November I made my first long cross-country flight with Brent in a twin-engine Beechcraft Baron. We flew from Amarillo to Green River, Utah, then to Grand Junction, Colorado to get fuel, and back to Amarillo.

At this point, I had a total of around 80 hours of flying time and only about three hours of that was simulated instrument flying. Brent let me fly the leg from Grand Junction to Amarillo completely.

For an entire hour we were in the clouds on instruments, and we were in icing conditions. I was a bit nervous, but everything went well. When we broke out into the clear, I was relieved. But that gave me a real boost, having just spent an entire hour hand flying an airplane solely on instruments, holding my altitude, and staying on course in icing conditions, no less.

IV

After the first of the year, in early February 1976, I went to the next flight school to get checked out in another aircraft, the Beechcraft V-tail Bonanza. I was doing everything I could to build my flight time.

After I got checked out in the Bonanza, I knew two guys who wanted to rent the Bonanza and have me fly them to Wichita Falls, Texas. Even though they wanted to pay the whole cost of the aircraft rental, I couldn't do that. The Federal Aviation Regulations require that a private pilot has to pay his *pro rata* share of the aircraft rental. I was more than happy to pay my share to be able to get the experience and add more time to my logbook.

In March, my flight hours were actually sufficient to get my instrument rating, and while I did study up once again and pass the instrument rating written test, I didn't want to start the actual flying lessons until the end of the school year.

I was taking a safety pilot to watch for other aircraft, any chance I got. Having them with me allowed me to fly "under the hood," which was a device worn that blocked my vision of everything but the instrument panel. We would go out and do ILS, BACKCOURSE, and VOR approaches at Amarillo International along with NDB approaches to Tradewind.

Back then it required 200 hours of total time, of which 100 hours were acting as pilot-in-command, to get that instrument rating. From what I understand, the requirements have been changed, and it's somewhat easier now.

About this same time, Brent got a new job flying a Cessna 414 for a company out of Pampa, Texas, so I would go with him many times and fly the aircraft. He would give me the left seat when his passengers had been dropped off somewhere, and it was just the two of us.

Another wonderful memory, at this time, was getting to fly my former boss from the Texas Agriculture Experiment Station, Gary Peterson, from Amarillo up to his hometown of Perryton, Texas. His mother and father still lived up there on the family farm. I really enjoyed getting to go out with him to meet them.

V

The first part of July I started instrument rating training in a Beechcraft Sundowner. Michael and my friend from church, Louis, whom I had encouraged to get his private pilot license, were my safety pilot several times when I practiced.

One month after starting the training, toward the end of August, I took the check ride, and H. R. Costello passed me, giving me the rating. About that time, I also took and passed the commercial pilot written test.

In September, Jim Sheppard gave me my flight prep for the commercial check ride, and Bob Meredith gave me the check ride. We got in a Cessna 150 for the commercial pilot, single-engine certification, and then we jumped in the Piper Seneca for the commercial pilot multi-engine certification.

I was on cloud nine. I was filled with enthusiasm as he filled out my commercial certificate, and Mr. Meredith was very encouraging, which gave me a tremendous boost. Here I was, barely eighteen years old, at the beginning of my second year at Amarillo College, with my commercial pilot certificate and my instrument rating. It couldn't be any better. My grades were good. I was flying every chance I got to build more time and was looking for any chance I could get to fly for hire.

I was also glad to donate some time to a useful cause. A special flight that autumn was to Taos, New Mexico with the Civil Air Patrol in search of a lost aircraft. Unfortunately, we never located that aircraft during that trip to help the family and friends get closure on what had happened.

VI

After the first of the year, when class started again, I made a new friend, Phil Atkinson, who had enrolled at Amarillo College. He was a mutual friend of Brent's, and he had an interest in learning to fly. They both had gone to Canyon High School in Texas. I found it shocking to learn that had I just lived on the other side of my street when I was in high school, I would have been making the seventeen-mile daily trek to Canyon High as well. Phil and I became very close friends. One of the things he still remembers is how I helped him learn the crosswind landing technique, which is something you have to be very good at up in Amarillo where the wind never seems to quit blowing.

The major event that took place very early in the year was being hired for my first flying job. Praise the Lord. There was a new company starting up to do infrared photography of farmland to reveal where there was damage to crops from insects and lack of water.

I initially flew around with the manager while they were contracting with the farmers for this service. We did that marketing via the crop dusters all over the Texas Panhandle.

Once March arrived, I was flying many hours per month with a photographer in a single-engine Cessna 210.

I would fly up to the field, slow the aircraft down significantly, and line up so that we were flying parallel to the field. Just before we came up parallel to the crops, we would pop the window open on the photographer's side, and as we flew along, she would snap the infrared photos.

After we completed the day's shoot, we would return to Amarillo, go to the office, and ship the film to Lubbock. There the film would be developed; all of the pictures would be evaluated, and a drawing of the field would be done.

The drawings would show where there was insect and drought damage. The printouts showing the potential damage would then be sent to the farmers so they could treat the problem.

While all of that was going on, I was still taking, pretty much, a full load of classes at Amarillo College. One of the classes in the curriculum was basically a ground school class to prep for the FAA written test for the instrument rating that I already had on my license.

I probably should have tried to take a CLEP exam to get credit for the class. It was rather humorous, though, that the instructor in the class knew I had the instrument rating on my license. He had something come up and asked me to be his substitute teacher for one class, which I did.

The sophomore year came to a close, and I graduated with honors at AC with an AD in Aviation Management. That was a relief. Now I could truly devote more time to Cindy and the life we had ahead of us.

WEDDING BELLS TO
MAYDAY-MAYDAY-MAYDAY

I

Just a little over two weeks later, June 17, 1977, Cindy and I had our wedding ceremony at her parents' home. It was very small with just close family. I was so happy, and my desire was to provide a good and joyful life for Cindy as we went forward in our lives. We had purchased a new mobile home and rented a space in a very nice mobile home park southwest of Amarillo. We went to our new home and celebrated our new union as husband and wife.

The very next day we jumped in Cindy's yellow Beetle to head for Red River, New Mexico for a short honeymoon. Once again, I was so happy and thrilled with what we had in store, but I was really wishing we could have stayed longer and had more time to relax and enjoy the time together, just us. As it always happens, though, as soon as you get home, you have to hit the ground running at work. Actually, Cindy hit the ground. I took to the sky.

Several months prior, Brent had been hired by a big company in Amarillo that owned and operated a twin-engine Beechcraft Queen Air, a single-engine Cessna, and a Cessna Citation Jet. Sometime in July, he told me there was a weekend ground school being conducted in Denver Colorado to prepare for the written test for the flight engineer certificate. He also said to stand a chance of getting hired by an airline you have to have that written test under your belt.

He wanted me to rent a Cessna 210 at Amarillo Flying Service where my company was renting them to get us there and to go to the class. I didn't feel real comfortable doing it, financially or schedule-wise, and I didn't really think I had a snowball's chance of getting hired at an airline.

However, with all the help Brent had been to me and his career-savviness, I thought I probably should do it. Phil had talked about going along as well, since he had lived in Denver for several years and would like to go back for a visit.

We flew up to Denver, went through the two-day class, and took the test. Boy, that was a doozy! I had done really well on all of my previous written tests scoring in the 90s, maybe a high 80 on one of them, but I was really concerned that this was not going to be a pass. Learning about all of the aircraft systems and how to figure weight and balance and calculate all the performance problems for the Boeing 727 in two days was something else.

By the time we got to the airport to get ready for the flight home, the weather wasn't looking good at all. I could see thunderstorms starting to roll in. I checked the weather, and to be in an aircraft with no weather radar to help avoid the stuff, it was "no go" in my book. Severe thunderstorms were almost to the field and extended a good distance along our route of flight. If that weren't bad enough, the forecast didn't look very good until late in the night.

I told Brent we couldn't go and had to wait.

He gave me a funny look and said, "We're going!"

I said, "No."

He informed me that he had an early-morning departure the next day and that we were going. He demanded the keys and demanded that he was in the left seat flying the aircraft. He had flown the leg from Amarillo to Denver, and it was my turn to fly the leg going back home. I should not have caved in, but with all the help he had been to me, I did and handed him the keys.

As we went down the runway in heavy rain with lightning flashing all around us, I was quite angry and half scared. On top of that, I was the one responsible for that airplane. It was rented under my name, and I was very concerned. I could just see us getting that airplane beaten to a pulp with hail, or even worse, a downburst, now known as a wind shear, driving that Cessna into the ground after we became airborne.

I didn't have anything to say all the way back to Amarillo, and neither did he. When we parked the plane he got out, tossed me the key, and took off walking without saying a word, no apology, no nothing. Phil sensed the tension but was still a newbie in aviation and didn't realize how dangerous what just took place had been. As I drove home, I didn't really know what to do with that.

I just tried to refresh my memory on things that I had read in the Bible to give me comfort, and I reflected back on how thankful I had been and gave praise to Jesus Christ for the blessing He gave me of graduating with honors. My grades had never been close to that good back in high school and prior. To top it off, I passed that flight engineer written test by two points. Praise Him.

Not long after all that, Brent was hired at one of the major airlines. Our paths never crossed, and I didn't see him or speak to him again until about nine years later.

My job had been a real blessing. It, along with some other side trips, had added over 600 hours to my flying time in nine months. Unfortunately, the business was losing lots of money, and the company had to let me go in September.

Oh no! Here we were, married less than six months, and I'm out of work except for the part-time office work I was doing on the weekends at the flight school.

II

I immediately started hunting for a new flying-related job. I went to the manager of the flight school who had been my flight instructor back when I was working on my Instrument rating. I practically begged him to allow me to do an occasional charter flight, which would require him to give me a check ride to qualify me. He wore quite a number of hats: instructor, manager, and examiner. I had the minimum hours required to be legal to do that, and I told him I would gladly pay for the time on the aircraft if he would give me the check ride and just give me a chance.

Now, I was just trying to support Cindy and me financially and was doing everything I could to make that work. The instructor finally agreed to give me the check ride, but he informed me that there wouldn't be much coming my way. I would be at the bottom of the ladder.

I went out to do the preflight inspection on the twin-engine Beechcraft Baron, and he came out to observe me as I did it. When I was done with the inspection, we climbed in, taxied out, and proceeded with the check ride. After we took off, he told me to call Amarillo Approach control and ask them for a clearance to do a VOR-DME Approach to Runway 22 at Amarillo International.

I was cleared to go directly to the VOR and was cleared for the approach. I flew to the VOR, crossed it, flew the outbound radial, did the procedure turn, caught the inbound radial, and continued the approach as published. At the final approach fix, I initiated the descent down to the minimum descent altitude.

When I reached the missed approach point, he just told me to go ahead and take the hood off and tell approach we are going back to Tradewind Airport. I did as he requested. We flew back to Tradewind, and he told me to just enter the traffic pattern, land, taxi in and shut it down. I was really confused. I thought that can't be an entire check ride with just one approach and you're done.

Well, I was right. I shut the engines down and he turned to me and said, "Do you know how far you went past the VOR before you were established inbound?" I couldn't remember exactly so I said, "No." He gave me the exact number which was over ten miles and then informed me that ten miles was the maximum allowed before you are procedure turn inbound.

He told me, "You failed the check ride."

That was pretty much it, no offer to redo the check ride later or anything.

I was devastated. Every previous check ride went well, and I was complimented by the examiners. I had passed every oral exam and written test with flying colors—well, the 71 on the FE written wasn't flying colors, but that one doesn't negate how well I had done on all the others. I got in the car to go home and was really down in the dumps. I actually had a few tears trickle down my face as I drove home. Here I was, nineteen years old, out of work, married, and not feeling really good about the situation.

I went home, and Cindy wasn't back from work yet. I just sat there on the couch and asked the Lord, "What now?" I was sitting there thinking about the approach plate that gives you all of the parameters of the approach. It popped in my head how nearly every approach I had ever seen in my short time of instrument flying has a 10-mile restriction between the final approach fix and completing the procedure turn inbound.

Wait a minute. As I sat there and thought and thought some more, the light bulb went off. That particular approach allowed fifteen miles, and while I can't remember now the exact distance that he told me I went past the VOR, it was well under fifteen. I guess in the stress of the moment, since ten miles is the standard, I just thought that was correct and apparently the examiner did as well, along with not really wanting to give me the opportunity to start with.

I ran out the door, jumped in my car, and headed back to the airport. I walked in and caught him in his office. I asked him, "Could you tell me again how far I went out before I was procedure turn inbound?"

He gave the number again.

I said, "Would you mind getting out the approach plate for that approach so we could take a look at it?"

He gave me a funny look and said, "Sure." He got to that approach plate and there it was, fifteen miles. He looked up with a much different expression on his face this time. I think he probably had to swallow really hard to tell me that I hadn't failed after all. He told me we could finish the check ride the next day if I were good with that.

I said, "That would be great."

I went home and told Cindy what had happened, and we were both thankful that the Lord had saved the day by bringing that approach plate back into my mind, allowing me to go and show the examiner. I went out the next day and passed the check ride. After that, I started searching everywhere I knew to search, and no flying jobs were to be found. Almost a month went by, and nothing.

III

As a few more weeks passed, I was starting to look for anything I could do to help pay the bills. I also put in an application at Santa Fe Railway, in hopes that potentially I could get into a career as a railroad engineer. My Uncle Clinton had been an engineer for Santa Fe his entire career. One of my flight instructors also had a full-time job as a railroad engineer. I thought that might be a possibility, but I really wanted to be a pilot. That was in my blood. I was really struggling with what to do.

I was about to the point of going back out to the Agriculture Experiment Station to see if I could at least get some part-time work and hopefully find another part-time job to keep us going. I was sitting at home with all of this going through my mind, and the phone rang. I answered, and the man on the line introduced himself as Leonard Hudson.

He informed me that he had an oilfield related business in Pampa, Texas and that he had just purchased a twin-engine Beechcraft Queen Air from a friend there who had upgraded to a Beechcraft King Air. He said another pilot that he knew there in Pampa had recommended me as a candidate for the position.

At that point, I was asked if I could come to Pampa for an interview. I asked when would be good for him, and he said, "How about this afternoon?"

I said, "Absolutely, I can head that way and be there in a little over two hours."

"See you then," he said.

Wow! I jumped up, ran and took a shower, put on my suit, and ran out the door to drive to Pampa. I walked in the office building and introduced myself. The lady at the desk told me to have a seat and said she would tell Mr. Hudson I was there. He came out right away and invited me into his office.

Once I was seated, he proceeded to tell me a little about his business and how he had survived the big downturn in the oilfield several years prior. He went on to share how well things were in the business now. He also told me that he had his private pilot license but had no instrument rating or multi-engine rating. He had no interest in flying an aircraft like the one he had just purchased.

He then asked me about myself. He wanted to know how in the world someone nineteen years old had gotten interested in flying and achieved the licenses and ratings that I had. Along with that, he asked about my previous job and what I had flown to get the multi-engine time. I went through everything I've already shared with you.

He asked me if I were willing to move to Pampa from Amarillo. I guess he had heard that Brent didn't mind the one-hour drive and would not move to Pampa, since he was well acquainted with Brent's former boss.

I told him I had no problem moving to Pampa, and I informed him that I was living in a new mobile home that I had recently purchased and would have it moved to Pampa as soon as possible if he were to hire me. The next thing he did was run a salary figure at me and ask if I would be willing to come and work for that amount.

I told him I would be quite satisfied with that.

I was thinking that the interview was about to come to an end. I was sure that Mr. Hudson was going to tell me that he would let me know what his decision was in a few days, and I expected he would be interviewing some more candidates for the position.

He stood up and said, "Let's go out here so you can give Martha all of your information to get you on the payroll."

Wow! I was shocked. I almost couldn't believe it.

I thanked him and told him how much I looked forward to serving as his pilot. I sat down with Martha and filled out all the paperwork. As that got wrapped up, I asked her where nearby mobile home parks might be. She told me about a couple, and I drove by to take a look at them before I left town.

As I drove home, I was so thankful, happy, and just stunned really. I thanked the Lord over and over, and I couldn't wait to tell Cindy. When I got home, she was home from work, and I jumped out of the car, went running to the door, opened it, and proceeded to tell her everything that had happened. She was very supportive.

IV

We jumped in the car to go share it with my parents. When we got there and I proceeded to tell them, I was shocked that my dad was not happy. He really tried to talk me out of it. I couldn't believe his reaction, but I just had to stand firm and try to reason with him on the good and the blessing in this. Dad and I had a great father-son relationship, and I guess he felt like I was moving to another continent even though we were only moving sixty miles. Mom pretty much kept quiet, but I could sense that she was fairly supportive in it. As we continued to talk, Dad finally ceased in his total rejection of it, but I could tell he still didn't like it.

When we got to Cindy's parents and shared the news, it was met fairly well. I could see that her mom was not really happy with it, but she didn't display any opposition to it. Her dad was always quiet, but he seemed supportive. So, at the end of the evening we went home and talked about the next leg of our journey in life. I felt such a relief and was so thankful to the Lord for giving me this opportunity.

The next day, I had to go get checked out in the aircraft that I was going to be flying for Mr. Hudson. The Beechcraft Queen Air he owned was pressurized, which was a bit unusual for that model. I had actually flown as co-pilot a few times in an unpressurized Queen Air for a company in Amarillo.

As Paul Lloyd, who was the pilot for the previous owner of the Queen Air, was teaching me about the aircraft, he shared with me that there were only forty-seven of the pressurized model produced from 1965–1969 because of the high price and the low useful load of the aircraft.

Basically, once you topped off the fuel tanks, you were a bit limited on passenger and luggage weight. From what I recall, six adults, pilot included, and luggage were right at the max gross weight. That left an empty seat that could usually not be occupied.

After Paul showed me how to do the preflight inspection, we got in and flew my passengers to Oklahoma City and back for my aircraft checkout. As we sat at the fixed base operator in Oklahoma City, waiting for our passengers to return, Paul went through the operating manual of the aircraft, showing me the critical items that I needed to commit to memory. I was elated when we got back to Pampa, and Paul told me I had done well.

V

The first major trip, two days after my aircraft checkout, was to Las Vegas with Leonard's son and some of his associates. We arrived, and they told me to get a rental car and meet them at the Las Vegas Hilton. They jumped in a taxi and took off.

I went to the rental car establishment, and when I gave them my driver's license they looked up and said, "We can't rent you a car."

I asked, "Why not?"

They said, "You're not 21 years old."

I said, "You have to be kidding me, I just flew an aircraft in here with four passengers and my boss told me to get a rental car." They basically said they were sorry, but they couldn't change the policy.

So, I had to get a cab, and everyone had a big laugh when I arrived at the hotel and explained what had happened. We only stayed one night and headed back late the next afternoon.

The day after we got back from that trip, I had to delve into getting our mobile home moved from Amarillo to Pampa. I had managed to get the lease signed to get one of the available lots. It wasn't nearly as nice as the place in Amarillo, but I was so thankful that I had another full-time flying job that I felt was fairly secure.

Dad helped me immensely in getting things moved. I was so thankful for him and all of his help. He was truly my best friend at that point in my life and would remain my best friend. Michael had been in Lubbock at Texas Tech and was moving to Weatherford, Oklahoma to get his degree in pharmacy. And while I had developed a very good friendship with Phil, no one could match Dad.

VI

Three weeks into the job, Leonard called me and told me he needed to go to Wichita Falls and Dallas. I checked the weather and called back to tell him it was a go. We flew to Wichita Falls, and I waited at the airport for them to return, to fly the second leg of the trip to Dallas Love Field.

When we got to Dallas, I parked the aircraft at Cooper Airmotive, the FBO. When it was getting close to our approximate departure time, I checked the weather, and it didn't look really good for our potential arrival time in Pampa. It didn't look good for our best potential alternate airport, Amarillo, either.

I filed the flight plan, and since Amarillo International was forecast to be at minimums for the ILS approach, at our time of arrival, I made Childress, Texas the alternate airport. It was forecast to be clear skies at the time we would potentially get there.

Leonard and his associates got to Love Field just after dark. I told him what we were looking at with the weather. We took off, and when we got to Pampa, it wasn't looking good. The weather report at every location close to Pampa was indicating that the cloud base was going to be below minimums for the potential instrument approaches that we would be flying.

I was going to have to fly a non-precision NDB Runway 17 approach to the Pampa Airport. If I broke out of the clouds and saw the airport, I was going to have to break to the right, keep the airport in sight and land back to the north, with the wind being out of the north, while maintaining the minimum descent altitude for a circling approach, which was right at 400 feet above the ground, in the pitch black night sky.

I flew the approach, got down to minimums, and when I reached the missed approach point, I could see absolutely nothing. I executed the missed approach procedure and contacted Albuquerque Center, which is the air route traffic control center that handles the Pampa airspace, requesting a clearance to Childress.

Albuquerque came back and cleared me direct to Childress and gave me the current Childress weather. Fortunately, the skies were clear, but the wind was straight out of the west blowing 40 knots. You've got to be kidding me. The only runway at Childress that was operational at the time ran straight north to south, and the wind was forty knots straight out of the west.

The maximum crosswind component to land our aircraft was twenty-seven knots, so the crosswind component was thirteen knots over the maximum. Here was my first experience with basically having to violate the rules due to an emergency. You're not supposed to exceed those limits, but when you've already flown to an alternate airport and don't have the fuel to go anywhere else, you have to play the hand you've been dealt.

In a crosswind landing, you come down final approach with the nose of the aircraft facing into the wind, so that you can remain lined up with the runway. If the wind is blowing from the right, as it was for me that night, just before you touch down, you apply left rudder to move the nose of the aircraft to the left to line it up with the runway.

At the same time, you do that, you apply right aileron to make the wing bank into the wind, so that it doesn't blow you off into the grass, or dirt, being unable to remain on the runway.

When we were still about thirty miles out, I looked back into the cabin and called out to Leonard to inform him on what was going on, and that it was not going to be a smooth landing. I told him I was going to have to just plant it on the ground as quickly as possible to prevent us from getting blown off the runway, no smooth landing tonight.

As you come down final approach you always line up with the centerline of the runway; you want to touch down in the center, but not tonight. I lined up as close to the far-right side of the runway as possible. I knew that I was going to run out of rudder and be unable to get the nose pointing exactly straight down the runway. And I had to have as much runway to my left as possible to prevent winding up off the pavement in the dirt.

That's exactly how it came down. I planted it firmly on the ground as soon as possible. I touched down at an angle with the nose pointing a little to the right, and the plane was a little left of centerline by the time we were firmly on the ground.

We parked the plane and found a payphone. Leonard knew that a friend had relatives in Childress and called to see if someone could loan us a vehicle to drive to Pampa. The relative loaned us the car, and I drove us to Pampa getting in around 2 a.m. The next day, I drove the vehicle back to Childress and flew the plane back to Pampa.

VII

About two months after that in the middle of January 1978, it was a journey to the New Orleans, Lake Front Airport for Super Bowl XII, Dallas Cowboys vs. Denver Broncos. They typically had a room for me at the same place they were staying but were unable to get me one this time. They told me where my room was, so I got a cab and told the driver where I was going. It turned out to be a place across the river.

As I rode in the cab, I just had an eerie feeling. I had never experienced anything like that, and I was almost feeling a bit apprehensive.

When we pulled up to the motel, not hotel, after he got my suitcase out, the cab driver put his hand on my shoulder and said, "Young man, you can go anywhere you like up and down this street, but do not go one block this way or one block this way." He pointed to the streets that paralleled the one we were on.

Holy Moly! Believe me, I thanked him and took his advice.

I sat there all the next day and just went a short distance to find something to eat. I couldn't even watch the game on TV since it was blocked for local viewing. The next day I was quite glad to get out of there.

I got to the airport a little over two hours prior to our scheduled departure time only to learn some bad news. The FBO was supposed to be providing a sandwich tray that I had called in and ordered, that Leonard had requested I get for them. The sandwich tray was not there, and there was no way they could get it in time for our departure.

Oh my, the next thing you know, my passengers show up an hour early. I had not filled the coffee pot in the aircraft yet, because I wanted it to be fresh. I had not filled the ice chest either, so it wouldn't be half melted when we left.

I told Leonard what happened with the sandwiches, and I went running to get the coffee and ice. He asked me why I wasn't ready. I explained my reasoning and that I didn't expect them to be that early. He wasn't happy with that explanation, and he made that very clear.

He was normally very congenial, but this was turning out to be a bit unpleasant. This certainly brought home that old saying that goes, "The best laid plans of mice and men often go awry." No matter how hard you try to work and plan, something can still go wrong. On the other side of the equation, the other passengers were glad to tell me about the Cowboys whipping up on the Broncos

VIII

Around a month after that trip, Leonard called and said he needed to go to Oklahoma City. There was some winter weather in the mix that day, and I told him I would check the weather and let him know.

There was something I greatly appreciated about him. The day he hired me he told me with great emphasis, "If I ever call you and tell you I need to go somewhere and the weather is unsafe, you tell me it's unsafe. There is no place that I, my family, or my associates will need to be that is worth risking our lives to get there." I had already heard plenty of stories about corporate bosses that didn't see it that way, and it ended in serous accidents and some fatalities.

When I checked the weather, not far to the east of Pampa, and all the way to Oklahoma City, light-to-moderate icing was in the forecast, and the cloud tops were right at 8,000 feet. Our aircraft was certified for flight into known icing conditions thanks to the de-ice and anti-ice equipment that it had.

Also, being pressurized, we would be cruising at 15,000 feet, well above the clouds and icing conditions until the descent and instrument approach into the Wiley Post Airport. That shouldn't be a problem, so I called Leonard and told him I would have the plane ready to depart in an hour and a half.

I called Roy at the airport and asked him to pull the airplane out of the hangar and gave him the amount of fuel that I needed. When I got to the airport, Roy had already brewed a pot of coffee for me to put in as well.

I called to check the weather one more time and filed the flight plan. Leonard showed up with some other passengers, and I was ready to go. We got in, I closed the door, started the engines and proceeded to taxi.

As we taxied, I went through the checklist and paid very close attention to the items pertaining to de-ice and anti-ice equipment. Everything was good. Once the engine oil temp got up, into the green, I did the engine run up, completed the checklist, did the three-sixty turn looking for traffic and made the radio call, "Pampa traffic, November Six Seven Tango is taking the active for take-off runway three five, Pampa." I applied takeoff power, and off we went.

Shortly after departure, climbing through 5,000 feet, I called Albuquerque Center and got our en route clearance. We were in the clear with no clouds during the entire climb to cruise altitude. Albuquerque handed us off to Forth Worth Center, and once we were forty miles from Oklahoma City, Fort Worth handed us off to Oklahoma City Approach. That seemed a little early, I thought. That usually didn't happen until we were about thirty miles out. Oh well.

I called Oklahoma City Approach and gave him the altitude I was at. He came back and told me to descend to 5,000 feet. I didn't want to do that yet. I wanted to stay above the cloud tops at 8,000 feet until I was a quite a bit closer because of the icing potential, and I requested he let me do that.

He came back and said, "Negative, I need you at 5,000 due to airline traffic going into Will Rogers."

I said, "Roger, descending to 5,000."

I entered the clouds and within just a few minutes the ice had built up on the wings to the thickness that required me to cycle the de-ice boots. The interesting thing is that in training they don't tell you exactly how thick the ice needs to be. They just say, that if the ice isn't thick enough and you cycle the boots, it can just create a bubble where the ice doesn't break off and depart the aircraft, and once that bubble is there, you are in trouble.

They also tell you that ice just one quarter inch in thickness can potentially cause a catastrophic aerodynamic problem. So, what's the correct thickness of the ice to cycle the boots? Anybody's guess I presume.

I monitored it very closely, and when it got close to a quarter-inch thick, I hit the switch to cycle the de-ice boots, and absolutely nothing happened: no bubble and no bye-bye to the ice. It appeared that the boots had not inflated at all. How could this be? Everything tested perfectly when I taxied out at Pampa and went through the checklist.

I hit the switch again and nothing. I grabbed the mic, called approach, and told him I needed to climb to get out of the icing conditions.

He came back and said, "I have to have you at 5000 feet for traffic; continue your descent and maintain 5,000 feet."

I came back, declared an emergency, and told him I was initiating my climb to get out of the clouds.

He responded, "Roger, tell me when you're clear of clouds and the altitude you will hold."

Pertaining to the declaration of an emergency, if an emergency situation develops, the pilot in command has ultimate authority, and air traffic control and the FAA have to step aside, even if what you are doing is a violation of a regulation under normal circumstances.

I pushed the throttle up to the climb power setting, raised the nose to initiate the climb, and the aircraft would not climb. *Good Lord!*

I lowered the nose to go back to cruise airspeed and hold the aircraft attitude for level flight, grabbed the mic again and informed Oklahoma City Approach that I was unable to climb and asked them for a heading direct to the Outer Marker for the ILS to runway 17 at Wiley Post Airport.

They said, "Roger," and then gave me the heading to take me directly to the outer marker. Now, that's not how it's typically done. They will normally vector you several miles outside of the outer marker to give you some distance to get established and lined up with the runway that you can't see when you're in the clouds.

The closer you are to the runway, the instrument you are following that lines you up with the runway becomes more sensitive, so it's really necessary to get established on the approach and get stabilized on the heading required due to crosswind some distance out.

I was holding the heading they gave me, and was keeping the nose level with the horizon, on the attitude indicator, to maintain altitude, unfortunately the aircraft would not maintain altitude. It was coming down, and I had no control over it.

I increased the power setting to the redline on the manifold pressure gauge, which was the maximum I could get without doing damage to the engine, in hopes of making it to the airport. The only thing I had control of was the direction the airplane was going; the rate of descent and my altitude were totally out of my control.

Just prior to reaching the outer marker I initiated the turn to line up with the runway that I could not see since we were in the clouds. When we crossed the outer marker, we were exactly at the prescribed crossing altitude, and we were right on the glide slope, and we stayed on the glide slope all the way to touchdown. In the stress of the moment, the significance of all this didn't come to mind.

Once the event was over, I thought about everything. It became very clear to me that the mathematical odds were astronomical of that aircraft going all those miles, with me having no control over the rate of descent, its crossing the marker at the exact prescribed altitude, and coming down the glide slope perfectly all the way to the runway. There had to be a divine intervention in this.

So, we broke out of the clouds at 300 feet with snow reducing the visibility to a little over a half mile. We were lined up with the runway perfectly and exactly on glide slope. I left the power set at max redline all the way to touchdown. I cleared the runway and called ground control for clearance to taxi to the FBO.

As I taxied in, the guide men came out to park me. I watched them as their mouths kind of gaped open, and they were pointing at our aircraft. That puzzled me, but once we got parked and I was able to exit the aircraft and look, I could see why they were so animated.

As I flew the aircraft and taxied in, I could see a lot of ice on the wings, but I was absolutely stunned when I turned to take a look at the entire aircraft.

It was covered from one end to the other with a layer of ice, well over a quarter-inch thick.

There is no telling how much weight that added to the aircraft and how it affected the aerodynamics of the aircraft and the lift of the wings. It was absolutely God's divine intervention that allowed us to survive that ordeal.

I had the FBO put the aircraft in their big heated hangar to melt all of the ice off to make it safe for our departure later in the day to return home. That's if the weather improved and the icing conditions were gone. The weather did improve, and we made it home.

The next day I made a beeline out to the airport to fly the aircraft to Amarillo to find out why the de-ice boots failed. This really had me scratching my head. You remember me telling you how I had tested the de-ice boots when I taxied out the previous morning for our trip to Oklahoma City? I tested it again that morning before I headed to Amarillo, and it worked perfectly.

When I got to Amarillo I went in and talked to the mechanics at Amarillo Aircraft and told them everything that had happened. So, they hooked the aircraft up to a device that pressurized the system for the de-ice boots to check it out. Everything seemed to be working, so they inflated the boots and went and examined them up and down each wing.

Holy cow! They discovered that each boot on each wing had about twenty to thirty tiny pin holes in them. The holes were small enough that they weren't visible, and when you tested the boots they would inflate and look normal, and the pressure gauge would give a proper reading.

But if you had a layer of ice running the full length of the wing to constrict it, the boots would not inflate. The air would run out those holes between the ice and the boot, and the boot would not inflate to break the ice.

They wound up putting patches on all of those holes, basically the same thing as a rubber patch you would put on a rubber inner tube to fix a flat bicycle tire.

This was an experience that really opened my eyes to how in aviation something can sneak up and bite you big time. This was something that the 100-hour or annual inspection would not detect, and your preflight inspection before each and every flight would not detect it either. It was a very humbling experience, and it strengthened my faith in my Lord and Savior even more.

Jay standing by the pressurized Beechcraft Queen Air in Aspen, Colorado

TURBINES AT TWENTY
AND THE ENTANGLEMENT

I

A couple of months after that trip Mr. Hudson had a trip to Los Angeles on the schedule. We took off that morning, and we couldn't make it non-stop to L.A., without fueling. As I flew the traffic pattern and made the turn to final for our fuel stop, I looked down, and there was some guy standing on the corner in Winslow, Arizona pointing at a flatbed Ford. OK, I'll bet many fans that love the Eagles song, "Take It Easy," and whenever in Winslow have said they did that or saw that, but not many could have the fun of seeing it from my vantage point.

I landed, parked the plane and everyone got out to go in the FBO to wait for the fueling to be complete. As I got off the plane, I glanced over to the right and saw something I did not want to see. There was a stream of engine oil running down the engine nacelle. Good grief! What next? I went in to tell Leonard what was going on and to find out if there were a mechanic available.

Fortunately, there was a mechanic, and he went out to look at it. When he discovered where it was coming from, he said it definitely needed to be re-paired. I told him my passengers needed to get to LA and asked him if the leak were serious enough to prevent us from making the short hop from Winslow to Phoenix, where I could get my passengers on a commercial flight to LA. The mechanic said that wouldn't be a problem to do that, so we paid for the gas, I finished the preflight inspection, and we took off for Phoenix.

We landed at Phoenix Sky Harbor Airport, and when we cleared the run-way, I told ground control we wanted to go to Cutter Beechcraft. I got out and went in to check on the possibility of getting a charter flight from Cutter or if that weren't available to get my passengers over to the terminal to catch a commercial flight.

Once I got that done, I would head over to their shop to get our aircraft in to be repaired. My hope was that it could be repaired soon enough to make it to LA in a few days to take my passengers home from the multi-day conference they were attending.

Unbeknownst to me, as we taxied in on the ramp at Cutter, Leonard had noticed a Beechcraft King Air sitting on the line with a *For Sale* sign in the windshield. As I was talking to someone at the front desk, he came over took me aside and mentioned the airplane he'd seen. He had recognized that it was a King Air. He told me he was interested in that airplane and said he wanted to take a demo flight in it to LA. My eyes about popped out of my head when he said that.

I went over to the lady at the front desk and told her my boss wanted to take a demo flight in that King Air on the ramp.

She said, "Just a moment." She got on the phone, and before you could sneeze, Bill Cutter, the owner of the business was there to greet us. Leonard introduced himself and asked the price on the aircraft. Mr. Cutter told him.

Leonard then told him that he wanted a demo flight in it to Los Angeles. Mr. Cutter asked him when, and Leonard said, "Right now."

Mr. Cutter said, "I'm sorry, Mr. Hudson, but we have a demo flight for that plane scheduled an hour from right now. I can't do that."

Leonard went on to basically tell him that if he put us in that King Air, took us to LA, and he, Leonard, liked it that Mr. Cutter could consider it sold.

I think Mr. Cutter's eyes just about popped out of his head too. I don't think he'd ever had a sale quite like that one. I could hardly believe it. Here I was, having just turned twenty years old around two months prior, and I might be flying a turbine-powered aircraft before this trip ended.

Mr. Cutter said, "OK, let's get your bags transferred over to the King Air, and we'll do it." He had me join him in planning the flight to LA and checking the weather. After we got the flight plan filed, we went out, and he showed me everything involved in the preflight inspection of this aircraft.

We loaded our passengers, I got in the right seat, and Mr. Cutter was the pilot in command in the left seat. He called clearance delivery, "Sky Harbor Clearance, November One Seven Six Two Kilo (N1762K), request clearance to Orange County Airport."

That was actually about a year before they had named it John Wayne Airport.

As we taxied out, took off, climbed, cruised, descended, and landed, Mr.

Cutter went through all of the check lists explaining things to me that I might not be totally familiar with.

When we parked at Orange County and shut down the engines, I was so impressed with everything. What an awesome aircraft this was. One thing that I was totally amazed at was how quickly you could stop after touchdown. You would pull the throttles straight up, which would allow you to pull them even further back to the next stop.

Pulling them back causes the propeller blades to rotate to an angle that has them blowing the air forward rather than the normal aft thrust. Then the further you pull the throttles back, you increase the reverse thrust until it hits the maximum setting.

Mr. Cutter shut down the engines, and I got up and went back to open the door. All the passengers got off with Mr. Cutter coming off last. We were all standing there, and Mr. Cutter looked Mr. Hudson in the eye and said, "Well what do you think?"

Leonard looked at him and told him to take me back to Phoenix and teach me how to fly this thing. He went on to say he would call his office and tell them to work with him on all the paperwork. Mr. Cutter told Leonard he would definitely get it all taken care of.

My gosh, I almost couldn't believe this was taking place.

We went in the FBO and planned the return flight to Phoenix, during which he gave me more instruction on some things pertaining to the aircraft systems that were different from what I was used to in the Queen Air.

When we got to Phoenix, he recommended a hotel and told me when to come back the next day for some flight instruction with another one of his employees who was a certified flight instructor and was qualified in the King Air. He also gave me the operating manual out of the King Air to take with me and study that night.

II

The next day I went to the airport to get started on some training. Mr. Cutter greeted me and told me that the insurance company was agreeable to insuring the aircraft with me operating it, as long as I was given ten hours of instruction in it before I was sent off on my own. They would include the time going back and forth to Los Angeles the previous day and the time to go with me one way back to LA. So, we were going to be spending about two and a half hours that day and the next in the air doing the training. I also had to schedule to go to Wichita, Kansas to the Beechcraft factory for their next available company ground school and flight training on the aircraft.

We went out and did a little over an hour of slow flight, stalls, steep turns, and short-field take-offs and landings. We came back for lunch, and as we were walking across the ramp to go somewhere for lunch, I couldn't believe it. I came face-to-face with my friend Phil Atkinson.

He and a friend had gone together to share the cost of renting the single-engine Beechcraft Sundowner there in Amarillo to make a trip to LA. Phil was wanting to proceed in a flying career as well and was trying to build his time. His friend needed to make a trip to LA, so they shared the rental cost, and he flew him out there and back. He was really surprised when I told him what was going on.

After lunch, the instructor and I jumped back in and did some instrument approaches and other in-flight training to complete the day. I went back to the hotel, did more studying of the operating manual, and called it a day.

The next morning, Mr. Cutter informed me that my boss was one lucky man and that he had just learned that an airworthiness directive had been issued by the FAA on the Queen Air. An AD is similar to a recall notice on an automobile except that the AD has to be followed to the letter, or the aircraft is grounded.

This AD on the Queen Air required that a fire detection and extinguishing system be installed on that aircraft's engines. Gee! The cost to do that would be astronomical, and now Mr. Cutter would have to have that done unless he found someone who wanted to buy an aircraft that could not be flown. I felt terrible for him.

That rest of the day was a repeat of in-flight training.

The next day, it was check the weather and file the flight plan. This time I was in the left seat, Mr. Cutter in the right seat, and he went with me to Orange County where he shook hands with Mr. Hudson and took off to catch a commercial flight back to Phoenix.

I loaded up the luggage and passengers and off we went in Mr. Hudson's new aircraft, the Beechcraft King Air E-90, N1762K to San Francisco. We were there for just a few hours, and then went to Albuquerque, New Mexico, where we spent the night and returned home to Pampa the next day.

III

What a week! One week later it was off to Wichita for the training at Beechcraft. That was a pretty intense school with five full days of systems training along with more in-flight training with an instructor. It was topped off with lunch, and our pictures were taken with none other than Olive Ann Beech, the co-founder, President, and Chairwoman of Beech Aircraft Company.

I was really thrilled with how everything was going, but Cindy seemed to be a bit unhappy. It appeared to me that the problems we started having seemed to intensify when she went to Amarillo to spend time with her mother. Her mother had never liked me, but Cindy was always supportive of me until we moved.

After this continued for months, I allowed it to upset me more than I should have. Unfortunately, I let it bring back bad memories from when Nana passed away. And sadly, on my side of things I had gotten slack in my focus on God's word and was not praying about the issues at hand and truly being obedient to how I knew Jesus expects us to live our lives and deal with things. That was a huge failure on my part that was going to have serious repercussions for a large portion of my life.

IV

The next two and a half years were quite an experience for me. Within a couple of months of my getting trained in the Beech King Air, we made a trip to Washington National Airport. It hadn't been named Reagan National yet. That was quite the experience. You had to get a reservation, no more than 48 hours in advance, to be allowed to land or depart there, as a Part 91 general aviation operation, and your arrival and departure time had to be accurate.

There were dozens of trips to Oklahoma City, Dallas, Houston, Midland, and other resort destinations that were great, but some weren't. On the male-only trips to Vegas and the fishing trips to Mexico, there was a lot of drinking. The fact that I did not drink alcohol made me the candidate to make sure my passengers didn't have their wallets stolen. I did not like that responsibility and being the only sober person in a venue like that was not a good experience.

Of all those trips to Vegas, there was one in particular that left a really bad taste in my mouth. On nearly all of those trips my passengers would include me in going to some of the shows and some very nice meals with them. That was great, but on this trip one of the guests had a very close connection at one of the casinos.

That person came up and told me one of the security guards had to go to another one of the casinos and would be going backstage to see—I'll just keep the name anonymous—a very famous musician-entertainer and asked if I would like to go.

I said, "Sure," and got in the vehicle with the security guard.

We drove to the other casino and just had a normal conversation. When we got there we went backstage, and there in the dressing room stood the famous musician with another well-known female who was performing with him. We walked over to them, and I was introduced.

The next thing I know, this security guard I was with pulled out a plastic bag that contained a white powdered substance and hands it to them. They were very appreciative, and we left immediately. At that point I was half-scared and absolutely livid. I was almost shaking over the fact that I was with the guy who just delivered cocaine to this star.

The thought of possibly being arrested with this dude, who was delivering an illegal drug, and the lifelong potential ramifications of it were just swirling in my mind. At first, I thought I needed to separate and get another ride back to where my group was, but then again what the heck would that put in this guy's mind? So, I rode back with him. I never mentioned what I witnessed to my boss and was frankly very glad when that trip was done, and I was back home.

V

Around this time Phil had attained his commercial pilot certificate, multi-engine rating, instrument rating, and a job up in Dalhart, Texas, flying a pressurized single-engine Cessna 210. He did that for a few months, and I got him to come to Pampa for an interview with Warren Chisum at J. T. Richardson Trucking. Warren had purchased a twin-engine Cessna 310 and needed someone to fly it. He hired Phil, and I was thrilled to have helped him in that and have him join me in Pampa.

In getting back to my experiences, one rather interesting trip was a result of a potentially catastrophic event at one of Mr. Hudson's drilling rigs. I was at home and got a call telling me to get to the airport pronto. I was told we had to go to the Houston Hobby Airport immediately.

Once we got airborne and leveled off at cruise altitude, Leonard came up and told me they had a blowout on one of the rigs, and we were going to Houston to pick up Coots Matthews and bring him back to go out and hopefully save the rig.

For those who don't know, a blowout is what happens when the drilling rig hits a very high-pressure oil or natural gas pocket, the drilling mud is not heavy enough to contain it, and the blowout preventer fails. When this happens, you have high-pressure natural gas or oil just blowing up in the air through the derrick.

I went out to the rig with them, and the roar of the natural gas coming out of the ground sounded like four turbojet engines set at max thrust for takeoff. I knew just one little spark would ignite that gas and melt that entire drilling rig posthaste.

It was a real treat getting to meet Ed "Coots" Matthews. He and his partner, Asger "Boots" Hansen, had been fired for the "umpteenth time" by Red Adair a few years prior to this, and they had started their own well control company, aptly named Boots & Coots.

About this same time period I had made another trip to Houston and spent several days in the hotel there. I didn't have any opportunity to do much of anything but read or watch television. I got to see the daily news coverage of the Camp David Accords.

I had a great deal of interest in the proceedings because Lindsey's book had really motivated me to keep an eye on what was taking place in Israel and delving into the Bible pertaining to Israel in the last days.

I was very disappointed to see what President Jimmy Carter was doing to pressure Israel. He was attempting to persuade them to give over land that had been miraculously restored to the Jewish people in the Six-Day War after they were attacked. From my vantage point, I felt that was a very unwise thing to do, and I will delve more into that subject a bit further on.

VI

Another fond memory pertains to my trips to United Beechcraft in Wichita, Kansas to get the 100-hour inspection done on the King Air. That was another thing I really appreciated about Leonard. We were not required to do inspections every 100 hours because we were not renting the aircraft out or using it in any commercial aviation capacity. He just wanted to ensure the safety of the operation, period. On those inspection trips I would be there about three days.

I called my dad and asked if he would like to go with me. I thought he would enjoy seeing some of what goes into aircraft maintenance and a tour of the Beechcraft Factory would be cool as well. He was very receptive to going. So, he drove over to Pampa for an early morning departure from Pampa to Wichita.

I couldn't believe it; this was the first week in May, and there was snow in the forecast, and the weather was solid clouds all the way to Wichita. I was glad that it hadn't started to snow while Dad was driving. That started right after he arrived at the airport. I had the aircraft out of the hangar and had the flight plan filed. We did the exterior preflight inspection and climbed into the plane to initiate our adventure.

We got buckled in, and knowing what was ahead of us, I thought I should brief Dad on what we would experience. I explained that as soon as we entered the clouds, I would be using the instruments in the aircraft to know if we were banking left or right, climbing or descending, what our heading, altitude, and airspeed was.

I showed him how the attitude indicator would work in helping me with that along with a short description of some of the other instruments. He seemed to be cool with it all, and we taxied out to the centerline. I applied take off power, and we went airborne.

Yes, within ten seconds we were in the clouds. A split-second after we entered the clouds, out of the corner of my eye, I saw Dad's hands come up and clench his armrests. I asked him if he was OK, no response. Oh my! When our altitude was 600 feet AGL, I initiated a turn to get on course, and once the turn was complete, I connected the autopilot, so I could look over at Dad and engage him to explain everything that was going on.

Wow, it had truly put the fear in him. He would not turn his head when I would try to get him to look at the instruments to show him how they were showing that we were climbing or turning or flying straight and level.

That's how it was all the way to Wichita. As I initiated the approach, I gave a play-by-play description of everything I was doing that was going to line us up with that runway and bring us right down at the very end of it, even though we could not see it.

When we finally broke out of the clouds about 400 feet AGL on the ILS Approach to Runway 1R, I could see that he relaxed immediately, and he blurted out, "How the hell did you find this runway and get lined up with it?" That was pretty humorous.

How funny indeed. I couldn't get a word out of him all the way to Wichita, and after I shut the engines down on the ramp at United Beechcraft, he couldn't quit talking about how incredible it was and how we found that runway having not seen the ground or the sky for over an hour.

That turned out to be a wonderful time with Dad. He really enjoyed seeing the Beechcraft factory and seeing the top-notch maintenance facility at United Beechcraft. And what a joy it was to have clear skies on the trip home.

VII

Not long after that, the company had a trip to New York City. This was a trip to train the office staff on the new computer system Mr. Hudson had just purchased. The people who coordinated the training told him we needed to fly into the La Guardia Airport and take a cab into Manhattan.

La Guardia was another of the few airports in the country that required a reservation in advance for a Part 91 operation to arrive and depart. So, I made the reservation, and the tricky part was that we would be making a stop in Mt. Vernon, Illinois to drop off Leonard's wife so she could visit family.

This was going to be a big challenge to make sure everything was timed right. Fortunately, it was, and the real issue was for this Texan to be able to understand the air traffic controllers, who were speaking a thousand words a minute with their New York accent. Praise the Lord. I got through it with no blunders.

Once we got to Manhattan, it was Leonard, the ladies from the office, and I. During the day I just walked around, had lunch, and spent some time in the room at the Waldorf Astoria Hotel. The first evening, all of us went out to eat, had a great meal, and went down to Times Square.

The group picked out a movie to see at one of the theaters there. We went in, and ten minutes into this thing it was so obscene and vulgar that I just leaned over to Leonard and said, "This ain't my cup of tea, I'll see y'all back at the hotel." I got up to leave, and one of the ladies "Arlene," joined me. She didn't like it either. She and I walked back to the hotel and had some very pleasant conversation along the way. I had always enjoyed visiting with her during their breaks back at the office in Pampa as well.

From then on, she and I stuck together when we were all out eating and sightseeing. This was a big mistake on my part with Cindy and me having the issues we were having.

The last night in Manhattan we went to see a play on Broadway, and Arlene and I sat together. I was really enjoying the conversations and found her to be attractive. What a mistake. I knew this was wrong in God's eyes, but I was turning a blind eye to how wrong it was. It went no further on this trip, but Satan had planted a seed, and I didn't stand firm and prevent it from sprouting. In other words, I could have done the right thing but didn't.

Not too long after the trip to New York, Leonard was in the break room discussing an upcoming trip to Canada. Arlene perked up and said how much she would like to go to Canada. I'm sure you'll never guess what my response to that was.

Shortly after she said that, Leonard got up and left the room. I told Arlene if she really wanted to go to Canada, she should ask Leonard if he would let her ride along as long as she paid her own way. What a foolish, stupid, and disobedient thing for me to do. I knew my thoughts were very wrong. I knew my Lord and Savior would not approve, but I frankly rebelled and did not think through what I was doing.

Arlene did make that trip to Canada, and I'm sure I don't have to tell the mistake and sin that was committed. Oh, how I wish I could have received half a clue of the intense pain and sorrow that would result from this. The pain that was dealt to Cindy, the secretaries' ex-husband, her daughter, and many others was intense. While the pain was intense for me, struggling with a deep self-hatred over the pain I caused, it was just a smidgen of the discipline I would receive for this.

How awful. I continued to have an affair with her and turned my back on Cindy, who filed for divorce and moved back to Amarillo within about six months. Arlene's husband divorced her as well. If what I've shared so far isn't bad enough, this next item frankly nauseates me when it comes to mind. I moved in with her before we got married. Thankfully, my friend Joe Warren suggested I rethink that, which I did. I moved back to my place, and we proceeded to just date for several months until we could be married.

A photo of the "blow out" that Coots Matthews contained after Jay flew to Houston and back to bring him to the well site.

THE CONSEQUENCES—
AND HOW 'BOUT THEM COWBOYS?

I

My affair and divorce also created tension at work which shocked me a bit based on some things I had witnessed. But the fact is, I was guilty in God's eyes, and I'm so thankful that His Son paid the price for our forgiveness when we are repentant, confess our sin, and truly desire to follow Him.

I flew for Leonard another year after all of this played out. Out of the clear blue I was contacted by someone who was a close friend of Lynn and Doris Odom, who owned and operated an oilfield service business in Pampa.

This friend of the Odoms' told me that they were purchasing a new Beechcraft Duke, which is a smaller, twin-engine, pressurized aircraft powered by piston engines, not turbine engines like the King Air. The friend told me the Odoms were wondering if I would be interested in going to work for them and said I should contact them if I were. With the way that things had changed for Arlene, and I at our current jobs, after wrestling with it a bit, I decided to visit with them.

I met with them, and they offered to pay me what I was earning and provide a company car similar to the one I had working for Mr. Hudson. They were well aware of what had taken place with Arlene and me and were not judgmental. That was a relief, and I took the offer. I had some new adventures in store, and it was going to be a real pleasure working for the Odoms.

The main part of their business was cleaning up the gas wells in Oklahoma after they had been fractured. This was serious business. They worked on wells that were expelling bauxite material, which at a 20,000-psi pressure would cut through regular steel like butter.

The valves had to be lined with tungsten carbide material that would have to be changed out and replaced multiple times in the clean-up process. They would have this material coming through heavy steel pipe that weighed thousands of pounds and had to be welded to anchors that were cemented into the ground. If that were not done properly, that steel pipe would go on a tear like an extremely light garden hose with a pressure nozzle on it. That would not be a pretty picture.

I got checked out in the Odoms' new aircraft, and they immediately put us to work. Within two weeks I made multiple trips to get Lynn to job sites in Oklahoma and back. Then I got a call to prepare to go to San Luis Obispo, California the next day and come back four days later.

This was a little different. One of the four days we would be there was Christmas Day. They were actually apologetic that I would be gone on Christmas, but this was a brand-new asset, and they had to fly out and spend Christmas with Doris's sister and family.

Her sister's husband was going to be working at the new Diablo Canyon Nuclear Power Plant. I found that very interesting, especially with all of the protests I read about during that time pertaining to the opening of that plant. It was also a real treat for me getting to see the Madonna Inn, famous for its Christmas Decorations.

II

Over the next month came a flight to a job site almost every other day with a ski trip to Durango, Colorado to top off the month. That was one of my few attempts at snow skiing, pretty unsuccessful this time since there was not much snow and what little there was had melted in a lot of places and turned to ice.

So far it looked like I was going to be logging time in the air a significant amount more than in the previous job, and I really enjoyed that possibility. I was getting even more excited, though, that a very special day was fast approaching; Arlene and I were getting married.

As that wedding day approached, I was thinking through a lot of things. Arlene had indicated several times that she was concerned that her being thirty-two years of age and my being twenty-two could be an issue. I couldn't see a problem with it and hoped that it wouldn't bother her. I was also going to be a stepdad to her daughter. I knew that could be a challenge from other people's experiences, but I had high hopes.

Over the previous year, in all of the pain, I had returned more of my focus to where it should have been, God. Arlene had been going to the First Baptist Church in Pampa for several years, so I had joined her, and I was really pleased with Pastor Claude Cone and his sermons. He really dug into the scripture and presented his sermons in a way that focused on the Bible and how we should live it out.

Pastor Cone counseled us over a several-week period on the biblical significance of marriage prior to marrying us. The wedding was just family, a couple of close friends, and my new stepdaughter was the flower girl. The honeymoon was quite short because I had to fly the Odoms and another couple to Hot Springs, Arkansas two days after our wedding, but I was very happy and joyful to be with Arlene and have a new stepdaughter as well. I had hoped to take a week off fairly soon to make up for that short honeymoon, but that option never materialized.

III

I wanted nothing more than to be a good husband and father for them and be able to provide well for them. I wanted Arlene to be able to stay at home and be there for my stepdaughter, just as my mother had been there for me for the most part. I really felt that was important, especially with my being gone for several days at a time. I was truly thankful to the Lord that she was able to stay at home, and we were able to achieve that in less than two years.

To me, a big part of being a good husband and father was to dig deeply into God's word, the Bible, and to be discerning in what I read and listened to in the Christian arena. A major asset in that was some teachers whom I discovered on the local Christian radio station in Pampa: John MacArthur, the pastor of a large church in Panorama City, California and Tony Evans, the pastor of a large one in Dallas, Texas.

I listened to them every night that I was home. They are great teachers of His word, and I soaked it up. One of Pastor MacArthur's books, *The Gospel According to Jesus*, has blessed me to this day with discernment and the importance of sound biblical study.

IV

Getting back to my job with Mr. Odom, I could see that he was a great father to his three boys. The two older boys were very active in motorcycle racing, especially enduro racing, which is long distance, cross-country, time trial. Lynn had purchased a brand-new Blue Bird Wanderlodge, and he would load their motorcycles up on the trailer and take off every Sunday with a race.

Five months into my new job, I took a number of the family members on a non-stop six-and-a-half-hour flight to Bellingham, Washington for a major enduro race. Lynn had driven the Blue Bird with the cycles all the way up there and would bring it back at the end of the event. The rest of us would have the pleasure of being home in six and a half hours versus two days or more.

They were so into the motorcycle racing that they wound up opening a KTM dealership there in Pampa. In relation to that new part of their business, flying them up to Loraine, Ohio to the KTM Headquarters here in the States was really cool for me. We got to meet some of the factory riders, which was very interesting.

I wound up purchasing one of Greg's used KTM 250s to whet my appetite a bit for the motorcycle racing I had enjoyed growing up. I just couldn't bring myself to do it like I used to, though. My health was too important in the career I had chosen.

In the discussion of my KTM, I have to take us down a short rabbit trail here that I find quite significant and beneficial.

I want to share more about my cousin, Curtis and his decision to go into Christian ministry.

As I started writing, I had a question on some dates, and when we communicated, he brought something to light about that KTM.

I had forgotten that I sold that motorcycle to him, and he shared a very special memory:

> The decision came August 1, 1984 on top of the continental divide above Telluride, Colorado sitting astride the KTM motorcycle that I bought from Jay Straub. Sitting in a snow drift watching rivulets of melting snow run off in opposite directions to end up worlds apart, I knew I must make a life decision that would send me and our family, and their families someday, in completely opposite directions. Neither

was bad, just radically different. But only one would be God's highest and best use of why and how He created me. I could continue my CPA career, serving God in the marketplace, or step out in blind faith following a deep sense of God's call to serve him vocationally.

We chose the latter, and the first big step in that journey was departing for Dallas Theological Seminary one year later in August 1985. Next was my very first mission trip. It was to Malawi, Africa in August 1987 that God then called me specifically to missions. Two years later in July 1989, I joined the fledgling Global Missions Fellowship as the second new staff member. Upon graduating from Dallas Seminary in May 1990, I led my first of hundreds of missions and training trips now spanning three decades and nearly fifty countries.

Through e3 Partners, we have been blessed to see over 5 million people make professions of faith in Christ through over 12 million personal gospel presentations. Over 1 million indigenous Christian leaders have been trained and mobilized to establish some 250,000 (and increasing exponentially) new churches among the least-reached people around the world, including in the USA. I Am Second has experienced over 100 million film and content views and over 1 billion media impressions since launching in December 2, 2008. Thanks for selling me that KTM motorcycle that took me to the top of the world and ends of the earth . . . and now countless others far further!

When I read what Curtis just shared, it was one more example that you just never know how God is going to use something as minuscule as a motorcycle to get you to the top of a mountain to bring something to fruition and glorify Him. I've already shared one near-tragic divine intervention in my life that gave Him the glory. And there will be more to come.

V

Around six months into our marriage I was absolutely floored. Arlene called me into the living room, sat me down, and gave me a three-hour session of complaints. On some of the things she was complaining about, I tried to be agreeable and said, "OK, I understand and will try to correct that" or "try to get that done in a timelier fashion."

On other issues, I tried to explain to her that they were things that caused me problems, being health related, and I did not want to risk doing something that could cause me to come down with asthma again. That could end my career, and then where would we be?

Her response indicated that she didn't really accept my explanation or concern on those items. I think what it boiled down to was the fact that she grew up on a farm; her father worked sunup to sundown seven days a week, and she thought that's how it should be, period. While she wasn't holding a job at the time, she was doing something that she considered work related where she was moving about all day long and couldn't see me doing otherwise.

At the three-hour point, with no end to the complaints in sight, I had to get in the car and leave to cool off. Once I cooled off, I came home, forgave immediately, and put it behind me. I planned to do everything I could to correct the things that didn't make me feel miserable to the point that I couldn't safely fly an aircraft or potentially lose my medical certificate and end my career.

About nine months later, when it happened again, I couldn't put her down like she was doing to me. I could find no reason for it, so I proceeded to curse and name call. That made me feel miserable, and I got up to do like I did the last time, leave the house to go cool off.

As I walked out the door to go get in the car that was sitting in the driveway, she followed, yelling at me. When I got in the car, she stood behind it where I couldn't back out. OK, I had no choice but to go back in the house.

After it went on for another thirty minutes, I felt trapped. My apologies for failing to meet her expectations and a desire to improve on my end wouldn't stop it. When it went to the cursing and name calling on my end again, that wouldn't stop it. I was at wits' end. I stood up and slapped her. That finally ended it, but I felt totally miserable, disgusted with myself, and sorrowful in what I just did, as I should have. There was no excuse for that.

As demeaning as Arlene was in those events, I loved her, forgave immediately, and put it behind me. Not so on her end. Unfortunately, a slap or physically pushing her back to get her out of my face were the only things that would end her verbal onslaught toward me.

Every time it happened; it crushed me and would break my heart. It would also, once again, bring back some very bad memories from my childhood: the women in the family attacking my mom, my mom attacking my dad, and my ex mother in-law who had despised me.

VI

Not long after that event, I ran into an attorney, a very outgoing and friendly gentleman whom I had come to know through Mr. Hudson. In our conversation, he was telling me about how he had been purchasing houses in Pampa as an investment. At the time he had around a hundred of them and was renting them out.

That was pretty astounding to me, and after I questioned him, I thought that might be a good thing to look into for an investment and future income for Arlene and me. Along with that, I thought the work I would be doing to maintain and take care of the properties would please Arlene and help me gain some love and respect. And I thought we could be working together, which I really would enjoy. I was in hope that she would as well. We wound up purchasing three different properties, and I had high hopes.

When I wasn't out on a trip with the Odoms, I was busy working on those rental properties. I knew going in that there were going to be more allergy problems from cleaning, mowing, and fumes from the paint, but I had high hopes this could bring the benefits that I just shared.

Unfortunately, that wasn't how it turned out on any front. We had no income, respect, or mutual enjoyment working together. I was praying and looking to the Lord, and He was my comfort. It was always a blessing and joy to read His word and hear some good teaching from Mr. MacArthur and others when things got difficult.

VII

Almost a year exactly after Mr. Odom hired me, he told me that he was about ready to fulfill a promise he had made me. I couldn't recall any promise and asked him what that would be.

He said, "I told you the day I hired you that you would be back in the left seat of a Beech King Air one day."

That really was good news. I much preferred the performance, room, and proven reliability of turbine engines that the King Air had over the piston type. He wanted me to be involved in the discussion with the salesman at the Beechcraft dealership at my old home base, Tradewind Airport, to share my thoughts on the avionics and some of the options.

They looked at some of the aircraft available and decided on the F-90 model, a new version that had a T-tail just like the King Air 200. It was basically an E-90, like the one I had flown for Mr. Hudson with the T-tail, 70 more shaft horsepower per engine, and the wingspan of 45 feet versus fifty feet on the E-90. It was a little hot rod. That was really a good feeling to be back in a King Air with turbine engines.

The first long trip in it made for a very long day. We went from Pampa to Prescott, Arizona to San Luis Obispo, California, and then back to Pampa. We spent nine and a half hours in the air that day, the most flight hours in one day for me at that point in my career.

Several months later I went back to Wichita to the Beech Factory for training in the F-90. The year and four months I spent flying the F-90 were pretty similar to what I'd done in the Duke for the Odoms. It was all over the oil patch, as they say, and another eight or ten long hauls to California, Colorado, and Ohio.

VIII

A couple of months after that, Arlene came to me and had some news to share. "I'm pregnant," she announced.

Oh my gosh! I was totally surprised. We had decided we wanted to have a child together, but I did not think it would come to be that quick. I was thrilled to learn this.

What a joy, and I was hoping that my stepdaughter would take it well. She was nine years old now, so I was in hopes that she would be happy with her new sibling. Arlene told me that December was the month. Mid-December was Dad's birthday so it looked like they might have the very same birthday. How cool would that be? I couldn't wait for this new member of the family to arrive.

About a month later, in April of 1983, I had a rather unusual trip. There was a brother of one of the Dallas Cowboys, who was promoting some of the Cowboys' coming to do charitable events.

A lady in Pampa heard about this, got with the brother, and arranged for this group of Dallas Cowboys to come to Pampa and play a fundraiser basketball game. They were supposed to spend the night and have breakfast with a bunch of the locals, who paid a pretty good sum for the privilege.

The lady running the show contacted Lynn, explained what they were doing, and asked if he would donate the use of his aircraft to transport these Cowboys to Pampa. He agreed to do it and told me when to be at Love Field to pick them up.

They refused to arrive any earlier than right when the game was supposed to start. So, I was asked how long the total time from engine start at Dallas to shutdown at Pampa would be. When I gave them that figure, they came up with the time that the Cowboys were supposed to arrive at the FBO for me to get them to Pampa in time for the game.

That day I arrived at Cooper Airmotive, the FBO where I always parked at Love Field. I got out of the aircraft, went in, checked the weather for the return flight, filed the flight plan for the return, and waited for departure time. That time came and went, and there were no Cowboys.

I waited about ten minutes and made my credit card long-distance call to the lady in charge of this event. Yes, credit card call, it's hard to remember the times before cell phones. I told her there were no Cowboys in sight. This was not what she wanted to hear. She told me to wait at least an hour, and if they hadn't shown up by then to call her back and let her know so she could give the bad news to everyone.

About five minutes later a couple of big dudes sauntered in. I've never been a big follower of football, so I wouldn't necessarily recognize the players, but it seemed pretty clear that these were some of my passengers. I was rather shocked to see them just turn and make their way up the stairs to the restaurant that was on the second floor of the FBO. It was now over fifteen minutes past our departure time, and because of their demand, we didn't have any time to play with.

I went up the stairs, introduced myself, and asked if they were my passengers who were going to the charitable event in Pampa, Texas. They basically glared at me and gave me an inaudible grunt that indicated yes. I told them we were supposed to be in the air already in order to get there in time for the game. They were clearly irritated that I brought that to their attention and told me they were going to get something to eat.

OK. I went back downstairs, and as the others trickled in, I told them where their teammates were. Fortunately, none of the others went up to order food. I made a call to set the lady in Pampa at ease, and when those up in the restaurant finally came down, we got in the plane and headed for Pampa.

When we landed, I parked on the ramp where a lot of people that brought their kids to greet these guys on their arrival, were standing in wait. As I walked through the plane, I was stunned by what I saw. These guys had trashed the plane. I opened the door, went down to the tarmac, and watched as these guys just walked by and blew off these fans who had been waiting to see them arrive.

I climbed back in the aircraft, started the engines and taxied down to our hangar. I put it in the hangar, got out the vacuum to clean up the nuts and crackers they had ground into the carpet, restocked all the alcohol and snack items that they had completely emptied, and closed everything up to go home. I was sure hoping that the experience for the fans at the game was better than what I had just witnessed. I was just glad to be home to sit down for dinner and relax.

I told Arlene everything that had happened when I got home, as she reheated our dinner. When we finished eating, I went in the living room and sat down to read. I had been sitting hardly any time when the phone rang.

I got up to answer it, and it was the lady who was running the charitable event. She told me I needed to go back to the airport and fly them back to Dallas. I said, "I thought they were having breakfast in the morning with the people who bought tickets." She informed me that they were refusing to do it.

I told her I would have to call Lynn to get his approval. I called Lynn and told him what was going on and how they had trashed the plane. He told me to take them back but to completely remove all of the drinks and snacks, which I gladly did. I called back and told the lady I was headed for the airport.

When I got there, I did just as Lynn had instructed. The passengers arrived, I loaded them up, and we took off. I had barely broken ground and someone in the back yelled, asking where the f&*@^#* drinks and food were. When I got a little more altitude, I turned and informed them there wasn't any. That was followed by a barrage of cursing. When I let them out at Love Field, I was very glad for that event to be over.

After that ordeal, I flew one round trip to Lawton, Oklahoma, and Lynn called me to come to the office. When I got there, he informed me that business had gone down drastically and that today was my last day and he was going to have to put the King Air up for sale. I was devastated and speechless.

I had sensed that things had slowed down, but I didn't realize it was that bad. I told him I would go get my headset and some personal items from the hangar and bring all the keys back to the office, which I did. As I drove to the airport, I was truly worried and concerned. Here we are with a baby on the way with no job and no health insurance. What am I going to do?

I certainly had no hard feelings toward him or Doris. I understood that he didn't have any choice in the matter. He had to let me go for a logical reason through no fault of his own. Nevertheless, I had truly enjoyed working for the Odom's.

It really surprises me that I never saw either of them again even though I lived in that small town for another thirteen years. I learned sometime in 2002 that Doris had passed away a few years after we had left Pampa. I called Lynn and gave him my condolences. It was a short conversation, but it was good to speak to him again after all those years.

HILLS AND VALLEYS?
WHERE ARE THE HILLS?

I

The next five months were going to be stressful. I would be doing any flying possible on a day-trip basis and anything else day-labor related that could pay the bills. Arlene was doing what she could as well. I was mowing lawns, and on one of those jobs I about did myself in. It was Bermuda grass, and it did something I hadn't experienced since junior high. It kicked in the asthma, and boy oh boy, did that put the fear in me.

I thanked God though that it went away within a couple of days and didn't return. I definitely wouldn't touch a Bermuda yard any more after that, and I was thankful that I had done well in following in Dad's footsteps with the beautiful Kentucky Bluegrass at our house. All it gave me was hay fever. Between all that, washing cars, lawn care, and part-time flying, we stayed afloat and met all of our bills.

There were a couple of businesses in Pampa that had bought airplanes but didn't want to hire a full-time pilot. So, I was flying for them at $100 per day plus expenses. Both of those were owned by members of the church we were members of, First Baptist.

One of them was a company, Energy-Agri Products Inc., which was owned by several of our church members, and the other was Malcolm Hinkle Heating-Air and Plumbing. What a surprise that the house I grew up in Amarillo was within walking distance of one of Mr. Hinkle's locations. I always saw his business vehicles drive by our house. I had always thought that he lived in Amarillo until I learned about his plane and need for a part-time pilot in Pampa.

During these five months, I was putting out resumes and doing everything I could to find another full-time flying job. Unfortunately, the very thing that caused the loss of my job, the oil boom going bust, had put a bunch of other corporate pilots out of work as well.

I had even put out a resume to the State of Texas. I had learned they had a flight department in Austin with a number of flying jobs. What a shock and joy when the Chief Pilot for the State of Texas called and asked me to come to Austin for an interview.

I went and did the interview. At the end of it, the Chief shared what the pay and benefits would be and that he would like to hire me. At that point I told him I found that acceptable.

He went on to say, "Why don't you bring your wife down to Austin to see what she thinks?"

I thanked him and told him that's what we would do.

I was ecstatic, and when I got home and shared this with Arlene, she was way less than ecstatic. I tried to explain to her that this was a government position, and they would probably have a large flight department for as long as we were living.

I went on to basically say that it doesn't matter what happens to anything else, as a matter of fact, when things get worse everywhere else, the government just grows even more. That was a fact that I was well aware of in my study of current events and history. My enthusiasm and what I said didn't change her view.

She agreed to go check it out, so we went to Austin immediately. We went to meet the chief pilot, then we went to Round Rock to look at some homes that were for sale there. We had lunch with the Chief, looked at more homes, and I called him to tell him we would go home, discuss it, and I would let him know within two days.

When we got home, almost immediately after we walked in the door, I got a call from one of the fellows at EAPI, telling me they needed me to fly them somewhere the next day. I informed him that I couldn't do that and went on to share what was going on with the job in Austin. I told him that Arlene and I would be discussing it, to let the chief pilot know by the end of the next day. He congratulated me, and we said goodbye.

The next day, Arlene and I were barely up, and the fellow from EAPI called and said they wanted me to come by and talk to them. Uh, oh! I had a bad feeling about this. Sure enough, I got there and several of the partners had me come back to talk. When I sat down, one of them mentioned that they had learned from the other partner that I had been offered a job in Austin.

I said, "Yes that's correct. I've been offered a job with the State of Texas, and Arlene and I have to make the decision today."

As soon as I finished that sentence, the one who was speaking basically told me that over the last five months, they had really appreciated my getting them where they needed to go in the Cessna 414. He went on to inform me that they had talked it over, and after learning that I might be leaving, they would like to offer me a full-time job with the same pay I had with the Odoms and a company car as well. But they wanted me to come work in the office also during the week when they weren't traveling. I told them I appreciated the offer and that I would add that to the discussion with Arlene and let them know.

As I walked out the door, I was fairly annoyed. I was thinking, here are my fellow church members, and they just took advantage of my situation. They let me sweat bullets for the last five months with a baby on the way, and now inform me they would like to hire me when I have finally found a good secure job somewhere else.

On top of that, I was going to be required to work in the office when I wasn't flying and out of town, which was not how it had been in my previous jobs. When I got home, I really thought Arlene would be as annoyed as I was. Wrong!

When I walked in, Arlene asked what they wanted. I told her everything that was said, and when I finished, I asked if she could believe how they had just taken advantage of our misfortune? She disagreed with my statement. I was flabbergasted!

"How is that?" I asked.

She went on to tell me how good it was and how wrong it would be to move my stepdaughter that far from her dad. She was emphatic that I needed to take that job and stay in Pampa.

I couldn't believe what I was hearing. I asked her how this response measured up with what Pastor Cone had taught us, and she just rebuffed it. There was no changing her mind. At the end of the day, I called the Chief Pilot for the State of Texas and informed him I had been offered another full-time job where we lived. I told him we would be staying in Pampa and thanked him immensely for his offer.

II

One of the partners at EAPI wound up purchasing a Piper Cheyenne, and the group sold the Cessna 414 and started using the Cheyenne. It had been totaled, but a dealer in Colorado purchased it from the insurance company, did all the repairs, and got it restored to airworthy status. I felt safe in it, but I was not sure how that would go for him if he had to sell it in the future.

I had made a new friend who was just starting his career in aviation and had moved to Pampa, John Gries, originally from Iowa. I asked if he would like to fly out to Los Angeles and back with me. I would let him fly and log the time. He joined me, and we flew out and dropped off our passengers. It was just he and I on the return flight. We got to cruise altitude and the heater quit working. In case you didn't know, the outside air temperature at our cruise altitude of 25,000 feet was around minus 35°F.

If we descended to a much lower altitude it was still going to be so cold that our teeth would be chattering. To top that off, with a turbine engine your fuel burn at lower altitudes is significantly more than up high at your normal cruse altitude. If we did that, we would have to stop for fuel. We decided to tough it out and continue.

That was three brutally cold hours, and no joke, our teeth almost were chattering from that ordeal. John still reminds me, with a big smile on his face, about our journey in the deep freeze.

III

I had been in this job for three months when that very joyful day arrived. We were blessed with our precious daughter. What a joy that was! That was such a joy standing out in the hall, after she was put in the bassinet, looking through the window at her, with my mom and dad. Her pretty red hair and her precious smile were absolutely adorable. I couldn't wait to get back to Pampa and show her off to everyone.

Another unexpected treat in all of this was that I had evidently started a Straub tradition. Back when I was just eleven months old, my mom entered a picture of me in a Valentine's Day contest with the Amarillo Globe Times. I won in the boy category and had my picture on the front page of the paper.

Well, Arlene and my daughter had to remain in the hospital a few days, and someone from the Amarillo Globe Times showed up wanting to take a picture of a newborn and relate it to the Christmas Season. My daughter was chosen, so we were blessed with a picture of Arlene and my daughter on the front page, following in Dad's footsteps, so to speak. She looked so sweet with her red hair in her little red Christmas outfit.

When I finally got to take them home, it was right in the middle of a multiday snowstorm. Quite a few people can't believe it snows in Texas. Believe me, you can have a full-blown blizzard up in the Texas Panhandle. I was so excited. I asked Arlene if we could stop at the office for just a minute as we pulled into Pampa to show our daughter to everyone. She agreed, and we stopped in for just a few minutes to show them our little bundle of joy. I was so happy to arrive home with them and enjoy another blessing in my life. My daughter was and is a true joy to me. I loved holding her and gazing at her as she slept.

IV

I was flying quite a bit with EAPI, but within a few short months, things started to look quite problematic. I had learned early on that they along with some other oil companies were referred to as "white oilers." The deal was that up there in that part of the Texas Panhandle, oil rights and gas rights are separate. That seemed a bit odd to start with.

The next thing in the mix is that the Texas Railroad Commission, who controls oil and gas production in the state, only allowed one natural gas well per section of land, in that area, but they allowed 64 oil wells per section.

If a well that met the production requirement to be classified as an oil well produced natural gas too, it could produce and sell 100,000 cubic feet of natural gas per barrel of oil produced, up to a maximum of 500,000 cubic feet per day, as a legal byproduct which was called "casing head gas" by Texas law. By the way, I still scratch my head on a railroad commission's controlling oil and gas drilling and production. Somewhere along the way, someone came up with the idea that if you drilled a well and put a refrigeration unit on it to refrigerate the natural gas as it came out of the well, it would produce a liquid hydrocarbon that should be classified as oil. If it produced enough of this liquid hydrocarbon to meet the amount required by the Texas Railroad Commission to be classified as an oil well, then, voila, you have an oil well, and you can sell up to 500,000 cubic feet of the "casing head gas" it produces as well.

That's what my employer and others were doing, and that's why things became problematic. After many of the white oil wells came into production and the natural gas was being sold by the millions of cubic feet, Big Oil, didn't like it. Phillips Petroleum in particular, which owned the majority of the gas rights in that part of the Texas Panhandle, became, as we say in Texas, "madder than a wet hen."

The lawsuits started to fly. Big Oil went to the Railroad Commission, which stood by allowing these wells to be classified as oil wells, which allowed the sale of the "casing head gas." OK, now you've done it. It's time to go to the federal government. That's what they did, and the Federal Energy Regulatory Commission came in and shut it down, and the Texas Railroad Commission finally found in favor of Phillips as well.

Along with all of this, the fact that the major oil boom had gone bust close to a year prior decreased the population of Pampa from around 30,000 to close to 20,000.

You can only imagine what Arlene and I were being dealt in the rental house arena. We had purchased that last property right before the bust. Property values were falling; no one would purchase them unless you sold them for next to nothing. To top it off, except for one house that we had, the rest of them just brought tenants who wouldn't pay and trashed the properties.

That third house that we had purchased had a woman living in it who was a problem from the start. It was a constant battle to get the rent from her. Right after she moved in, I had to go over and fix the toilet one time, and the house was already a wreck, but I had no idea what was coming. Finally, after being there almost a year, and her not paying for two months, I sent the eviction notice.

When I got word that she was gone, I went to the house, and I could not even get in the front door. I went to the back door and could barely squeeze my way in. There was a layer of trash bags and junk, including a few pieces of her furniture, two feet deep, throughout the entire house, except for one bedroom.

I had to hire a company to come clean it all out, and they wound up hauling off an entire dump truck full of trash. I don't know about you but that sent shivers down my spine. To this day I haven't figured out how a human could live in that squalor, and she was an RN at the local hospital.

Additionally, the EAPI job ended after about a year and two months because of the FERC ruling. Here I was, back to day trip flying, yard work, car washing, and I even threw in window washing this time. I was pretty well, as we say in Texas, chapped.

Let's see now, we could be in Austin, and I could be in a secure government job, doing what I loved to do and could probably hold that job until retirement. Hmmm? I stewed on it a few days, but it finally sunk in that God has it all in his hands, and I needed to be thankful and content. He will bless us all in His timing, and I can truly testify to that.

"LONESOME DOVE"—BLOODY 98— MY DREAM CAME TRUE

I

As I'm sure you recall, the last time the job loss took place, I had done some day trips for Malcolm Hinkle, who was also a member of the same church we were. He heard what happened, contacted me, and offered to pay me considerably less than the $2,000 per month I had been making.

He just wanted me to be on call and give him first priority when there was a trip that he needed to make. I could also fly for anyone else or do any other odd jobs, as long as I put him first if he had a trip. I certainly agreed to that. I knew I would at least be able to make the house payment and have food on the table. I didn't have the company car any longer, but Dad came to the rescue and, bless his heart, bought me a little, used standard-shift Toyota pickup.

I had spread the word over in Amarillo that I was available to fly day trips, and I got a call offering me an opportunity to fly with Montgomery Harrison Wadsworth Ritchie, AKA Montie Ritchie, in his Beechcraft King Air, N743JA. I had heard that name before, but I couldn't place who he was.

I asked the person on the phone, "What's his business and what exactly do you mean, fly with?"

The person informed me that Mr. Ritchie was the owner of the JA Ranch. Well, holy cow! How's that for a play on words? JA Ranch—holy cow? Sorry about that; I couldn't resist.

Mr. Ritchie owned what was once the largest ranch in that part of the Texas Panhandle. At one time it contained 1,335,000 acres (2,086 square miles) with 100,000 head of cattle.

Mr. Ritchie was a fully licensed pilot with all the appropriate ratings, but he was in his late 70s, and even though he passed the medical, the insurance company would not let him fly alone. He had to have another pilot in the right seat who was qualified in his aircraft.

The person I was speaking with went on to inform me that I would just sit there and not touch anything unless it were a life-or-death necessity. OK, this should be interesting, I thought, and it really was. When I met Mr. Ritchie, his British accent, mustache, and demeanor were intriguing. He had a statesman's air about him as well as the cattle rancher temperament.

I flew a number of trips to Phoenix, Denver, and a few other destinations with him and really enjoyed it. On one of the trips, he was returning from one of his visits to England. I wasn't available when he flew out, to West Palm Beach, Florida, but I was on his return.

He got me an airline ticket to fly to West Palm and do the return trip with him back to Amarillo. When we got to our seats and were all buckled in, he opened his little briefcase and pulled out a box of Bacci Chocolates. He handed them to me and said, "Here, you might enjoy these, and save some for your wife." That was very kind and thoughtful.

He didn't talk a whole lot when we flew. When he did, it was usually something relating to the flight or something aircraft related. It was rare to get anything out of him pertaining to the ranch. Years later, I really regretted not trying harder to initiate a conversation about the ranch.

With history being my favorite subject in school, I had a brief knowledge of Charles Goodnight as one of the initial co-owners of the JA Ranch. When Larry McMurtry's Lonesome Dove, came out, and I learned that Gus and Hall in the book represented Oliver Loving and Charles Goodnight, I was truly kicking myself that I didn't talk more about it. At that, I really started digging into his history and that of the JA, Goodnight, and Loving. That made those trips with Mr. Ritchie an even bigger treat to think back on.

One last note on this subject, back in 1960, Margaret Harper contacted Pulitzer Prize-winning playwright Paul Green. She informed Paul that an outdoor amphitheater was being built in the Palo Duro Canyon and asked him to consider writing a play on the history and beauty of the canyon. Other people in the area funded Paul's first trip there, and when he spent some time, he devoted himself to telling the story. His play, Texas, has been seen by several million people from all over the world, including me at least six times.

The play is set right in the middle of the JA in its heyday. Between the fireworks, the fantastic song and dance, seeing the star-filled night sky, along with getting to see Comanche Chief Quanah Parker meet up with Goodnight and the cattlemen, who are raising a ruckus with the farmers, it's a night to remember!

II

During that time, I flew one trip truly etched in my memory bank. Mr. Hinkle had a close friend, Eddie Duenkel, who had a brand-new Beechcraft Bonanza. He flew it himself quite often. He wanted to take his whole family on a vacation trip to Destin, Florida, however, and he couldn't get them all in his Bonanza.

To solve that problem, he worked out a deal to rent the King Air that Phil's boss had purchased, and he asked me to fly the family down to Destin. He would follow in the Bonanza and have me leave the King Air, jump in his Bonanza, and take it back to Pampa. A week later, we would do it all in reverse.

That's what we did, and a week later I was en route back to Destin. I had been in the air close to four hours, and I looked over at the oil pressure gauge. It was sitting on zero. I reached over and tapped on the gauge expecting it to pop back up in the green. That didn't happen.

OK. I thought I would pull the power back to take some stress off of the engine and find the closest place to land. I pulled the throttle back, just a tad, and the engine quit immediately.

The weather was clear that day, so I just had the ARTCC tracking me on radar to keep me posted on potential air traffic. That's a procedure known as flight following. Memphis Center was the ARTCC facility tracking me.

I grabbed the mike and said, "Memphis Center, November four-four-four echo delta, I've experienced engine failure and need a heading to the closest airport."

They came back and said, "Roger, four-echo-delta, turn right heading one eight zero."

I said, "Roger, what airport am I going to?"

They came back, "Mobile, Alabama."

I said, "Roger, how far?"

They said, "Forty miles." I was flabbergasted and asked them if there weren't a closer airport, and they told me there wasn't and immediately handed me off to Mobile approach control.

By the time I got the new frequency for Mobile approach, dialed into the communication radio and called them, Memphis Center had already informed them of my situation. They immediately asked me what my rate of descent was. I came back and told them 1,000 feet per minute.

They could see my groundspeed on their radar and came back fairly quickly to say they thought that I would make it to the airport. I was definitely in hopes that they were correct, but I didn't think there was much of a chance that I could glide forty miles from a cruise altitude of 11,500 feet.

I immediately initiated the engine restart procedure and was thrilled when the engine came back to life. When you do the restart, you have the throttle back at the idle position. As I thought it through, I was just going to barely push the throttle forward to produce enough power to get an extra four or five miles, hopefully.

As I inched the throttle forward, *bang!* The propeller stopped completely. It had been wind milling as I glided through the air. Smoke came in the airplane. Oh my! Fortunately, the smoke stopped and cleared out fairly quickly.

As I continued to glide, I was looking for a road or an open field, anyplace that would make a decent spot to put this thing down reasonably safely. As I looked, all I could see was big trees below. That was a very bad prospect. It wasn't much longer before the runway at the Mobile Airport came into view.

I could tell immediately that I was not going to make it. I called Mobile Approach and told them I had the runway in sight, gave them the bad news, and asked if there were a road anywhere that I could get to and land this thing. They told me that highway 98 was just a few miles ahead and that I was coming up perpendicular to it. Sure enough, it came into view fairly quickly. I was headed straight south, and it ran east and west. It wasn't dark yet, but some cars already had their lights on, which helped me spot it.

As I approached the road, I looked to the right and it had a slight curve to it, to the left it was perfectly straight. I made a left turn, was lined up with the road perfectly, and was less than a thousand feet above the ground. For some strange reason I got the urge to make a one-eighty, go back, and land the other direction.

I put the aircraft in a fairly steep bank to keep the turn as tight as possible due to how little altitude I had to play with. While I was in the turn, I put the landing gear and flaps down and turned on the landing lights. Thank goodness those were all electric and the battery was still well charged.

As I proceeded to line up with the road, the cars coming toward me immediately maneuvered into the bar ditch. The last car that was going the same direction as I was had no idea I was there. I cleared them by about fifty feet and set it down right in front of them. I got on the brakes and was able to make a right turn into the parking lot of the Second Baptist Church of Semmes, Alabama. Whew!

I sat there for about a minute with my heart pounding then took a deep breath and slid across the seat to open the door. An ambulance had already pulled up behind me. Approach control had notified them. As I proceeded to climb out, the EMT came running and yelled at me, "Sit down! Sit down!"

OK, I turned back around and got back in the seat.

He climbed up beside me, strapped the blood pressure cuff on and took my blood pressure. It was way high. He said, "You better sit here for ten or fifteen minutes before you get up."

We sat and talked, and after the time was up, he checked it again. It had gone down enough, so he allowed me to get up.

I got out and went to the left side of the engine cowling, where the oil dipstick was to check the oil. There was no oil, absolutely none. What in the world? How could that be? It was completely filled when I left Pampa. How could this basically brand-new engine burn all of that oil in four hours? I was dumbfounded.

As I had sat there talking to the EMT, the news media had arrived and were setting up their video camera. Many of the passersby had pulled in to talk to me as well. One of the first who came up to talk said, "You don't know how lucky you are. Our nickname for this road is Bloody 98 due to all of the traffic fatalities." He went on to tell me how it's usually bumper-to-bumper along there at that time of day and there's no way I could have had the room to land without hitting an automobile.

The folks from the television station interviewed me, and I shared with them basically everything I've shared with you up to this point. As the people started to clear out, I was talking to someone, and the next thing you know, I feel something tugging at my shirt sleeve.

I turned to look, and there's a little lady, barely five feet tall, if that. I'm guessing she was in her late 70s, maybe 80 years of age, and she points up at me, kind of shakes her finger at me, and says, "Young man, Jesus Christ has kept you here for a reason."

I thanked her and told her I agreed with her whole heartedly. Actually, when the first fellow had told me how lucky I was, inside I was telling myself that the Lord had intervened somehow, just as He had back in the icing incident a little over seven years prior, and it had nothing to do with luck.

The pastor lived in a house behind the church, so he was there to witness all of this. This happened on a Saturday evening and here sat this aircraft at the entry to the parking lot, blocking the way for the church members the next day. I got the little hand-held tow bar out to steer it, and he and I pushed it to a corner of the parking lot.

After we got that done, he took me to a hotel and went in with me to see if they had a room available. While we were driving, I had asked him if he thought anyone in his congregation would mind bringing me to church the next day. He informed me he would come and get me personally. I thought that would interfere with his duties, but he was insistent. He told me when he would be there to pick me up, and I thanked him profusely.

I went up to the room and thinking that Eddie was probably wondering why he had not heard from me yet, I called him immediately. His daughter answered the phone and as soon as she heard my voice, her voice went shrill, almost in tears and she said, "Dad, Dad! Jay is on the phone!" That shocked me, and I was wondering why she was so emotional.

When he got to the phone, I learned that they had already seen my interview on the news in Destin. I couldn't believe a city over hundred miles from Mobile had already run that on their news. When he asked me what happened, I shared all that I knew and told him I didn't have a clue how that much oil could have been used. At the end of the conversation he said he would charter a plane in Mobile to bring me to Destin the next day. I thanked him and told him I was going to church first. He was very agreeable to that.

The next call was to Arlene. She answered the phone, and I said, "Well, you'll never guess what happened."

She asked, "What?"

I said, "Well the engine quit in Eddie's plane, and I had to land on a two-lane highway in Mobile, Alabama.

"Oh?"

"Yes, that's what happened."

And that was it.

I went on to tell her that I was going to church in the morning, and Eddie was going to charter a plane to get me to Destin. I told her I would call the next day and let her know approximately when I would get home. We always talked about my stepdaughter and daughter when I was out flying, and as always, I said, "I love you," at the end of the call. After the call ended, I just sat there for a bit. I had just come within an inch of death and her response was, "Oh?" That was a tough one.

When I got in bed, I could not sleep. I didn't sleep one single minute. The reason was, I couldn't stop thinking about how I had been lined up with the road, less than 1,000 feet above the ground, and I made that one-eighty to go back and land in the other direction. I had barely completed that turn before I was on the ground. I was thinking that had to be the stupidest thing I could have done, and even thought the FAA might question my cognitive ability if they knew how it all transpired.

I watched the clock all night and got up at the time I had planned. I showered, got ready, and got in the car when the pastor arrived at the hotel. As we drove down the road that I landed on the previous day, I could see the area where I probably would have touched down had I continued and landed on the perfectly straight part of the road.

Coming back that way in broad daylight, when we got to the place which would have been the approximate touchdown point, something caught my attention. Where I would have touched down, there were high line wires crossing the road.

If I had hit those things, I would have truly been a dead man. I've personally known two pilots who hit high line wires, and they are no longer with us. Once again, there was divine intervention that saved my life, and that elderly lady the night before had definitely sensed it.

It was a blessing to attend church that morning and give God the glory. After the service they took me to the Mobile Airport. I thanked them and jumped in the charter plane to head to Destin.

I have to share a humorous side note. It wasn't long after this that the pastor sent me a letter. In the conclusion of the letter, he said, "Drop in anytime." I loved it and hoped I could do that someday in the future.

When I got to Destin, we loaded up the King Air, and Eddie had to be the co-pilot this time. What a shame that there was no Bonanza for him to fly home in. Shortly after I got home, I sat down to document everything in preparation to file the aircraft incident report. This is required by the FAA. There were no problems; they never even contacted me to ask any further questions.

One really amazing thing was that the engine for that Bonanza was manufactured at a Continental Plant right there in Mobile. They hauled a new one out to the church parking lot, changed out the engine and just a few days after the incident, the police blocked off the road and someone flew the plane out of there.

When I got home and shared about God's divine intervention that had saved my life, the pastor at our church asked me to share it with our congregation in the main morning service. I was more than happy to give God the glory in that. I went up to the pulpit and proceeded to share everything.

I was about halfway through it and looked out where Arlene was sitting, straight out and halfway back in the middle section. I was expecting to see joy on her face with God getting the glory in all of this. When I spotted her, I gave a big smile, but as I focused, there she was, sitting there with a sour look on her face. In seeing that, I don't know if the absolute pain I felt showed up on my face. I would be surprised if it didn't. She disliked anything that gave me joy, even giving glory to God.

Sometime after all this, I learned from Eddie that he had been informed that some abnormality had caused the engine crankcase to pressurize, which blew all of the oil out of the crankcase through the breather tube. That tube was mounted where the oil ran right down the belly of the plane and could not be seen.

I also learned that shortly after my adventure, the same thing happened to another Bonanza that had taken off from the Addison Airport in Addison, Texas. Fortunately, it did it immediately after takeoff. They saw the oil pressure gauge drop to zero and made an immediate turn back to land with no problem.

III

Immediately after the Highway 98 event, Mr. Hinkle's flying increased significantly, so he raised my pay a little, probably because he was keeping me so busy that I couldn't get any other day trips. It was still less than I had been earning, so I informed him that I still couldn't make ends meet and would have to continue looking for full-time employment. He said he understood.

That very same month, my friend Phil had put in an application with American Airlines. After the oil boom went bust and fuel prices had dropped significantly, the airlines had started some major growth and expansion. Phil and I had been discussing the possibility of getting hired by an airline, but I was dragging my feet a bit.

In the not-so-distant past, the airlines basically only hired military pilots whose commitment was up and so were free to come on board. The few that weren't ex-military definitely had to have a four-year degree. All I had was the AD in Aviation Management, so I wasn't that optimistic. What a mistake that was.

A month later Phil got called in for an interview. Now, that got my attention. So, I set out to get my resume typed. Mr. Hinkle was keeping me so busy it was another full month before I got my resume completed and sent to American.

I had another big event in August along with all of this. It was my ten-year high school reunion. It was a real treat getting to see some of my classmates. I basically hadn't seen any of them in that entire ten years except for Michael and maybe a couple more.

I think it was the first night of the reunion that I ran into a classmate, Rick Husband. I'm not exactly sure when he had started taking flying lessons. What I do recall is seeing him at Tradewind Airport a few times in our senior year at Amarillo High. While we were never in any classes together at school, we recognized each other at the airport and said hello to one another.

When I spotted him, I was anxious to find out if he had done anymore flying. Boy, was I about to be surprised. When I asked, he told me that he had and that he was in the Air Force based at Valdosta, Georgia flying F-4s. Wow! That was my favorite fighter jet, and I would never forget when Michael and I went to Canon Air Force Base in Clovis, New Mexico with his dad to watch the Thunderbirds do their show in F-4s.

We had some good conversation. I shared what I had been flying along with my emergency landing on the highway in Semmes, Alabama. I went on to share that I had just sent my application to American Airlines. He wished me the best. I thanked him and told him how thrilled I was with what he had accomplished.

Getting back to my job pursuit, I was really surprised how things were going. The interview process at American came in three phases. In September, I got called for phase one, and Phil got notified that he was hired. I was totally shocked at all of this.

As always, I was upfront and honest with Mr. Hinkle. I told him I had been called in for an interview, and he was fine with that. American provided the flight from Amarillo to DFW, the hotel room, and all of the transportation.

The next morning, I had on my navy-blue suit, tie, and well-shined shoes, for the ride to the American Airlines Flight Academy. I nervously waited for my turn with HR. As I sat and listened to all of the rest of my competition, it was clear they were all former military. Boy, that seemed to be some mighty tough competition. At least, that's how I perceived it.

My turn came, and he sat me down and proceeded to ask me some of the typical questions about education, how I got into flying, more questions about my flight training, and some of the equipment I had flown. He asked if I had ever had any disciplinary problems in school or legal problems.

The final question was, "Why do you want to fly for American Airlines?"

I shared that I was impressed with how they were at the top of the industry in IT with their Sabre Computer System and how they were also at the top in growth. I went on to share that I felt they were the absolute best to commit myself to in a lifetime career move. At the end of that, I felt that it went well.

From there I was sent to the Medical Department for a simple physical exam: things like blood pressure, temperature, weight, height, hearing, eyesight, and a simple blood test. After that it was jump on the next van to the airport for the flight home. That was quite the experience. I had never seen such an immense operation, and it truly humbled me.

A month later I was blessed with being called for the second phase interview. It consisted of a major medical like I had never experienced. They did the cardiac stress test, an EEG, more blood tests, X-ray, and one I had never experienced before, which I was not prepared for, the prostate exam. From there I went on to have an aptitude test and the Minnesota Multiphasic Personality Inventory Psychological Test, which was over 500 questions and took about an hour and a half.

What a day.

What a joy, after another month I was in for phase three. On this one, they put me in a Boeing 707 simulator and just had me do some fairly simple stuff, take off, landing, and steep turns. After that it was in to be interviewed by two American captains. It was sort of a good cop, bad cop scenario. One of them was very cordial and asked some normal questions. The other had a rough air about him with his questions.

It appears that one of my former employers, Mr. Hudson, must have had some negative things to say, pertaining to the affair most likely, when they contacted him because of the questions he asked me pertaining to that job. I was just honest and up front in response to all of the questions. This was the easiest and most relaxed of the three phases. Now it was back to Pampa and wait.

I had been given a date to call in and check on the end result of the third phase of my interview. That date came, and I dialed the number. When the lady answered, I gave her my name and told her I was calling to check on the final decision. She put me on hold, and as I sat there waiting, I knew it was in the Lord's hands. I was so hopeful that He would find favor and bless me in this.

When she came back on the line it was, "Congratulations, Mr. Straub. You have been chosen to be a future pilot for American Airlines." She went on to tell me they were so far behind on training all of the new hires, that my class date would be at the end of May, which was five months away.

I was ecstatic. I was thinking someone needed to pinch me; was I awake? I was so thankful it was hard to contain my feeling of excitement. I told her, "Thank you for that wonderful news. I look forward to the opportunity to make everyone who was involved in this pleased with the decision they made."

When I got off the phone, I was so excited. In my wildest dreams I would have never expected to achieve this. I felt fairly confident that within eight years or less, I was going to be a captain at American Airlines.

I went running to find Arlene. When I found her, I wrapped my arms around her and told her the news. I said, "We have to get dressed up and go out to dinner tonight and celebrate."

I didn't sense the extreme joy in her that I had, but I thought this was my dream not hers, so I can't expect her to be quite as excited as I am.

After I told her, I went back to the phone to call Phil and tell him. After we discussed my good news, he told me he was going down to Groom, Texas to see John Gries and Craig Howard. He invited me to join them, and I told him I would love to. At that he shared he would come get me in less than an hour. I went to Arlene to let her know what was going on and went on to inform her I would be back, in plenty of time, to get ready for our dinner celebration.

Phil got me back home by five. I went into the house, gave Arlene a hug, and started getting ready for our celebration. I was completely ready with coat and tie on and was just waiting for her to finish getting ready. The next thing you know, she came in the living room where I was, and with an angry tone she proceeded to question if I remembered what I told her I would get done that day

I immediately knew what she was talking about, and I apologized for failing to get it done. I went on to tell her I would definitely do it the next day. No, that was not good enough, and she proceeded to launch into the usual. I said that next to her becoming my wife this was the happiest and most important day of my life. I asked her if she could show me some grace and be happy with me in that accomplishment.

What I said, pertaining to the joy of her becoming my wife, meant nothing to her. I had been blessed with a job and an opportunity that only a handful of people in the world attain, and she was tearing into me over some menial, non-critical chore that in my excitement I failed to get done.

It didn't stop. That celebration dinner didn't happen, and there was never any apology for destroying one of the happiest days in my life. As painful as it was, however, deep down Jesus Christ gave me peace and joy in spite of the pain.

The next day came, and I got that chore done. The next thing on the list was to go and tell Mr. Hinkle the news. I went in his office and sat down in the chair across from his desk. I said, "Mr. Hinkle, I learned yesterday that I have been hired by American Airlines." I went on to tell him that I wouldn't report to them until the end of May, another five and a half months.

I went on to say, "I'll be glad to share my thoughts on anyone that you talk to or that approaches you to take my place when May gets here." He thanked me, we did a little small talk, and I departed.

Just a few days later Mr. Hinkle called me and asked me to come by the office. I went right over, walked in and sat down. He said, "Jay, I've found your replacement. Please give me the keys to the hangar and the aircraft. The office manager will have your check."

I couldn't believe it. I could hardly speak. After a few seconds, I said, "OK." I stood up fished my key ring out, took the keys off, handed them to him, and said, "Goodbye."

I don't recall any response from him. I headed to the office manager, got my check, and went home.

I walked in the house, sat down on the bed, and was asking the Lord lots of questions. As I sat there running it all through my mind, I just couldn't help it, there were a few tears streaming down my face. I had been sitting there, probably fifteen minutes, and Arlene came in the house.

She looked at me and asked, "What's going on?"

With my voice a bit shaky, I shared what had just happened.

Apparently, it was still visible that I had shed some tears, and she said, "Well, crybaby, what are you going to do now?"

I couldn't believe it. I was feeling so devastated I couldn't even respond. As always, I forgave and continued to love her.

The next five months were tough. The oil bust was eliminating almost everything flight related, even day trips. There were so many other pilots available that I got nothing. And I was obviously not going to get a full-time job anywhere with it known that I'm headed to American Airlines five months down the road. I was just doing any kind of odd job I could find to keep us afloat.

Another event took place at this point. The gentlemen whom Phil had been working for threw him a grand going-away party out at the airport, and I was invited. Boy, was that difficult. Arlene refused to go with me, and I felt totally alone. I tried to keep a smile on while Phil's soon to be former employers were celebrating his success, but it was way hard with what Mr. Hinkle had just dealt me with my achieving the same thing that Phil had.

An incredible surprise was awaiting me, however. Phil's soon-to-be-former employers, while I barely knew them, presented me with a gift at the end of the party along with the one they gave to Phil. Wow! That was so very kind of them, and truly lifted me up right when I was in great need of it.

Of all the trials I had in the job loss arena up to this point, I had never filed for unemployment. After a short period of time it looked like I was going to have to do that. I did, and you will never guess what happened. Denied! I had never been late on a bill in my entire life up to this point, but now I was going to be unable to make a payment on one of the rent houses.

I went to the bank to inform the vice president of the predicament I was in. He was most unkind and informed me that I had three months. If it weren't up-to -date by then he was going to take action. I managed to do that before the three-month period had transpired. Praise God.

I really don't know how, but we made it through the five months, with only that one bill being behind. On second thought, I do know how. It was more of God's grace and provision. Now, the next twelve months will be another pay cut from where I was for most of the last eight years to $1,800/month, and I will be on probation in the new job at American Airlines. I was truly in need of the Lord's help.

DRINKING OUT OF A FIREHOSE

I

That day in May finally came. I showed up at the American Airlines Flight Academy in my suit and tie ready to go. It was an intense day, and they made it clear it would not be a cakewalk. To earn the flight engineer certificate on the Boeing 727 and learn the company procedures in six weeks were going to be grueling.

A part of that day was spent filling out paperwork and getting my picture taken for the company ID. In spite of the five months of trials that I just shared, I felt I was ready. The Lord had given me peace and some confidence. I was glad to be there with my five fellow classmates.

The second day was a bit unnerving on a front that I never expected or experienced in life prior to this. I had certainly been around lots of people who didn't put their faith in Jesus Christ, but I had never experienced this type of attitude personally. The instructor made more than one comment that indicated his dislike for people who give any credence to the Bible.

Given the fact that these guys could potentially have you terminated, made it even more stressful on my end, since I was not going to deny my faith. Fortunately, nothing happened, but whether it did or didn't, I knew deep down that Jesus would lift me up as He had time after time.

It was almost five weeks of ground school, learning the systems and operating procedures of the 727 and the FAA regulations. That part ended with an oral exam, where an FAA designee would sit down and ask questions on all of these items. The final week to ten days would be in the simulator with hands-on learning to do the flight engineer duties in normal and emergency procedures.

If you were successful, your instructor would sign you off for the simulator check ride with another FAA designee. You would go through a check ride with normal and emergency procedures to evaluate your skill. If you passed this one, you were issued the FAA Flight Engineer-Turbojet Certificate.

I went through it all and passed the oral exam and check ride. The designee told me during the debrief that I came mighty close to busting the check ride. I can't remember exactly which one it was, but he saw me reach for a particular switch that would have done me in. Thank the Lord, I caught the error before I did it.

In wrapping up my training as an American Airlines new hire-flight engineer on the Boeing 727, something that I had heard around 2003 came to mind. It was a supposed quote from a former new hire. You know how that can be. You don't want to rely on hearsay, so I set out on a mission to verify it. It was truly a pleasure when I got in touch with the person quoted.

The gentleman I'm referring to is Curtis L. Brown Jr. (Colonel, USAF, Ret., former NASA astronaut). When he returned my call, I told him what I had heard. When I finished, he basically affirmed it. He shared that he came on board at American in 2000 and that the aforementioned training was the most intense and difficult training that he had ever experienced, USAF and NASA-shuttle commander combined.

He went on to tell me that one of his classmates at American was a former captain on the 727 at another airline. That gentleman didn't make the grade and was dismissed. That pretty much confirmed what one of the instructors told my class on the first day. We were informed that the ground school was going to be like drinking water out of a fire hose, and our brains would be close to a max amperage overload. I can certainly vouch for that.

II

The next event was the initial operating experience (IOE). That's where a line check airman flies with you during an actual revenue flight to help you learn the ropes and sign you off to be on your own when he finds you capable. The IOE went well, and the check airman was very helpful, thought I did well, and signed me off. I was ready to go to work.

Now, the tough part was the fact that a week or so into ground school, we made a list of crew bases that we preferred to be based at. They told us that for months every new hire had been getting their first choice.

I naturally preferred Dallas. Well, wouldn't you know it? My class was the first in months that didn't get their first choice, and where do I wind up? New York City. As a matter of fact, my entire class got sent to New York. That was a good thing for two of them because that was their first choice, not so much for me and the other three.

I and the other three decided it would be good for us to stick together. We would find a place to stay until we got transferred to our desired crew bases. We reported the first day for our indoctrination, being done by the New York Chief Pilot.

After that, we set out in search of an apartment. We found a place shared by other crew members that would let us stay for just a few nights. They really didn't have any room to spare, but they were all out working that week.

We were all on reserve, which meant we had to have a pager. If crew schedule called with an open trip that needed to be filled, we had to call them immediately to find out what was going on. It could easily be a trip where a pilot was scheduled to fly and called in sick at the last minute. There were any number of scenarios where something could happen, and they had to call a reserve pilot to fly the trip.

At our indoctrination the chief pilot was emphatic. When crew schedule calls you, don't mess around in returning the call. We would typically have to be at the airport within two hours. Most of the crew bases wanted you there in an hour, but the New York crew base covered three airports, La Guardia, Newark, and JFK, so we had an extra hour.

There we sat, the four of us anxiously awaiting our first trip. Bob's pager goes off. That was peculiar. When crew schedule had a trip open, they were awarded by our seniority number. In our class, Bob was the lowest on the seniority list, and I was just above him, so I was wondering why his pager went off and not ours.

All four of us took off down the street to a pay phone. I know it's hard to believe, but this was 1986, still no cell phones, and there was no phone in the crash pad apartment. Bob made the call, and the rest of us were standing there, anxiously hoping there might be a trip for us as well.

Bob says, "Yes, he's standing right here."

Bob hands me the phone.

I take it and say, "Hello."

On the other end the crew scheduler says, "Flight Engineer Straub, why did you not answer the page thirty minutes ago?"

I said, "I'm sorry, sir. My pager didn't go off, and I have no idea why it didn't. It's turned on and has been the entire time. When Bob's went off, all four of us came down here with him to talk to you and see if there were any trips available for us."

He told me about the trip available for me.

I said, "Yes sir, I will take it."

Then the crew scheduler informed me that I did not respond to my page and he had already submitted a message to my chief pilot of my failure to respond. At that, the phone went *click* in my ear. I couldn't believe what just happened. When I told the others, they were about as shocked as I was.

It's two months into this, and I'm starting to wonder, a bit, what I've gotten myself into. My Christian faith has been attacked by someone who had a good deal of power over my potential future at American Airlines, and now I'm being accused of being unavailable when I was sitting there, just chomping at the bit waiting for a trip.

III

The next morning, I was up way early to be ready for my first revenue trip. You have to sign in on the computer one hour prior to the departure time, so I made sure I was at La Guardia an hour and a half prior for sign-in. I met the captain and first officer and headed to the aircraft to do the first flight of the day origination preflight inspection. Not only was the initial training to be a flight engineer on the 727 a major challenge, the actual job itself was equal to that for some time. It was intense.

It was a real challenge to get the inside part of the origination preflight done in less than twenty-five minutes. You have to check and set everything on the flight engineer panel, the flight engineer side panel, the flight instrument panel for the captain and first officer, the pedestal between the captain and first officer, and the overhead panel above the captain and first officer.

After all that, you go outside and do the exterior inspection, looking for any damage or anything that is not right on the exterior of the aircraft. Then you go back up the jet bridge staircase to get to the flight deck to complete the flight engineer part of the preflight. It's not easy, and I'll just leave it at that, especially when the ground crew doesn't get the aircraft to the gate until forty-five minutes prior to departure, as they did that morning.

I have a couple of memories from that first three-day sequence that I flew on my own as a flight engineer for American. The first was going into Harlingen, Texas late in the evening on the second day of the trip.

American's expansion was taking them into smaller airports that a number of the captains and first officers had never been to. Due to our late arrival time, the FAA Control Tower at Harlingen had closed. The captain or first officer had never experienced landing at an airport where the tower was closed and were a bit flummoxed. The captain was basically asking, "Well, how the heck does this work?"

I had done this numerous times in my eight-plus years of general aviation flying, so I responded, "Captain, we are VFR, so just fly the traffic pattern on the CTAF [Common Traffic Advisory Frequency] that you will find on the approach plate. Announce when you are on the downwind leg for the runway, then announce the base leg, and finally announce turning final."

He was still a bit concerned that we didn't have a clearance from the tower to land, but I assured him that we were good with this. He was really appreciative of my input and thanked me after we had parked and shut down the aircraft.

The next day was quite interesting. The first officer was brand new in that seat acting as co-pilot. He had been a flight engineer for eight years or longer. I didn't think much of it until we went into Baton Rouge, Louisiana that day. The runway we were landing on was somewhat short. Once again, I didn't think much of it, since the runways at LaGuardia were about the same length.

It was the first officer's turn to fly the leg going into Baton Rouge. Usually the captain and first officer alternate the legs on a trip. The captain always flies the first leg, then the first officer flies the next, and on and on it goes.

We were on final approach, we completed the checklist, and I announced, "Before landing check list complete." Now, I'm sitting in the middle, right behind and between the captain and first officer, and I'm sitting up a little higher than they are. I've got a real bird's eye view there.

We cleared the runway threshold, then we crossed the 1,000-foot touchdown zone marker. I was thinking, no problem. Next, we crossed the 1500-foot zone marker, and I'm starting to squirm. Then we cross the 2000-foot marker still floating, and the first officer is doing nothing to plant this thing on the ground. Those markers tell you how many feet have passed since you crossed the end of the runway, and you are supposed to touch down no more than 1000 feet from the end.

Now, I am seeing the end of my career, if not worse, flash before my eyes.

At this point the captain reaches down and pulls the speed brake handle, which kills all of the lift on the wing. The plane immediately fell the last five to ten feet and hit the ground like a ton of bricks.

The captain slammed on the wheel brakes, and when we came to a stop, I couldn't see any of the runway in front of us with the nose gear of that plane located basically right below my seat. We were just a few feet from having that nose gear be in the dirt. That was way better than what I thought was about to happen,

A new hire, "moi," going to a hearing after an event like that would not have been good. It was supposed to be the first officer making the landing at La Guardia at the end of our trip that day, as well.

I was relieved when the captain took that landing in place of the first officer. In my twelve-plus years of service at American Airlines, that event on my first trip was the co-winner of the, as they say, "hours of boredom followed by a moment of sheer terror" award.

The captain was very complimentary of me as we gathered our things to leave and complete the three-day trip, after we parked at the gate and completed the shutdown and checklists. After we shook hands, the captain and first officer headed for home.

Now, I had the joy of heading to the flight office to report to the chief pilot for not answering that page that I never received from crew schedule. I went in and told the secretary who I was and that I needed to speak to the chief. He called me into his office and told me to have a seat.

After I sat down, he asked me why I was there. I went through the whole spiel, giving him all of the details of how Bob's pager went off, mine didn't, and the crew scheduler still turned me in when it was evident that I was there just "chomping at the bit" to go to work and fly my first trip on my own.

At the conclusion of what I shared, he gave me a stern look and just told me not to let it happen again. I thanked him for his time and told him I would be doing my very best. As I left the office, I was just wondering how I was going to prevent a pager from malfunctioning, but rather quickly it just came to mind, that all I could do was my best, and all those other things were in my Lord's hands.

IV

After that I got to go home for a few days. While I was there, my classmates found us an apartment owned by a fellow American employee. He offered us a good deal if we would do some interior paint and improvement for him. He knew we probably would not be there long; now it was back to New York for handyman and flight engineer duties.

One of the days when it was pretty clear that none of us was going to be called for a last-minute departure, we all went into Manhattan to check it out. That was quite fantastic for a guy from Amarillo; topping if off with an awesome meal from a New York Deli was over the top for me.

After two months, thank goodness, I got to transfer to DFW. I was in hopes that I would be able to move our family to the Dallas-Ft. Worth area, but Arlene wasn't going to give on that one iota. We had learned that a lot of crew members commuted to work, using their travel benefits; some came from very long distances.

So, it was just as it was when I had the job offer from the State of Texas. We were not moving, period. Phil had gotten an apartment just south of the flight academy in Euless, Texas, so I stayed at his place when I was on call until I was able to get a trip. Then, once the trip was completed, I would use my travel benefits to fly to Amarillo and drive home. I was sure thankful that I was able to get an employee parking pass at the Amarillo Airport.

I went through the six-month probationary review. That involved going into the flight office to be questioned and evaluated by one of the chief pilots. I was glad that my review went well. All of my probationary reports submitted by the captains I had flown with were good, and I answered all the questions that the chief threw at me.

I could have upgraded to a first-officer position well before my one-year probation period was over, but I was advised to not do that, if I could avoid it. The reason was the lack of having any union support if you had a problem in your training while you were on probation.

There were some who didn't have the choice. If your seniority were low and a first-officer position opened up, and nobody senior to you bid for it, then you had no option. Going through the flight academy twice in one year under the probationary microscope was not at all desirable.

V

I was anxious to upgrade to first officer and get back to hands-on flying, but I enjoyed the time "riding sidesaddle." Another of my monthly schedule of trips that comes to mind was one which the captain I flew with all month was a former US Navy Blue Angel. We would get our bid schedule for the next month around ten days prior to the end of the current month. When I saw that this was the captain whom I would fly with and learned of his previous career, I was really looking forward to that.

In my conversation with some fellow former corporate pilot new hires, I was starting to hear that he was a good guy until he learned you're a former corporate pilot and not military. The word was that you better look out when that comes into the equation. That first three-day trip I flew with him that month went really well, and my job history never came up. I was relieved at that. The second three-day had a layover in Amarillo on the second day. I had called Dad and told him we were going to layover there, and he met us in the terminal. That was pre-9/11, back in the day when you could do that as you came off the aircraft.

As we met my dad, I introduced him to my fellow crew members. The captain proceeded to tell him he should be proud of me and went on to tell him what a great job I was doing. Wow! I was not expecting that. That was a relief. The rest of that month was great, and I was pleased to have flown with him a full month. After that experience, I learned not to sweat the rumors that float around and to just put it all in the Lord's hands. That entire year I never had a bad experience with any of them.

VI

Around the same time frame of what I just shared, I was commuting home from a trip one day and was still wearing my uniform. After we arrived at Amarillo, a gentleman who had been on the flight came over to talk to me. I recognized him as a professor at AC back when I was attending there, and he had recognized me as a former student. He saw that I was now a pilot at American Airlines. He congratulated me on my achievement and said he would like for me to consider something.

As we walked along, he asked if I had seen any of the billboards in Amarillo that had pictures of successful AC alumni. I told him that I had. He went on to say that they would really like to have a picture of me in my uniform on one of those billboards.

At that point our paths were about to change in getting to our cars. We stopped walking, and I extended my hand and thanked him for considering me for that. I told him I would give it some thought, discuss it with my wife, and get back with him. At that point he gave me his business card, and we shook hands again and bid one another goodbye.

As I drove home, I was certainly pleased that he recognized me and my accomplishment, but I wasn't feeling very enthusiastic about it. When I got home, I shared about it with Arlene, but I didn't go into my lack of enthusiasm. I just wanted to hear her thoughts. I frankly wasn't even finished with sharing the whole discussion, and I could see an irritation building on her face. She wasted no time in expressing her total disapproval.

When I tried to get a logical reason for her to be so against it, it became quite clear that once again she just couldn't stand the idea of me being given credit for anything. I guess, at the very least, that made it fairly simple to make the decision. I sure didn't want to experience her sour disposition every time we drove to Amarillo and she would see my picture on a billboard.

I called the professor and thanked him for seeing the value in me for that, but after discussing it with my wife, I decided not to do it. He told me to call back if I changed my mind, and I thanked him once again.

VII

It's stunning, the timing of things. Within a few months of when that meeting with the professor took place, I was working a trip, and we were about ready to depart. We had a policy where we could allow fellow pilots from other airlines to ride in our flight deck jump seat free of charge, and typically the captain would just send them to an empty seat back in the cabin if one were available.

The union policy was that we, the pilots, were not to allow any scabs from other airlines on the jump seat, and one of the captains that I had flown with actually had a printed-out list with the names of pilot scabs from other airlines that he carried in his flight bag. When we had a pilot from another airline request our jump seat, he would whip out that list and check before he would approve.

What's this all about, you ask?

I was sitting there, preparing everything on my end for our departure to Amarillo no less, when I sensed someone stepping into the flight deck. I turned to look, and there stood Brent, whom I hadn't seen or spoken too since that bone-chilling departure from Denver in the thunderstorm.

We were both a bit stunned to see each other, and we shook hands. Brent told me he would like to ride our jump seat if possible. At that, I turned my seat and leaned up to the captain to tell him what was going on and introduce him to Brent.

Here's the troubling part of this turn of events. As you recall, he was hired by a major airline shortly after our Denver departure ordeal, and the pilots at that airline went on strike several years later. Brent crossed the picket line, went to work, and was a scab. In spite of what he did to endanger me and Phil that night in Denver and all the rest, I couldn't bring myself to tell the captain that he was a scab.

BACK IN THE SADDLE AGAIN—
THEN HANDS BEHIND MY BACK

I

It wouldn't be long until I went to the flight office for my twelve-month re-view. I was all studied up and ready for whatever they might ask me. It turned out to be fairly laid back. I got the congratulations, the handshake, and welcome aboard. What a joy, and what a relief.

Not long after that, I put in my bid for 727 first officer at DFW. This was only going to be four weeks of training versus the six weeks for flight engineer. The ground school was easy since I already knew the plane quite well from being a flight engineer on it. The simulator part was not quite as laid back. I recall having a bit of a struggle the first couple of days, but then it smoothed out.

I absolutely loved everything about flying the 727. I nearly always hand flew it from takeoff until reaching cruise altitude. Then after level off, I would engage the autopilot. On reaching our destination, I would usually disengage the autopilot and hand fly it after we had slowed to the 250-knot speed limit to descend below 10,000 feet and be vectored for the approach to our landing runway.

When it came to landings, the 727 could bite you. The swept back wings and center of gravity played a role in that. I think the Lord truly blessed me in that arena. In the hundreds of flights I did there was only one that was really bad. We were going into Birmingham, Alabama in one of the 727-100s that we lovingly called "the shorty," as its length was considerably less than the 727-200s'.

That day we were light. We had more empty seats than filled seats, and the weather was great, so our fuel load was very light. When I pulled back on the throttles it floated, and when it touched the ground it was so light it just bounced back in the air. The second time it touched down it bounced again. The third time was the charm, but this time it was with a *thud*.

Gee, I got on the brakes, and when I finally handed the aircraft over to the captain, I turned to him with a sheepish look, and he just cracked a big smile and said, "Probably wasn't the first time and sure ain't gonna be the last."

Well, I can honestly say it was the first and last, but I don't take all the credit in that. That's truly a blessing from above.

Another fond memory was going into Milwaukee, Wisconsin one night. The weather was down to minimums for the Category 1 ILS Approach—200-foot ceiling, a half mile of visibility, and we had a cross wind that was just barely under the maximum to legally execute the approach. We were allowed to hand fly the Category 1s down to minimums, and I really enjoyed doing that to keep my skills fresh. That was truly serious business, and I loved it.

We went through the approach briefing where we look at the approach plate and verbally lay out all of the parameters of the approach, things like the ILS frequency, initial approach altitude, marker crossing altitude, approach course, and minimums. After approach control gave us the final heading to intercept the localizer, the needle started to move, and I initiated my turn to intercept while I maintained the initial approach altitude.

After a few miles the glide slope needle started to come down, and the outer marker (light and audible) came on. When the glide slope needle was centered, I initiated the descent to follow the glide slope down to our decision height of 200 feet. At that point, we would either see the runway and land or initiate the go-around.

As we came down the approach, I kept the localizer needle centered as well as the glide slope needle. The right cross wind also required that I was holding a heading a little bit to the right of runway heading, to keep us lined up with the center line of the runway. Just a little bit above the 200-foot decision height, I was starting to see the flash of the runway centerline lead-in-lights, that we call "the rabbit," lighting up the clouds.

When the captain called, "Two hundred feet, decision height."

I glanced up from the instruments and called, "Runway in sight."

From there he called, "100, 50, 40, 30, 20, 10." Those were callouts of our actual altitude, above ground, in feet, that he was reading off of the radar altimeter.

As we passed the ten foot callout, due to the cross wind, I started to put in a little left rudder to line up the nose of the aircraft with the runway, and a little right aileron to put it in a slight right bank, to prevent us from drifting off to the left, brought the throttles to idle, pulled back for a little nose up elevator, and we were on the ground.

From there, I deployed the speed brakes, engaged the wheel brakes, and put the engines into reverse thrust. When we reached the required airspeed, I disengaged the reverse thrust and announced to the captain, "It's all yours."

At that point he took control of the wheel brakes, steering and throttles.

When we got to the gate, the aircraft was done for the day, just as we were. We went through all of the checklists and shut it down for the night. As we walked through the terminal headed for the crew van, the captain shared that he almost asked me to reengage the autopilot after I disengaged it.

He said that he was a bit concerned with my doing that, since I was fairly new in the first officer seat and with the weather being at minimums. He went on to tell me, however, that I did a great job, and he was glad to have me on his crew. The flight engineer chimed in and said it was really good. I was glad to hear that. It built my confidence and made me even more thankful to our Lord.

II

Back in Pampa around this same time, I was still dealing with the rental property dilemma. One of the properties had a two-story apartment on the back side of the lot. I rented it furnished, and wouldn't you know the refrigerator on the top floor unit went out? Once again, Dad came over to visit right when I was in the midst of dealing with that, and he jumped at the chance to help me with it.

I got a new refrigerator, a two-wheel dolly, and now the fun begins. There was a fairly steep staircase up the side of the structure that led to the entrance door. I went up, opened the door, and secured the screen door open. After we got the refrigerator strapped and secured to the dolly, I took the position of going first, steering and pulling it as we went up the stairs one step at a time.

The Texas Panhandle is well known for several things. One is that as you drive down the highways, it's flatter than a pancake. I think Kansas lays claim to that saying, but it fits the Texas Panhandle as well. Another saying during the winter is the only thing between us and the North Pole is a barbed wire fence. And, last but not least is, it's so windy we use a log chain in place of a windsock. Well, this was one of those "log chain in place of the windsock" days. Just as I got to the top of the stairs the whipping wind managed to blow the screen door shut. I'm sorry to say I can't repeat what flew out of my mouth at that juncture.

Going back down the stairs and back up with that thing was a miserable thought. As I stood there and looked things over, if I could tilt the refrigerator back just a little further, that would give me the few inches I needed to reach the screen doorknob and fling it open.

Once that was done, I could pull the refrigerator over the last step and block the screen door from going closed again. I told Dad to really push on that fridge to prevent it from rolling in his direction and going back down the step we had just cleared. He told me that he had it under control.

I tilted the refrigerator back, and just as I was about to get hold of the screen doorknob, the dolly wheels rolled off that step. When that happened, it jerked the dolly right out my hand. I whirled around to watch my seventy-five-year-old dad tumbling backwards down that steep staircase with a 300-pound projectile in hot pursuit.

Oh, my God! I just knew this was going to be the worst, and I went flying down the stairs after him. To this day I can hardly believe that 300-pound monstrosity didn't flip over and come crashing down on top of him. Praise the Lord it didn't.

When I got to him, I was sure his back was probably broken from the multiple times it slammed into those steps as he tumbled. If that weren't the case, I thought other bones would be broken or a severe concussion perhaps. Who knows what awaited this tragedy? His eyes were closed as I proceeded to kneel down to him.

But before I got to my knees his eyes flew open, and he yelled, "Damn!" He started to get up.

I said, "Hey, stay there until you have a chance to sense whether or not something is really hurt or broken."

He said, "Aw bull," and proceeded to roll over and work his way to standing up.

I reached for him, and he grabbed my hand and said, "Thanks."

Unbelievably, he insisted on trying again. I said, "No way!"

After that I needed to let the refrigerator set upright for twenty-four hours before plugging it in to see if it still worked. Thank goodness it did, and I got some help the next day to get it up there.

III

As you can already tell, Dad was really a wonderful father. I had missed out on some things growing up due to his work schedule and probably his age when I came along, but he more than made up for it. He loved to help with anything he was able to do. He would drive to Pampa to help with something even if I were working and couldn't be there.

Sometime after that refrigerator ordeal, Dad came down with some internal problems that were related to an ulcer he had a little over ten years prior. His small intestines twisted and caused a blockage. The twist had cut off the blood supply, which resulted in emergency surgery to cut out a portion.

He was recovering from that, and I was visiting him and Mom after he got home. I discovered a problem with their kitchen faucet that needed repair. So, I went and got the parts to fix it for them. When I went out to the water meter to turn off the water to do the job, I couldn't get the valve to turn.

I went and got a two-foot pipe that I could slide over the crescent wrench to give me some leverage. It still wouldn't budge. I was down on my knees, and I finally decided to give it everything I had. I pulled as hard as I could, and all of a sudden, I had a bad sensation down in the area of my groin. I wondered what just happened and was concerned that it wasn't good.

It popped into my mind how the Aviation Medical Examiners did the test to check for a hernia right in the area where I had had that bad sensation. When I went in the house to replicate what they did, I wasn't happy with what I felt.

That ended my repair work, and I went home to get an appointment with my doctor. Yes, sure enough, I was informed that I had a hernia. I knew that I couldn't fly with a hernia, so I asked for a referral to a surgeon to get it fixed immediately.

I got in to see Dr. Mohan, and he examined me, advised me on everything involved, and set up the surgery. I got it done, and everything went well. The downside was that this wasn't done laparoscopically. I got the big cut, and holy cow, it hurt to stand up straight. It was going to be six long weeks before I could return to flight status.

As I sat at home recovering from that I spent some time on an old hobby, just sitting there playing my guitar. Arlene was disgusted with that, just as she was with my other few hobbies.

IV

Things continued to go downhill with Arlene. I had moved out a couple of times for a few weeks, trying to get her to see some value in me, which she never did. But I always came back because I truly loved her with all of my heart. I just convinced myself that, somehow, she would eventually see a value in me and love me for who I was.

One day I was coming home from one of my usual three-day trips. On the drive home to Pampa I was just thinking how I couldn't wait to get home and wrap my arms around her, give her a kiss, and spend time with her.

I walked in the door and said, "I'm home." I sat my bags down and set out to find her. She came into the room, and I stretched out my arms to hug her, but I could see nothing but a scowl on her face.

She said, "We need to talk."

Oh, I couldn't believe it. It turned out to be another of the many three-hours-plus sessions.

I asked her, "Why can't you just show me some respect? That's all I ask."

"You have to earn my respect," she continued. As usual, there was no point in trying to leave, to cool down, since she would follow me out to the car yelling and standing behind my vehicle. One of those was enough. And once again, I couldn't go anywhere in the house to get away from her verbal abuse. She followed me from room to room.

That was it. As you already know, when these had occurred previously, it would not stop until I slapped her or physically pushed her away as she chased me around the house. This time, having been so excited to get home and be with her and being bombarded with this, I lost it. With her in my face, I mouthed some profanity at her and pushed her so hard she fell to the ground, hard. That was it. With her unjustifiable verbal abuse and my absolutely unjustifiable physical response, which this time actually hurt her, I decided we had to divorce.

The next day I filed for divorce, packed my things, and moved to Amarillo. I was going to stay at my parents' house until I found a place in the Dallas area that I could rent. My remaining two days off were over, and I had to return to work. I flew another of my typical three-day trips.

It was not a pleasant trip. I felt totally beat and was not my usual self. The captain and flight engineer could tell I wasn't my usual cheerful self. I finally told them that I had just filed for divorce and how devastated I was feeling. They were very empathetic. The trip ended, and little did I know what awaited.

At the end of the trip I got on the last flight home from DFW to Amarillo. It was already dark when we landed and taxied in. I was in the last row where the company computer usually put the non-revenue passengers. That was certainly a good thing on that night. I got my suitcase out of the overhead and was the last passenger getting off.

When I got to the front of the airplane and made the left turn to exit the airplane, there stood the gate agent, whom I recognized and smiled at. The next thing you know, she pointed at me. I glanced to the left, and there stood a deputy sheriff.

He said, "Mr. Straub?"

I said, "Yes."

He said, "I have a warrant for your arrest. If you agree to be calm and collected, I will not put the cuffs on you until we get to my vehicle. Do I have your cooperation? Do you agree to that?"

I said, "Yes sir."

We walked through the terminal and just exchanged some small talk. When we got to his car, he put the cuffs on, hands behind my back, and put me in the back seat.

We got to the station, and they took me in and went through the standard procedure. I didn't call anyone. I was just going to sit in the cell and wait to get the bail bondsman to allow my release. I had not been there over a couple of hours, and the next thing you know, I look up and there stand Mom and Dad. Oh my gosh, how humiliating. I couldn't believe this.

I asked, "How in the world did you know I was here?" They told me they were worried when I didn't arrive at their house within a reasonable time. I had not even told them exactly when I would be getting back, so that was puzzling.

I asked them if they had talked to anyone at the airport, and they said, "No."

To this day I don't know what in the world led them to go there when I had never in my entire life had any contact with the police other than a traffic ticket.

If I weren't stressed out enough, the next day was an even bigger dose. I called Arlene to thank her for having me arrested at my place of employment. She proceeded to swear up and down that the Sheriff in Pampa, where she had reported this, told her they would just call me to come in.

She said that she had told them she didn't want anything like that to happen. Any truth to that? Who knows? She then proceeded to inform me that if I dropped the divorce, the charges would be dropped. Yes, that I was feeling stressed was quite the understatement.

I called my attorney and told him everything that had taken place. He pretty much insisted that I needed to get out of that mess and proceed with the divorce. Oh, my Lord, what do I do? I loved this woman, but it was absolutely clear that she did not love me. I can't please her. I am doing everything possible to provide for her, my daughter, and my stepdaughter.

She has not had to work outside the home for at least six years, other than the help with maintaining the rental houses we had invested in. The only way I can get any respect from her is to earn it. I'm clueless as to how to earn it without working sunup to sundown and then some. And if I don't drop it and lose in the courtroom where will I be?

I spent a day and a half just running it over and over in my mind, and I finally called my attorney, and told him to drop the divorce. It was clear he thought I was making a big mistake. I planned to proceed and do everything possible to improve the situation and keep this marriage intact. I would read more books on marriage, and hopefully she would too. More than anything, I wanted to make this what it should be, a God-centered marriage where we put each other first. Oh, how that was my true desire.

V

One thing I truly needed to do was to get us out of the rental properties. It was going to be a pretty substantial loss, but I hoped it would be a true gain in the long run and perhaps earn a little respect. That would be a relief to finally have that noose removed from around our necks. What a stress those things had been for us with keeping things afloat with that debt burden and the thousands of hours we had spent in keeping them going.

I had something in mind to help with the situation, but it was going to require a change in my position at work to increase my earnings. Before I share that thought, however, I have to share another experience right around this time that was a blessing and a huge surprise as well.

I was on a flight from Amarillo to DFW, headed to work, wearing my uniform. After we had taken off and were in the climb to cruise altitude, the lady sitting next to me struck up a conversation. She asked me what I thought of Donald Trump's attempt to buy American Airlines. I told her that it was certainly a concern, considering what had happened fairly recently with other hostile takeovers of airlines by Carl Icahn and Frank Lorenzo.

The lady proceeded to tell me she had a nephew who flew for American, and she had heard that he was concerned as well. We continued to talk, and she asked me if I were going to work. I told her that I was. She went on to ask if I had lived in Amarillo very long. I shared that I had grown up in Amarillo but was living in Pampa. When I said that, I could see that really piqued her interest for some reason.

After that, she asked where I had lived in Amarillo. I told her that I had grown up on the southern end of the city on Hillside Road. When I completed that sentence, her eyes got really big. The next thing you know, she asked if I were Jay Straub by any chance.

Wow! I couldn't believe this. How could a perfect stranger know who I was based on the street I grew up on? What in the world? When she could see how shocked I was and that she was obviously right, she explained, "You and I are cousins. I'm Patricia Clark."

This was over the top, and I was so pleasantly surprised. I knew her name, but I couldn't recall ever meeting her.

I asked her, "Who's your nephew who flies for American?"

"Brad Wheeler."

OK, now it was starting to come together. I remembered seeing Brad once or twice when I was around four years old. I actually remembered his being at my home and the two of us playing on the swing set in my backyard.

I hadn't seen him since then and had only seen his parents once. That was when my parents and I ran into them in, of all places, Red River, New Mexico. That was one of the few vacations we ever took.

With this being someone from my mom's family, considering the big break-up, I was very glad to finally make contact with one of them. To learn that Brad and I were both pilots, much less for the same company, was a complete shock. Since I didn't know a thing about them since the family break-up, I had to ask her how she figured out who I was so easily. She went on to share that somehow the family had learned a long time ago that I flew and gotten a job over in Pampa.

So, it all added up quite easily for her. That was a real treat and opened up the opportunity to mend one fence in that fiasco, at least. When we arrived at

DFW, I wished we could have had more time, but it was definitely a blessing having that time to get to know one another and open that door.

About a year after that I was able to meet up with them. Aunt Connie outlived both of her husbands, and I joined them at the funeral service when her second husband passed away. That was certainly sad, but it was also a repair of a family tie. It was great to meet family that I had not seen, or heard about, in over twenty years. My dad was really glad to see them and make contact as well. Sadly, Mom had gotten to the point where she would not leave the house for the most part. She wasn't there. I sure wish she could have been.

ON TO THE WIDEBODY—RECONNECTING

|

Advancement for an airline pilot many times comes by moving to bigger planes. For me that meant moving to a Boeing 767. But that increase in respect and income came at a cost. It meant that I would switch from domestic flights to international flying.

Making this change meant going back to school. I had several new things to accomplish. I had to get certified in the 767. I had to learn the duties of an international flight first officer. And I had to get type-rated on the 767, which authorized me to serve as a 767 captain. Also, I could not hold that position at DFW. I was going to have to transfer and commute to the Miami, Florida (MIA) crew base to hold that position.

On international flights there is one captain and two first officers. When the captain goes back for his rest break one of the first officers is in the captain's seat, doing his work.

Early in 1990, I put in the bid for the position and got it: Miami, Boeing 767 first officer, international. I couldn't believe it. I was going to be flying a 767 wide-body. Now it was off to the flight academy, or schoolhouse, as we call it.

During ground school a gentleman introduced himself to us. Captain Cecil Ewell was the new fleet manager of the Boeing 767. Keep that name in mind.

The 767 was a big change from the 727. Along with being a larger aircraft it contained more technology (i.e., automation). Only on longer international flights was a crew of three required. Domestic flights only needed two pilots.

I sailed through the training. Ground school was great, and I passed the oral exam. Then it was off to the simulator for the in-flight part. I was getting qualified for the 767 and 757. Some of the simulator training took place in a 757. For the final simulator check ride, we moved to a 767 simulator.

I showed up for the check ride and was feeling a bit tense because this was for a type rating in the aircraft. The check airman came in the briefing room and introduced himself. As he looked over my paperwork, he said, "Straub, I don't guess you would have known a George Straub, would you?"

I said, "Well as a matter of fact I had an uncle named George. I didn't know him all that well since he lived a good distance from us."

He asked, "Where did he live?"

I told him, "Carlsbad, New Mexico."

His eyes flew open, and he told me he was from Carlsbad. He went on to share that they were great friends with George and Ruby. He went on to elaborate that his kids and George's were best friends and spent the majority of their spare time together. That was really cool. What a small world it truly is. I felt a lot more comfortable, and the check ride went quite well. Now I was type rated in the Boeing 767/757 and international qualified.

II

Now it was time for the IOE down at MIA. The initial part was done in a 757. We flew from MIA to Lima, Peru then from Lima to Santiago, Chile. We did our twenty-four-hour layover in Santiago and did the reverse going back to Lima and MIA. Then I had to do another sequence in the 767 to Europe and back to complete the IOE. It all went well, and I was now qualified to fly to Europe and South America.

I was really excited about the possibility of going to these foreign destinations, especially Germany, to see the land that my grandfather emigrated from. I bid for a trip where I would be flying there for an entire month. It wasn't long before I was blessed with an entire month of trips to Frankfurt and back.

I flew that first trip to Frankfurt. What a deal that was, to call ramp control and announce that American Seven Zero Heavy is ready for pushback. You tack on the "heavy" classification when you call ATC if your takeoff weight is over 300,000 pounds. When the aircraft is a heavy, ATC has to put more vertical and horizontal separation between the heavy and the lighter planes, due to the serious wake turbulence created by the heavy.

We would be arriving about 8 a.m. local time. When we got there, I was so excited. I couldn't wait to see the place. We got on the crew bus, which took us to the city of Darmstadt and our layover location, the Maritim Hotel. It was about a twenty-minute bus ride to the Maritim, and the view was fabulous as we rolled down the Autobahn.

We were laying over twenty-four hours, and then it was back to MIA. I wasn't sure how this was going to work. It was close to 1 a.m. or 2 a.m. on my body clock and around 10 a.m. local time. Nevertheless, I had to see something in Darmstadt. I loved every minute of it and couldn't wait to get home and talk to Dad about it.

I met the captain and the other first officer for dinner then went to bed and slept fairly well. The next morning, when we got to the Frankfurt Airport, since I was the number two first officer, I had to go to ops and prepare the old-style paper maps that showed our route of flight and all of the flight information. They were hung back in the cabin for our passengers to look at.

That's hard to believe now when we have video screens in the seat backs to view all of that information in real time. From there it was off to the aircraft to do the preflight setup of the flight deck, including the flight management system (FMS) and the exterior inspection. When departure time arrived, it was back to MIA.

That early morning departure out of Germany with a United Kingdom flyover was over-the-top fantastic. When we got to MIA, I had to take off running to get through customs, then to flight ops to drop off my flight bag. From there, I hurried to catch the next flight back to DFW and then on to Amarillo with the drive to Pampa. Whew!

I had to go to Mom and Dad's to tell them all about seeing Germany.

I went in the house and immediately told Dad about the trip. When his father passed away in 1937, all contact with the family in Germany had been lost from what I knew. So, I was asking Dad if he had any idea where I might find family members there.

He shared that a couple of years ago my grandfather's youngest sister passed away, and the family there went through her stuff and found his old mailing address in Umbarger, Texas.

They had mailed a letter to the postmaster in Umbarger, and that person forwarded it to Ann, Dad's sister. He told me he would check with her to see where the letter came from and the name of the person who sent it. I thought that was fantastic and wondered why in the world he never mentioned that to me. Regardless, I couldn't wait to get the information.

III

Dad called me the day before I left on my next trip with the name and the return address on the letter. In two days, I would be back at the Maritim Hotel to make the first verbal contact between family members since at least 1937.

When I arrived, I went to the concierge and asked if he could assist me in getting a phone number for the family member in Freiburg. He helped with that, and I went to my room to make the call.

I dialed the number and was a bit anxious as the phone rang. After several rings a gentleman answered.

I said, "Hello, this is Jay Straub from Amarillo, Texas."

Before I got any further, I could tell that he had turned his head from the phone, and there was a great deal of excitement in his voice. He was speaking in German to others in the room, and I could hear several different voices responding.

The next thing you know, a young lady's voice came on the phone speaking very good English. It was his daughter, Irene. What a joy it was to find these long-lost relatives and speak to them.

I learned a little about them, and toward the end of the conversation she asked where I was. I told her I was at the Maritim Hotel in Darmstadt. She said she lived within walking distance of that hotel, and she went on to say that she was just visiting her parents.

Once again, what a small world. Unbeknownst to me, when I was there the previous week, I had a cousin who was within walking distance of my hotel. As we finished our call, she asked me when I was returning.

I told her it would be a week. She gave me her phone number and told me to call when I returned so we could meet. I was just thrilled with this new chapter in my life, getting to know family who has been out of the picture since 1937.

As I did the last time, when I arrived in Amarillo at the conclusion of my trip, I had to drive over to Mom and Dad's to give them an update. I told Dad that I spoke to his first cousin, Hans, and his daughter, Irene. I encouraged him to fly over there with me to meet his family and see the beautiful land that his dad had left to come to America.

I was stunned, that as I talked about it, he didn't really seem to show much interest in it. I could only surmise that he really wasn't feeling all that great after the intestinal problem that he had. His health seemed to be going downhill a bit. I worked with him quite a bit, but sad to say, he never got to go there.

The next trip was another real joy. When I got to the hotel, I changed clothes and immediately called Irene. She gave me a good time to come to her apartment, and I counted it down. She had given me directions to her apartment from the hotel, so off I went. I knocked on the door, and it opened to the sweet young lady I spoke to on the phone the week before. I introduced myself, and she was very happy to meet me. We went in, sat down, and proceeded to have a great conversation. Her English was very good.

Irene was in school to become a nurse and had two brothers, Ralph and Rainer. Ralph was an attorney in a small town, Singen, down near the Swiss border, and Rainer was a medical doctor at the University in Regensburg. Her father, Hans, was retired from an equivalent of a credit union in Freiburg, and her mother's name was Ruth.

I was thrilled to learn all of this, and I shared a little of my life and family history with her, which she appeared to find very interesting. We talked for hours, and she shared a meal that she prepared when her boyfriend arrived. It was such a joy visiting with them, and I hated to leave. As we said goodbye, I told her to tell her parents that I was going to rent a car and drive down to Freiburg to meet them on my next trip if that would work for them.

When I got home, I went straight home and shared over the phone with Dad. It was such a blessing seeing family that hadn't been contacted in just shy of sixty years. The next trip, when I arrived at Frankfurt, it was straight to Hertz for the rental car. Wow. Driving down the Autobahn was one of many things I had never dreamed I would experience. It was about three hours down the A5 from the airport to Freiburg. As I pulled up at their home, I couldn't wait to meet them.

I knocked. The door flew open with Hans reaching out saying, "Herman, Herman, come in, come in." Next, he's calling Ruth. He said my name and then he went into the German language that I couldn't understand, obviously telling her I was there. Ruth came right to the door to greet me.

They brought me in and sat me down at the dining table, and Ruth started to feed me immediately. She lavished me with black forest ham, cheese, muesli, a soft-boiled egg, their version of Nutella, and on and on. I was amazed at their hospitality. Their English was pretty good too. They seemed to understand what I said quite well, actually much better than I expected, and when they spoke in English it was really quite good.

They had lots of questions about my side of the family, and I had many pertaining to theirs. Neither of them had ever been to the United States, so there were also lots of questions about my homeland, and once again I had similar questions for them. We got in the Audi, and Hans gave me a brief tour of Freiburg. It was such a pleasure getting to know them and spend time with them. I was definitely wishing that the layover were more than twenty-four hours.

The time flew by, and with the three-hour drive back to Darmstadt ahead, I had to leave much sooner than I desired. As I got up to start the drive back, Hans said, "Herman, one moment." He went scurrying off to another room and came back with a book that he gave me to keep. "This is a 150-year history of where I worked."

He opened the book and showed me a picture of him in his younger days. Then he went further back to a picture that really brought empathy on my part. It was obviously World War II related. He pointed at a young lady in the back of a group of people who was smiling. She was his dear wife, Ruth. On a table that all of the people were standing around was a box that was being opened. In big black letters the box had *CARE* written on it, and under that was *USA*. In the background of the picture was rubble where Freiburg had been fairly recently bombed.

I thanked him and told him I would cherish the time and this precious gift that he had given me. I went on to share that I really looked forward to more visitation with them, and they told me they would be looking forward to that as well. I gave them both a hug, got in the car, and headed back to Darmstadt. This had been a wonderful trip that gave me some fantastic memories that remain to this day. It made for some good discussion the next day on the flight back to Miami as well as on the phone with Dad when I got home.

IV

Over the next year I made a number of trips down to Freiburg. On one of them, my fellow first officer expressed an interest in joining me, and I was more than pleased with that. He really enjoyed meeting my family. On another, I was able to meet Hans and Ruth's two sons. Ralph, the attorney, shocked me when he asked me about the Cadillac Ranch. Egad! I couldn't believe anyone in Germany would have heard of the Cadillac Ranch.

For those of you who don't know, in Amarillo we had a rather eccentric fellow and prankster, Stanley Marsh 3. (He used the numeral 3 in place of the Roman III.) Mr. Marsh did a number of off-the-wall art projects, but probably the best known was burying a number of old Cadillac automobiles sticking straight up out of the ground in a field west of Amarillo.

It had been out there since 1974, the year before I graduated from high school, and I had never ventured to check it out more closely, even though I drove by it hundreds of times going to work at the Agriculture Experiment Station. Ralph couldn't believe I'd never gone out to take a closer look.

It was amazing to learn of the snow that they got there in the Black Forest. I was planning to go down on one trip, but Hans told me not to come, the snow was too deep. When summer finally arrived, I couldn't wait to take Arlene and my daughter there to meet the family and see the beautiful countryside. When we arrived, my daughter absolutely loved Hans! She thought he was the greatest next to her Pa-Pa, my dad.

We stayed with Hans and Ruth a few days. During that time, the highlight for me was Hans taking us out to see the old family farm. I was entranced as I learned about it. I was told that this property, where my grandfather, John Straub, grew up, was in our family over two hundred years. I couldn't fathom that. When I asked what happened, as our family no longer owned it, Hans didn't seem to understand my question. So, I just dropped it.

Anyway, it was truly a delight getting to go in the old house that my grandfather grew up in over a hundred years prior. I learned that it had caught fire long ago, and part of it had to be rebuilt, but a large part of it was still original. It was intriguing that it was a house-barn. The bottom floor was where the animals lived, and the second floor was for the family.

The rest of the trip we drove through the Black Forest seeing the House of 1,000 Clocks in Triberg. What a place! Then it was on to see Neuschwanstein Castle, built by Ludwig II back in the 1800s, right in the middle of the southern tip of Germany. I had seen it in pictures many times, and what a treat it was to see it for real. From there we made it over to Munich to see a few of the sites there, including the world-famous Hofbräuhaus, where Mozart and many famous and infamous individuals had imbibed the brew.

After Munich we continued up to Dachau. Walking through Dachau, one of the main prisons of the Holocaust, was heart wrenching. Curtis's dad, Clinton, was in the Rainbow Division of the US Army in World War II. They were one of the US Army divisions that liberated Dachau at the end of the war.

As we walked through, we saw the gas chambers, the ovens, and the rail-cars that were used to attempt to exterminate God's chosen people, the Jews. It made me tremble at the thought of how evil mankind can be. While Stalin, Mao, and others have exceeded the number of lives that Hitler destroyed by tens of millions, the truly troubling thing is how there were many Christians (in name only) who justified that evil act against the Jews.

It was truly difficult discussing all that had taken place in the location that we had just seen with my sweet little daughter, who was around ten at the time. Also, it was a bit sad to basically end our journey in the land of my ancestors on that note. All in all, though, I loved it. It was an absolutely wonderful week, getting to introduce our families to one another and to have a great time and many conversations together.

As we flew back home, I sat there wishing that my stepdaughter could have been there with us. She had moved out of our home and in with her dad. She was at the age, though, where it would have probably been completely insignificant to her, especially with her having no real connection to it. At least my daughter seemed to enjoy it, and that gave me tremendous joy. I was looking forward to hopefully doing that again, and I really hoped that some of the family over there would come and visit us.

V

There's one other thing that sticks in my memory: a trip coming home from Buenos Aires, Argentina. I was the FB on that trip, so I was the first one to go back for a rest break. FB is the designation for the second first officer that goes on the international flights.

Ours was the right seat in the center section of first class, second row back. I left the flight deck, walked back, sat down, and buckled my seat belt. After getting settled in, I just glanced over to my right, and there sat Billy Graham. What a pleasure!

I didn't say anything, but Mr. Graham obviously could tell that I recognized him. He immediately stuck his hand out to shake mine. I introduced myself and told him that I had seen posters up in various places around the city that shared about the ministry event he had just completed. I went on to ask him how it went. You could see the joy on his face as he shared about all the people who had come down and put their faith in Jesus Christ.

Before he got too far, he asked me if had ever given my life to Jesus. My response was, "Absolutely, when I was around seven or eight years old."

He obviously took joy in hearing that. He went on and talked to me close to twenty minutes. That was one of the most memorable events in my career, getting to meet and talk with him.

VI

If you recall, I mentioned earlier that I was going to hopefully increase my income and attempt to earn her respect, as Arlene had put it. At this point I was ready to give it all I had. The house was a big deal to Arlene, and my working on something pertaining to the house was primo.

There had been an event several years prior that had given me an idea of something that could be truly beneficial relating to the house. I was sitting in the living room reading on one of my days off between trips. Arlene was in the kitchen cooking dinner and she said, "Jay, it's looking pretty dark outside. Why don't you check the weather?"

I got up and walked over to the stereo system and turned on the AM radio to the local channel to find out if there were any weather alerts.

After doing that, I thought I would go out the front door to take a better look at things. As I stepped out from under the awning and glanced up, about four blocks to the west of us there was a tornado coming down, and it was only a few hundred feet above the ground.

I whirled around and ran back in the house. I yelled, "Everybody, get to the bedroom! There's a tornado headed this way!"

Arlene wasn't buying it.

I yelled, "This ain't no joke."

I grabbed up our still-little daughter, got everyone to the bedroom, and pulled the mattress on top of us for protection.

We lay there what seemed like a very long time, and our daughter actually fell asleep. After about fifteen minutes, I'm guessing, we got up, and we went out front to take a look. Everything on our street appeared normal. We noticed some people at the end of the block walking west, so we decided to join them.

We walked about a half block to the end of our street and turned left with the other people. We got about halfway and saw what the others saw. The first house on the next street was missing its entire roof. All that was left were its walls. That was the home of some of our friends from church, Ray and Jane Mouhot, and they were out of town. What a close call and what a tragedy for our friends that was.

VII

Having thought about that for a few years, I felt that it would be beneficial to have a basement to go to when the weather was questionable. Basements in our area were scarce, I might be able to add on a sunroom to the back of our house with a basement under it. I approached Arlene with the idea, and she seemed somewhat open to it. It didn't take long until we looked into it seriously. I wanted to do as much of the work as I could personally to earn that respect hopefully and may save some money.

The first thing was to learn if a solid concrete basement could be done in our area with our clay soil. The most highly recommended concrete guy in the area convinced us that it could be done. He explained what he would do to make it sound, to keep it dry inside, and to have a nice open staircase down into the basement from the sunroom above. It would have a nice decorative wood railing with spindles to prevent anyone from falling into the basement.

Next, we found a framer in Amarillo who could frame the walls and tie in the sunroom roof to the existing roof. Along with that we wanted to change the existing flat ceiling in our living room to a two-layer recessed ceiling. After we got the bid for that, we went in search of getting the electrical work done and getting a bid for the Anderson Windows that would go all around the sunroom. We would be the general contractor and would be doing most of the finish work as well. When we totaled it all up, we were well within the budget we had decided on. We committed to getting it done.

We also had to switch out the wood paneling in our living room to textured walls. The old exterior door would be replaced with French doors that opened into the sunroom. Since we were doing so well on the cost, we decided to go ahead and refinish our kitchen cabinets and retile the kitchen floor, the front entry hall, and the bathroom floors. We also put crown molding in the bedrooms and recessed the ceiling in the living room.

I did the crown molding and learned from a trim carpenter how to actually do it by hand with a coping saw, not the electric miter saw. It was tedious but well worth the effort. I laid the ceramic tile in the sunroom, kitchen, and baths.

Arlene helped with stripping the kitchen and dining room cabinets and doors and refinishing them. She also did a lot of the painting and stripping of the wallpaper. To top it all off, I created an octagonal frame out of 2 x 6 wood and had a stained-glass piece done to fit in it. I mounted it in the wall between the living room and the new sunroom.

It took almost a year to get it done. Doing the commute to Miami entailed getting up at 3 a.m., showering, and driving an hour to Amarillo for the first flight to DFW at 6 a.m. Then I hurried to catch the next available flight from DFW to Miami. I would arrive in Miami usually around noon.

If I were going to Europe, those flights would leave late in the afternoon. The South America flights would go in the evening. I would time it to get about three or four hours of sleep in the crew lounge recliner before I had to sign in for the trip. Then it was the nine- to ten-hour trip with a typical three-hour sleep/rest break on the flight.

The typical layover was twenty-four hours, and the flight back usually arrived in Miami at sunrise. After we parked the plane and did the checklists, it was a run to get through customs, catch the first flight to DFW, and then on to Amarillo with the drive home to Pampa. When I got home, it would typically take me a day to get over the jet lag and get some energy back. Then I would do more work on the house.

When it was all done, I thought it was really worth all of the effort, and the price was a real blessing. Our house went from 1,500 square feet to 2,100, and we had a wonderful finished basement with a nice carpet, cabinets, and wooden desk along with a sleeper sofa, treadmill, and bookcase. It never got damp or musty like the typical basement, and we were able to get air conditioning down there as well.

Sadly, in the midst of the downright brutal commute to Miami, all of the manual labor I did on that addition and remodel, I gained nothing. When I would get home from a trip, it would take me a day to get over the jet lag or loss of sleep and get the energy to take on the work. Arlene made no effort to hide her irritation at my resting an entire day.

One day she had been hammering away at me, and I was in the kitchen cooking something at dinner time. She popped off and said something when I was there dicing some vegetables. I had taken enough for one day and proceeded to spout some profanity at her. With that knife in my hand I pointed it in her direction, with the intent of it being like me pointing my finger at her and told her she needed to knock it off. I certainly should have laid it on the counter and used my finger to point rather than what was in my hand, but in my irritation, I just didn't think it through too well. Wouldn't you know, my daughter was standing in the doorway and saw that.

She and my stepdaughter were always at school, and never at home to witness the three-plus-hour sessions of verbal abuse that I received. That ordeal that she saw is what was, and I think still is ingrained in her mind pertaining to me.

As always, though, I would forgive and put Arlene's unkind, and disrespectful insults behind me. For years prior to this it would be gone from my mind within hours. At this point it was starting to take a day or two, but I always forgave, loved her, and did put it behind me. It was not so with her. She would not forgive, and anything I did that was actually wrong would be added into the verbal abuse sessions.

Jay on final approach at Sao Paulo, Brazil

The family farmhouse in the Black Forest, Germany, where Jay's grandfather grew up

Jay's grandfather and grandmother: John and Elizabeth Straub

Jay's great-grandfather Johann, 1841-1910

Jay's great great-grandfather Mathias, 1791-1865

DREAMS FULFILLED—DASHED—RESTORED— MIXED WITH THE MOST PAINFUL LOSS!

I

While I was completing that project, I was thinking about bidding to become a captain; it was apparent I could be awarded that position in MIA. The only drawback was that I would be in the on call-reserve position.

It would be several months before I could actually hold a line and have a confirmed monthly schedule of trips. I mulled that over a couple of months, checked on the possibilities of a place to stay down there, and decided to put the bid in for captain on the 727 in MIA. They did the bid run, and—hooray!—I got the award. I was going to be a captain at American Airlines.

I was awarded the new position, but the company needed me in my current position more than they did there. When that happens, they withhold you from your new position, but they pay you at the rate of your new position. Whenever they can take you out of your current spot and move you on to the new one, they do.

I certainly had nothing to complain about on that. I immediately got my pay increase and would just have to wait a little longer to go to the left seat. I was withheld about three months and got notice of a training date to report for the captain upgrade training.

That date finally arrived. I was so excited and couldn't wait to be in the position that I had dreamed about. I didn't have to report to the flight academy until the middle of the day to start training, so I would stay home the night before and catch the first flight to DFW the next day.

I went to bed early, so I would be well rested the next day. About 2 a.m., I awoke with a terrible abdominal pain. I couldn't be still, and it got worse and worse. It was finally so bad that I decided I had to go to the emergency room.

I woke Arlene and told her what was going on. Our daughter had a friend spending the night, and Arlene told me she didn't really want to wake them.

I said, "Fine. I'll get there."

I got up and dressed, made a beeline to my pickup, and drove to the hospital in the blowing snow. I'm sure you recall my previous mention that it truly does snow in Texas.

When I got to the emergency room, I went in and begged them to stop the pain. They asked if I had a doctor they could notify. I gave them Dr. Mohan's name since he had done my hernia surgery there a few years prior. They drew some blood to run some tests, and I just lay there in pain on the stretcher.

Wouldn't you know this was on a Saturday? Things weren't moving quite like they probably would on a weekday. Something showed up in the blood test indicating a potential problem in my circulation, a possible blockage in the arteries, so the first doctor who got involved was a cardiac surgeon.

When Dr. Mohan finally got there, I got something for the pain. He wasn't inclined to the view of a potential problem with my arteries. He said there were other things that can elevate that enzyme or whatever it was that showed up in the blood test. Plus, the horrendous abdominal pain was certainly not heart related.

He told me that I would have to wait for more tests to be done Monday morning. Great. I should be boarding the flight to go and start my captain training, but I'm lying in the emergency room and have to wait two more days to find out what's potentially wrong. If that weren't enough, the cardiac surgeon insists that I be tested to check this potential cardiac issue.

Wow, back then a cardiac issue could be the end to your career as an airline pilot. That just added more stress to the issue. The pain was finally starting to subside, though. I thanked the Lord for that and prayed that this would not be heart related.

When Arlene got there, I asked her to please call the training department and let them know I would not be there and to give them an explanation why. I had a book at home with the phone numbers for her. Saturday rolled by, and Sunday did as well. Monday finally arrived, and they took me in and did a sonogram. Shortly after that I was moved to another part of the hospital and given a stress test.

Gee whiz! I was not really up to that.

Dr. Mohan came in and informed me that I had a stone in my gall bladder, and that was what was causing the horrific pain. He went on to inform me that it was so large that it was going to be potentially problematic to remove the gall bladder laparoscopically. If it were too large, he would have to do the old-style long incision. That would require a six-week recovery. Oh my, I hoped that would not be how it came down. That was my prayer.

What next? Well, the cardiac doctor came in later in the day and informed me that something went wrong on the stress test. He went on to say I would have to have an angiogram done and concluded with telling me that he was leaving town, and I would have to wait about three weeks for his return to do it.

The next time I talked to Dr. Mohan and shared that with him, he didn't say it verbally, but I could see he wasn't really on board with that. He also told me that he didn't think I needed to worry about the results.

If that weren't enough, Arlene came in that afternoon and informed me that one of the chief pilots in Miami had called. She said that he spoke in a very rude and irritated tone, wanting to know why I did not show up for training. When she told him why, his response was just an OK, and the call ended.

I found that totally unacceptable. I got on the phone and called the Miami Flight Office. I asked to speak to the chief whom Arlene had spoken to. I informed him that my wife had called flight training to tell them what had happened and why I would not be able to make it. He just nonchalantly told me that they never notified him. That was it, no apology for the rudeness to my wife and absolutely no concern for my well-being.

The next day they put me under, and when I woke up the good news was that Dr. Mohan was able to remove the entire gall bladder laparoscopically. But I also learned that my gall bladder had gangrene in it. Yikes! If that had spread to my pancreas, I would most likely have been a goner. But thank the Lord, it was just in that part of the gall bladder, and that was it.

I had actually experienced those severe abdominal pains twice before just not quite as bad, and they went away within two or three hours. I went to get medical help both times, and the doctors just said, "It must be something you ate that disagreed with you." I was sure glad to have found the problem.

I went home the next day and had a couple of big items to resolve. I had to find a doctor in Amarillo to do the angiogram. Since that cardiologist in Pampa wouldn't sign me off, I could not fly again until it was done, and I was not going to wait three weeks for his return. I got a recommendation and went in for an evaluation right away. The doctor set me up to go to a hospital in Amarillo for the angiogram within two days. That was a relief.

The other big item that I had to delve into was my training reschedule. I called flight training to see when they had rescheduled it. They told me that they didn't know yet and would call me when they knew. They also informed me that, for now, I was back in my previous position as first officer.

The time came to go to Amarillo for the angiogram. I can't remember what the reason was, but once again Arlene couldn't take me to the hospital in Amarillo for this day procedure. I wound up calling my neighbor and asking him if he could take me. He was more than happy to.

It was a cold, dreary day, and even though the surgery had been laparoscopic, I wasn't moving at a great clip. My neighbor picked me up and dropped me off at the hospital in Amarillo. I went in, did all the paperwork, the doctor did the angiogram, and everything was in great shape. Praise God, I could clear medical now and return to work. I waited a bit, and Arlene arrived to take me home.

II

I think I only missed working one trip in all of that mishmash of things. I went to MIA to resume my duties and flew the trip. When I got home, I was thinking surely it's been long enough to hear from flight training on the reschedule of my captain upgrade training.

I called them, gave them my name, employee number, and asked them the date and time they had me down for the reschedule of my captain upgrade training. They put me on hold, then came back and informed me that I failed to qualify, that my captain bid was cancelled, and that I would remain a first officer at Miami with first officer pay.

What? I was flabbergasted! I asked, "How can you say I failed to qualify?" That would apply to someone who went through training, failed, and would have to remain in their current position. I never even got to training. I wound up in the hospital prior to my training start time.

They said, "That's all I can tell you."

I couldn't believe this. As I thought about it, I concluded that this had to be some mistake. I decided I would talk with one of my bosses in MIA when I reported for my next trip. That day came, and I went to MIA. When I arrived, I went straight to the flight office and asked to speak to one of the other chief pilots, definitely not the one who had so rudely called asking why I hadn't shown up for training. The one I spoke to couldn't believe what I was telling him. He told me that was nonsense; he would check into it and get it taken care of. I thanked him, flew my trip, and went back home as usual.

I hadn't heard from him when I went back to MIA for my next trip. So, I went back to the flight office to see if he had learned anything. When I walked in, he had me close the door and told me to have a seat. I did as he requested, and he proceeded to share that he had made several calls and told me his hands were tied.

He went on to tell me that I needed to keep his next remarks between the two of us. I agreed, and he told me I needed to go to the union, the Allied Pilots Association, and file a grievance. I tried to get him to give me the company's explanation for this, but he just told me again to file the grievance. I thanked him and said that I would definitely follow his advice and keep it between us.

III

When I got home from the trip, I started the grievance process immediately. I thought this would be a piece of cake and get accomplished in no time. Sad to say, but it was not. While all of this was taking place, my dad was in the hospital with a repeat of what I shared earlier.

When I would return from trips, I would always make a run to the hospital to see him before I went home.

When I would walk in his room he would ask, "When do I get to see that fourth stripe on your jacket?" His desire to see me accomplish that was very strong. I couldn't share what was going on. I would just tell him it would be soon, hoping that I was right about that.

A few months into this, it became clear why American Airlines did what they did. At the time I was supposed to report for captain training, they had determined they were going to start furloughing pilots. That made it all perfectly clear. That position that I was awarded three months prior under contract really wasn't going to be needed after all, which made my illness and missing training the perfect opportunity to violate the contract and deny me what I had been awarded. They just had to find something in the contract that they could twist to fit their desire.

This mess rocked along for a year. I had a hearing with an APA attorney present, who basically just indicated my odds were not all that good. I couldn't believe this. My boss, no less, had told me it was outrageous, and my union attorney was basically conceding defeat on this.

IV

On the home front, Dad wound up back in the hospital for a third round of losing another piece of his small intestine. At this stage, he didn't have enough small intestine left to get the nutrition he needed to survive. Almost every time I went to the hospital, when he was coherent, he would ask that same question. Sadly, he never got to see that fourth stripe on my uniform. He was my best friend, and I loved him and cherished him as my father. It truly grieves me that he never got to see it.

I had finally been able to transfer to DFW shortly before this. Dad's funeral was going to happen in the middle of a trip I was scheduled to fly. I called one of the DFW chiefs and told him that my dad had passed away and I needed to drop the trip to attend the funeral.

This guy started reciting, you can do this; you can do that; you can't do this; and you can't do that. Then it was: do you understand, any questions?

I frankly couldn't believe how this was going down.

I said, "No questions."

As we proceeded to hang up, he interjected a cold, "Oh by the way, sorry to hear that." Unbelievable.

Over the next few days, I was truly kicking myself with all that was going through my mind. Here are just a few of those things that swirled in my mind. While I had spent a great deal of time at the hospital and at Dad's home a good deal of his last year, something kept gnawing at me. At the end, he had just been moved to hospice, and I had been told that it would most likely be a couple of weeks or longer perhaps. A friend had called me and suggested I take a long weekend to go with him and his father to ride motorcycles and camp out in Colorado. I was really not at all keen on doing it. I was afraid that it wasn't the time to do that. But I gave in and went.

On the drive home I had a bad feeling. When we pulled up at my home, I noticed my friend's wife's car was in our driveway. That didn't seem logical. I expected he would drop me off and head out immediately to go home, unload all of his stuff, and relax from the long drive.

As I walked up our drive and sidewalk, Arlene came out and met me. Now

I knew something was up. She never came to meet me when I returned from anything. We walked in the door, and she said, "Let's go back here." She led me to our bedroom and closed the door. By the time we got there, the tears were already streaming down my face. I knew what was coming. She closed the door and told me that Dad was gone.

I burst out sobbing. My best friend, the man I respected more than anyone on the face of the earth, the man who had given so much of his time for me and my family, whom I loved and respected, was gone. And I hadn't been there to hold his hand and tell him how much I loved him when he departed. I had certainly told him that before, and he knew it, but I wanted to be there for him on that day. I just couldn't quit thinking about it. There were many more things swirling in my mind as I mentioned, but I'll just conclude it here.

Over the next two days family and many people whom Dad had worked with expressed their sympathy and shared their friendship and love for him. That helped, but I was having a tough time with the pain of seeing his cold, lifeless body in that casket. The day for the funeral came, and as painful as it all was, I was certainly glad to have everyone there to honor him and have that US flag draped over and then removed from his casket and handed to me.

The funeral service ended, the graveside service ended, and now the day was about to end. In just a little over twenty-four hours, my wife, stepdaughter, and daughter were taking off on a trip to Hawaii that they had planned for themselves.

I stayed in Amarillo and went a time or two to the cemetery between Amarillo and Canyon where we buried him. I spent a good part of two days straightening up his old shop, the place where he had spent thousands of hours working. Along with that, I would walk into the old house where we had lived when I came into the world to reminisce.

As I stood there at the door to his shop and gazed to the west, I could see the five lots that had been just raw land when I was a child. I remembered Dad using his walk-behind Sears garden tractor with its five horsepower Briggs & Stratton engine. He would plow, harrow, and create perfectly straight raised beds with his cultivator attachment. Then he would hook up the planter attachment and sow his black-eyed pea seeds. It wouldn't be long until those five lots were loaded with black-eyed peas for harvest. There's no telling how many people I watched out there being blessed with the fruit of Dad's labor.

What a memory. I love you, Dad.

V

In this same time frame, there was a tragic accident in the upper management team at American Airlines. Chief Pilot and Vice President of Flight Captain William James suffered a snow skiing accident and lost his life.

His successor, Captain Cecil Ewell, immediately went around to all of the crew bases introducing himself and sharing his vision. He came to speak at the MIA crew base the very day I completed a trip. I went to listen to him, and after he concluded, he was waiting to catch the same flight back to DFW that I was on my journey home.

I stood there at the gate and questioned myself over and over, "Should I go present my case to him?" I was really concerned that I was overstepping my bounds. I finally decided, it's worth a shot. I went over and introduced myself.

He shook my hand and asked, "What's on your mind?"

I proceeded to share everything, as quickly as I could, since it was getting close to time for them to start boarding the plane. When I finished, he told me he was going to be snowed under in his new position. He told me to call him and refresh his memory if I didn't hear from him within three months. I thanked him for his time and said I certainly would.

After the three months I made the call. When Captain Ewell answered, I gave him my name and reminded him of everything we discussed in Miami. He told me he would have to do a little investigation and would get back to me by mid-afternoon. I thanked him for his time.

Just as he had indicated, at mid-afternoon the phone rang. It was he, and he recognized my voice. He said, "Captain Straub." When he said that, I was shocked. He went on to tell me I had a check in the mail for all the back pay I should have received as captain and that I would receive a call shortly to schedule my training.

I was almost speechless. I gave him my immense thanks, and he told me he was sorry for what had happened and how it was handled. What a man of true integrity!

Oh, and in case you don't recall the name, he had become fleet manager of the 767 when I was going through that training who would bless me in the future. This was not the last time Captain Ewell blessed me and was gracious to me. You will have to read a bit further to learn about the next one.

Going back to the egregious actions at American Airlines, most of you who have heard about it, including my boss at the time, find it shocking. I would certainly echo that. If I were to compose a song about it, I think I would have to borrow the title to a Bachman Turner Overdrive tune, "You Ain't Seen Nothing Yet." So, as we say in Texas, "just hang on to your hat."

VI

After Captain Ewell's intervention, the folks in training did call that afternoon, and I was going to the flight academy in short order. When I showed up for ground school, from what I recall, it was just the instructor and I. As I went through it, everything came back to me quite well. It had only been a few years since I was flying this equipment.

At the completion of the ground school, the instructor started to prepare me for the oral exam. He told me the name of check airman who would be giving me the exam, and said, "We have to get you well prepared!"

Once we finished the prep for the oral, he indicated that he was confident I would do fine.

The next day I showed up early, met the check airman, and he introduced me to the Federal Aviation Administration Inspector who oversaw the pilot training for the entire Boeing 727 fleet at American Airlines. The check airman shared that it had been so long since they had done a 727-captain upgrade that the FAA Inspector wanted to be there to observe my oral exam.

Holy cow! I've been basically warned that this check airman was a tough guy, and now the federal regulator was here to check me out as well. Those things were always a bit stressful, but that just added more.

At the end of the day, everything was good. This wound up being similar to when I flew with the former Blue Angel that others had portrayed as bad news for us non-military aviators. I was expecting a minimum of two hours in this oral exam. I think we had barely reached the one-hour mark, and the check airman looked at the FAA Inspector and said, "I think he's demonstrated proficiency in his knowledge of the aircraft. How about you?"

The FAA Inspector agreed.

They shook my hand, told me it was a pleasure, did the paperwork, and took off. What a relief it was.

I ran into that check airman a year later when I came in for recurrent training. I shook hands and said, "You probably don't remember me. You gave me my captain's upgrade oral exam a year ago."

He said he remembered me quite well.

I was a bit shocked. He said he had never had a captain upgrade candidate who knew the aircraft as well as I did. He continued that after I had only missed one or two non-critical questions after an hour, that it had been time to call it a day. That was a true blessing, and I gave thanks to the Lord.

The simulator went well too. The only thing that I had not done as a first officer on the 727 was the single-engine landing. The captain was the only one who was tested on losing two of the three engines and making a successful visual approach and landing with only one engine operating.

There were a lot of variables in that, one being which engine you had still running. But regardless, you had to depressurize the plane and turn off the air conditioning, fly at a much higher approach speed, cut the safety wire on the pneumatic brake handle that was for emergency use only, keep a close eye on your electrical loads since you only had one generator putting out the electricity, plus a whole slew of other items. You sure didn't want to mess up and have to do a go-around on one engine in the 727.

The V1 cut (when you lost an engine at your calculated V1 airspeed on take-off roll) wasn't so bad in the 727. You didn't get near as much yaw in it when you lost an engine as you did in one of the aircrafts that has the engines out on the wing.

If you reached that speed and lost an engine, you would continue the take-off and check your essential electric power switch position in case it was set on the engine generator that you just lost. Your flap retraction airspeeds were a bit different from normal, and once you reached 600 feet above the ground, if you had cleared all obstacles, you would level off and accelerate to 200 knots indicated airspeed, then accelerate to 220 knots indicated and continue your climb. After that you would go through the engine failure checklist and return to land.

What a joy it was to complete that check ride and now be type rated in my favorite aircraft, the Boeing 727, and be a captain for American Airlines. From here, it was off to do the IOE. I was also headed back to MIA as my crew base again.

The only downside was that when I bid for this position the company was growing. It looked like I wouldn't be on reserve very long and could hold a line schedule. I would have been able to commute to work the same day my trip started and come home the same day it ended in most cases. Now they were furloughing pilots, and I might be in Miami on reserve for a long time.

VII

Back before my captain training started, I searched for a place that I could stay while on reserve in MIA. I found a fellow pilot down there who was single and owned a home in Fort Lauderdale. He rented out his extra rooms to pilots who commuted, and he had a vacancy. I was glad to find it and signed up for that.

Just a few days before I was supposed to report on a Saturday for my IOE, I got a call from him. He had just completed a trip at MIA and wanted to do me a favor by going to my mailbox in MIA to get my mail for me. He knew I would have a whole month of manual revisions to do to get caught up and be legal for the IOE. If he did that, I could fly into FLL and have a much shorter journey to get to his house directly rather than having to fly into MIA to get all of my revisions first.

But then he called and told me that I had no mailbox at MIA. He said he looked everywhere just in case they accidentally got it out of alphabetical order. I thanked him for the information and said I would call the flight office, which I did immediately.

The person who answered transferred me to the lady who oversaw the mail for the pilots there, and I shared what I had just been told. In a very gruff tone she said, "Your mailbox is there. I remember your name, and I have been putting your mail in your box."

In a very polite tone I said, "He told me he looked over every single mailbox, and there was not one there with my name on it."

She came back with, "It's there!"

I said, "Would you please just go double check, I won't get to MIA until late Friday; my IOE is on Saturday, and if it's not there, I will be sunk, since no one will be at the flight office on Saturday.

She came back, this time actually raising her voice, "It's there!"

I said, "OK, thank you."

Thursday night I was starting to sense some sinus problems developing. I had flown many times over the years with sinus problems, but it never caused a problem with flight safety. My ears never plugged up or anything like that, so I wasn't really worried about it. Friday morning it was worse but didn't appear to be bad enough to interrupt my IOE. I got up and packed, took care of some things I had to get done, and left the house for the commute.

I got to MIA and went to the area we called operations, went to the mail room looking for Straub, and found nothing. I did as my fellow pilot had done, looked high and low, and nothing could be found. What the heck do I do now? There's usually a person in operations to help with a few things like this. As a matter of fact, they keep some loaner manuals there that are current in case something out of the ordinary happens and someone needs to borrow one. For cryin' out loud, though, I need every manual I am required to carry, and this person has apparently left for the day.

I went to the train station at MIA and caught the train to FLL, and from there I got a cab to the place I would be staying. I went in and told him everything that had transpired. He couldn't believe it, and neither could I. Meanwhile, the sinus thing was getting worse, and I was going to have to get up way earlier the next day than I should have to attempt to get this lack of current manuals issue resolved. So, I went to bed early.

I got up the next morning and was feeling even worse. It was getting to the point I was a bit hoarse. I thought I might call in sick, fly home, and avoid all problems with the mail and everything else. The company was not cool with calling in sick, and with all of the ordeal I had been through to get this far, I didn't feel comfortable with that. I decided I would just persevere and get it done. I caught the cab and train and showed up at flight ops with lots of time to spare. I found the person to get the loaner manuals that I needed.

When I explained the situation to him, he set out looking. I needed the two manuals with all of the domestic approach charts for the domestic airports we served along with the potential alternate airports. Along with that I needed the Part 1, the book of regulations, and the minimum equipment list for the 727.

He found everything but one of the approach chart manuals. He searched and dug and dug and searched, all to no avail. Now, what the heck am I going to do? I tried to get a phone number for the check airman to call him ahead of time and see what to do. That didn't work.

Next, I sat down where I could watch the area where we store our flight bags there in flight ops when we finish our trip. I was in hopes that I would catch another captain dropping off his bag at the completion of his trip, go explain my situation, and ask to borrow his book of approach plates for three days, returning it to his bag at the end. That didn't happen.

141

Now I was just in hopes that the check airman would get there early enough to get a reserve crew for the, flight to depart on time. He finally arrived, not all that early, and I proceeded to give him the scoop.

By now I was getting quite horse and was not felling very well. When I finished, he glared at me, and his total manner of communication indicated he was irritated with me and not the person who had caused this problem. As he stood there, I could tell the wheels were turning in his head. He decided that we would share the approach charts that he had.

Wouldn't you know it, the manual that was unavailable for loan was the one that had the charts in it for the first two destinations on our trip that day, the New York La Guardia Airport and the Toronto Canada Airport. You might be wondering, when I previously said charts for domestic airports, how could Toronto Canada be a domestic airport? That's just how it is. American Airlines and probably all the others classify Mexico and Canada as domestic.

Is that because the pilot pay rates are higher for international than domestic flights? I think how they handle baggage fees for the customer can answer that question quite well. Nowadays, they classify even Caribbean flights as domestic so they can charge baggage fees because international flights don't have the baggage fee.

This sharing-the-approach-chart didn't set well in my mind. If one of the FAA Inspectors showed up on our trip to examine us, we were both going to be in hot water. When I presented the concern to the check airman, his eyes bored a hole right through me. I started printing all of the paperwork, and about that time our flight engineer showed up and came over to introduce himself. He left immediately to head to the gate and do his walk-around inspection and preflight duties.

The first thing I looked at was the La Guardia weather. The ceiling was just barely above minimums for an ILS approach, and the visibility was slightly above minimums. There was potential for it to be snowing, and the airport already had snow. The braking action on the runways was reported as good.

The next thing I checked was the fuel load they had given us. I did all the calculations, and the alternate fuel and reserve fuel looked good. The flight plan, all the load information, and everything else looked good, so I signed my first flight plan as a captain at American Airlines. The Miami–New York LaGuardia flight was good to go, except for the fact that we were flying into instrument conditions and we were going to have to pass that approach chart back and forth. I did not like that.

We got to the aircraft, and I introduced myself to the flight attendant who held the number one position in the cabin crew. I shared what to expect along the route of flight and our arrival.

At that point, I got in the left seat and set up everything on my side: all of the airspeed bugs, nav-radios, and all the rest. The check airman, acting as first officer, got our clearance from clearance delivery. From there we went through the required check lists, and I gave my first crew briefing. When departure time came, the gate agent closed the door, and off we went. I'll skip through a lot of our activities at this point. You'll get a more detailed description of all this a little further in the book.

We made it to the end of the runway and received our takeoff clearance, and I taxied out to line-up with the runway centerline and applied take-off power. We went airborne and weren't even 400 feet above the ground when the check airman turned his head at me and yelled, "Check your airspeed!"

I looked at my airspeed indicator, and it was only three knots above the airspeed that was called for at this stage. That was within the parameters that you are allowed to deviate.

He was belligerent all the way to LaGuardia, and between my sinus problem, my hoarseness, and his attitude and demeanor, I was not feeling well. What a deal to make your first landing in the left seat, on a revenue flight, with a short runway, weather at minimums, getting sicker as the day wore on, and this guy in the right seat.

I flew the approach well; we broke out of the clouds just slightly above minimums, and the snow was flying by with the landing lights making a good spectacle of it all in the pitch-black sky. We touched down, I pulled the speed brake handle, went into full reverse thrust, and got on the brakes firmly.

When I parked the brake at the gate, I was ready for this day to be over, but unfortunately it was one more leg to Toronto. The weather was better there, and it was a relief for this day to end at the Toronto Pearson International Airport. I was so thankful to crawl in bed at the layover hotel.

The next morning, I got the wakeup call, and oh my gosh, I felt miserable, and my throat was horrendously sore. After taking a hot shower and everything else to get ready, it became clear that I had full blown laryngitis. I could barely talk.

When we met in the lobby and I tried to speak, the check airman did a double take and that was about it. I told him I was calling crew tracking when we got to the airport to inform them that I was checking out when we got to

DFW. They would need to put me down as sick there, and I would commute home to Amarillo. He basically said OK and informed me that I would get a call to reschedule the completion of my IOE.

The flight from Toronto to DFW was long. I felt totally miserable and could barely talk. When we got to DFW, it was a relief. At least he hadn't been quite like he had been the previous day. When I parked the plane, we finished all the checklists, and I took off to make the next flight to Amarillo.

By the time I finished the drive to Pampa, I was beat. Arlene was shocked when I walked in the door and asked me, "What's going on?" As I proceeded to talk, she knew. I got to the doctor the next day, and when I recovered, I cleared the sick list and got the next session of IOE scheduled.

VIII

When I got back to MIA and went to flight ops, what do you know? There was a mailbox for *HJ Straub* packed full, with a note to come to the office, to get the rest that it wouldn't hold. That took a good deal of time to catch up on.

I went to Fort Lauderdale, spent the night, and returned for the IOE continuation. The new check airman was truly a good one. He had a good attitude and made it clear that he was there to not only evaluate my performance, but to assist me and do anything to help me do my job better. How nice!

It was another three-day trip, and everything went smoothly. When I made the landing in Sarasota, Florida with the short runway as I turned off the runway, the check airman gave a thumbs up and said, "Great job!" The flight engineer chimed in as well. It was all-around a great trip.

At the completion in Miami, after I parked the brake, shut down the engines, and completed the checklist, the check airman stuck out his hand to shake mine and said, "Congratulations, Captain Straub."

I had to go to the flight office for something and followed him in there. When we walked in, one of the chiefs were standing there, and the check airman proceeded to tell them what a great job I did. That was sure good to hear after that last ordeal, and I was very thankful to that gentleman and our Lord as always.

THE LEFT SEAT—THE COMMUTE
FINALLY ENDS—THEN . . .

I

I'm about to share my very first revenue flight on my own as captain. I already shared about my first flight as a flight engineer going into Baton Rouge. Somehow, this flight in the left seat matched my first flight engineer trip in a number of ways.

I started off with my captain's briefing. This was going to be the first one on my own where I was truly the captain. I did this one just as I did them all.

I told the first officer and the flight engineer that this would be a team effort. I emphasized that if either of them witnessed me performing in a way that did not meet the Federal Aviation Regulations or the company procedures in how we were trained to operate the aircraft to be sure to bring that to my attention. I went on to inform them that I would do the same. From there I told them I was completely open to any other input they might have and would appreciate it, evaluate it, and make a decision from there.

After that I discussed our departure procedure and the clearance we had received. I closed the briefing with an emphasis for making this trip as safe, smooth, and enjoyable as we could for our customers and our fellow crew members in the back. At that point I asked if they had any questions, and that pretty much wrapped it up.

On the second day of the trip the first officer was flying the first leg. We were cleared to fly the published standard instrument departure from our departure airport at Hartford, Connecticut. When I did the briefing before takeoff, I told him to be sure he stayed right on course at the point in the procedure where we had to make a significant course change.

I emphasized that, because the FAA had filed a violation several years prior on a fellow captain when he flew this very SID. Air traffic control said that he didn't maintain the prescribed course, which caused him to get too close to another aircraft.

That wound up being an ordeal that dragged on for months, and the FAA wanted to levy a big fine and suspend his license for more months. I certainly didn't want to entertain that possibility.

As he flew the departure, and we approached the point where he needed to initiate his turn for the course change, he didn't do it when he should have. I bit my tongue for a bit and finally said, "You need to make the turn." He started a real shallow turn. As the course needle started to move, and we just proceeded to blow by the prescribed course, I said, "I've got it."

I grabbed the yoke and had to increase the bank angle considerably past the standard bank angle to hopefully keep us from exceeding the prescribed distance from the course centerline.

When I had it stabilized on course, I asked him if he could see the problem that we were about to be in. He said he did and apologized for the error. I asked him if he would like the aircraft back to finish that leg of the trip. He indicated that he would.

I gave it back to him and said, "It's all yours; you have the aircraft."

We proceeded on to our destination, and things seemed to be going well. He initiated our descent, and I could see that there were some thunderstorms in the area close to where we were headed, so I turned on the weather radar. It was clear that there were some cells close to our inbound route of flight. As we descended, I requested a heading change several times to dodge some of the weather.

As we proceeded on, they vectored us to intercept the ILS approach for our runway, which put us on a very long straight in final. The first officer intercepted the localizer, and we were lined up with the runway. The airport had another runway that ran parallel to the runway we were using, and ATC did simultaneous approaches to both runways. That meant that a fairly short distance from us there could be another aircraft flying an approach to that parallel runway at the same time. ATC staggered it so that we weren't side by side, but it was still somewhat close.

On the radar was a cell up ahead, but it was a reasonable distance to the left of our course, and it wasn't very intense. The radar wasn't showing any heavy contours in that cell, so I was comfortable with passing it by and proceeding on to complete the approach and landing.

I had folded up my en route chart, and as I reached down to put it in my flight bag, I had my head down for a short time. When I sat up straight again and looked at the instruments, I discovered that the first officer had turned the aircraft about thirty degrees to the right. Good grief!

I asked, "What are you doing?" At the same time, I grabbed the yoke again and said, "I've got it," just as I had to do back on our departure.

I asked, "Why on earth did you turn us toward the other runway when there could be a simultaneous approach taking place to that runway? You never make a course change like that without notifying the other pilot!"

With that barely out of my mouth, approach control came on the radio, called our flight number, gave us a heading to fly, and instructed us to turn to it immediately, which I was basically already doing. After giving the new heading, they were questioning why our heading had changed, and I told them I would call them on the phone once we landed and parked the aircraft at the gate.

As I flew the plane and got us back lined up to complete the approach, the first officer said, "We were getting too close to that cell, so I had to turn to avoid it." I said, "Our distance was quite sufficient, and you never make a turn or course change or altitude change or anything of the sort without notifying the other pilot."

Not long after that I intercepted the glideslope, completed the approach, and landed the aircraft. After we taxied in, shut it down, and completed all of the checklists, I got to go into flight ops and call approach control to explain what had happened. Gee, on my first revenue flight as captain, my entire flight deck crew was going to have to file an Aviation Safety Action Program report. Here's what the FAA says:

> The goal of the Aviation Safety Action Program (ASAP) is to enhance aviation safety through the prevention of accidents and incidents. Its focus is to encourage voluntary reporting of safety issues and events that come to the attention of employees of certain certificate holders.
>
> To encourage an employee to voluntarily report safety issues even though they may involve an alleged violation of Title 14 of the Code of Federal Regulations (14 CFR), enforcement-related incentives have been designed into the program. An ASAP is based on a safety partnership that will include the Federal Aviation Administration (FAA) and the certificate holder and may include any third party such as the employee's labor organization.

If there were a potential violation of the FARs and the entire crew submitted the ASAP report within a specified time period, documenting what took place, the FAA would waive the potential fines and disciplinary action.

It was done to help both sides learn what was going wrong and how to improve training and improve safety. In my years as a first officer and flight engineer, I had filed a few ASAPs before, but this happening on my watch, my first revenue trip as captain, wasn't a pleasant experience. It was memorable but not the type you want.

I finished out flying all of the remaining legs of the three-day sequence myself. Along with that, when I got home, I sat down and submitted a report to the Professional Standards Committee at APA. That is a group at the union that evaluates potential problems to help crew members get the help they need to fix any potential problems that could possibly result in anything up to termination.

My gosh, submitting that report on my very first sequence as a captain was the absolute last thing I wanted to experience, but having seen two major goofs on one leg of a trip by this first officer put a big concern on my heart for his career and other things.

II

My next six years as a captain were truly wonderful and a blessing, in spite of the challenges in getting there. I could not have been happier in achieving this. I suspect there are not that many people who are as happy and can't wait to go to work, as I was. That was what I experienced in my entire aviation career. It was truly an absolute joy.

On another end of the spectrum, during those years as captain on the 727 I actually had to declare an emergency four times. Of those four, two of them were really just to protect us as the flight crew.

One of them was on a flight from MIA to Houston Intercontinental. It was a beautiful day with clear skies and smooth air. The chime went off. I picked up the cabin crew phone, and the number one flight attendant informed me that a passenger was experiencing severe chest pains.

I asked if she had made a PA to ask for a physician's assistance, and she informed me that she had, and there was a doctor with him right then. I told her to keep me posted.

In just a few minutes she called back and shared that the doctor had informed her that the passenger had to get to a hospital as soon as possible. He was suffering a major issue with his heart. We were out over the Gulf of Mexico, and our destination, Houston, was the closest place to get him to a hospital. I told her we would increase the speed and gave her the new arrival time. Quite often, just getting there a few minutes quicker can save a life.

I called ATC, explained the situation to them, asked for direct Houston Intercontinental, and told them I was going to increase our cruise speed to Mach .86. They were very cooperative. As we went through our descent and came up to the 10,000 feet MSL altitude, I realized I really needed to declare an emergency.

The FARs limit your indicated airspeed to 250 knots below 10,000 feet. As we got close to that altitude, I told Houston Approach I was declaring an emergency to maintain max airspeed well in excess of the 250 knots. They came back and acknowledged that.

We landed, got expedited to the gate, did the shutdown, and finished the checklists. By the time we opened the door to the flight deck, the medical team was already on board and in back doing their duties. We almost never hear how things turn out for our passengers in cases like this, and this was one like that. I prayed for him and certainly hoped that everything turned out well.

III

The second event also happened coming out of Hartford. What is it about Hartford? Well, this wasn't really a true emergency. This was basically "a cover your you-know-what" type of deal in case something goes awry. The first officer was flying this leg. We completed our take-off and were going through the flap-retraction phase.

When we got to the two-degree setting, the first officer called, "Green light flaps up."

I reached over and put the flap handle in the full up position. The green light is then supposed to go out to indicate that all of the leading-edge devices have retracted.

The green light didn't go out. I asked our flight engineer to check his panel back there that shows the position of all the leading-edge devices. He checked, and sure enough, one was not retracted. This is a problem. With one of those extended, you are limited to an indicated airspeed of 240 knots, which means you won't be going to Miami.

I called departure control, told them we would have to return to Hartford, and explained the situation. Next thing on the roster was making a decision. Our landing weight was going to be over the max landing weight allowed, 150,000 lbs. This is a structural limit weight. In prior years, we would have just opened the fuel dump switches and dumped enough jet fuel to get us below that limit weight.

Times had changed, though, and for environmental protection, the word was that if this happens, you were just to make an overweight landing, doing your best not to hit the ground hard, and write it up in the logbook to have the aircraft looked at for any potential damage from the overweight landing.

So, I declared an emergency, which requires that the captain takes control. The first officer handed it over to me and said, "You have the aircraft."

I made a PA to give a brief explanation of what was taking place and that there was absolutely no reason to worry. I informed our passengers that they would see fire trucks and ambulances waiting as we went by, but that's just a normal thing, and once again, no worries.

The weather was nice, so we just did a visual approach, and it was a nice, smooth landing. We were quite heavy, so it was max reverse power and solid braking. As stated, the fire trucks and ambulance were there. After we passed them, they pulled on the runway full speed ahead to follow us in.

We went to the gate and parked and went through all the shutdown procedures. I got up to speak to the gate agents and tell them what was going on. Now we were waiting on maintenance to get there to hopefully fix the problem that brought us back and to also do that inspection. I was hoping that it wouldn't cancel the flight, and it would go fairly smoothly.

The next thing you know, an FAA Inspector comes into the flight deck. As it turned out, the FAA has a Flight Standards District Office—fizz dough, as we pronounce it—right there at the Hartford, Connecticut Bradley Airport. He introduced himself, showed his ID, and informed me that he heard our radio calls on the scanner and my declaration of emergency. I explained the situation to him. After that he asked for all of our pilot licenses, medical certificates, and the aircraft logbook.

When he completed that, he was cool with us, but when the maintenance guys showed up, he was on them like a basset hound. It was clear that if maintenance weren't spot on, there would be a "that dog don't hunt" coming at them from this inspector. He followed them and examined everything they did until it was all complete. They signed off the logbook and told me we were good to go.

As it turned out, the leading-edge device was coming up properly, but the sensor wasn't detecting that it was right where it should be. That was an easy fix, and the inspection was fairly simple and didn't take too long. I could see that inspector had all of the maintenance guys a bit nervous and they were glad to get us outta there.

The agent had taken care of the connecting flight problems for everyone while we sat there those two hours, and I think we departed with nearly all of the fine folk whom we left with initially. I apologized for the inconvenience, and within a few minutes we were back airborne, Hartford to Miami. The rest of the flight was nice and uneventful.

IV

Emergency number three was truly a potential emergency. We were cruising along en route from Cleveland to Miami when the flight engineer tapped me on the shoulder. When I turned to look at him, he pointed up at a lit light on his panel. The lower-aft-body-overheat light was on.

For those of you who remember the Boeing 727 well, the number one engine was hung on the left side of the fuselage back at the tail; the number two was in the center of the fuselage, and the number three was on the right side of the fuselage.

A staircase dropped down to the ground right under the number two engine. That's the staircase that the infamous D.B. Cooper let down in-flight to jump out with the money he received in his hijacking escapade.

Getting back to business, in the tail of the aircraft you have "bleed air" coming out of all three of those engines into the tail area. Bleed air comes straight out of the jet engine at a temperature of 250°C, 482°F.

That air is then transferred to a heat exchanger where it is used to pressurize the aircraft, provide heat and air in the cabin, and be used for anti-ice on the wings and engine nacelles. With it at that temperature initially, you can see that it could melt and burn some critical things, which would result in a very unhappy ending.

We went through the checklist procedure for this, and with the light still on, we were required to land at the nearest suitable airport. I immediately pulled the throttles to idle, pulled the speed brake handle, and lowered the nose to achieve a max rate descent. While doing all that, we called ATC, declared an emergency, and informed them that we had initiated an emergency descent to land at the Fort Myers Airport.

Fortunately, it was a nice clear day, we could see any potential air traffic, and we would not have to delay the landing by having to fly an instrument approach. Next, I called the number one flight attendant to tell them what was going on and to prepare the plane for an immediate landing.

At that point, I used the PA and told the passengers there was no need to worry and it was just something that could become more serious if we didn't act on it immediately. The number one chimed us to ask if they needed to instruct the passengers to assume the emergency position. I told her that it wouldn't be necessary.

We went from our cruise altitude of 31,000 feet to configuring the aircraft for the landing in right at five minutes. ATC had vectored us and had us lined up with the runway. We completed the before-landing checklist, and when we touched down, I could hear the cheers through the door. The passengers were quite happy to be on the ground safe and sound. And once again, the fire trucks were there to follow us in.

With an issue this serious the aircraft was taken out of service to find the problem and correct it. The gate agent had to get all of the passengers off the plane and get them rerouted on flights to get them from Fort Myers to Miami. As I stood there at the door to say goodbye, they were all very appreciative of how we handled it. Some wanted to know what happened, so I gave them a very brief synopsis.

While we waited to find out what crew tracking was going to do with us and what was going to happen to our flight sequence, I went out with the mechanics as they ran some tests. From what they could tell me the leak was very minor but was enough to set off the warning. Now they had to find where the leak was. At that, I bid them adieu and set out to learn what was up with our status. Our sequence was terminated, and we were going to deadhead home.

V

The last emergency declaration event I want to talk about occurred while we were going from DFW to Mexico City. The traffic was getting backed up going in there, so they gave us a holding clearance. After we evaluated our fuel, I came back and told them we could make two patterns in the hold, and then we would have to proceed to our alternate, which was Guadalajara. They replied and indicated that they would work us in where that wouldn't be necessary.

In my entire career, I had never had ATC do anything to get me in a bind, but I had an uneasy feeling about this. The expect further clearance time they originally gave us would involve much more than just the two patterns in holding. As we approached the end of the second pattern, I called and said, "We have to proceed to our alternate."

They came back immediately and informed me that wasn't necessary and gave me a heading for vectors to land at Mexico City.

I want to share a little about the crew on this flight. Our flight engineer was a new hire, and he was doing his IOE. The flight engineer check airman evaluating this new hire was a good friend of mine, Carter Jordan. Back when I had just made captain down in Miami, Carter was the flight engineer on several of my trips.

This holding procedure and getting close on our fuel were giving the new flight engineer a bit of a challenge, but Carter was doing a great job in showing him how to manage it. Once the en route ATC handed us off to approach control, we received a heading to put us on the downwind leg, but they went on to tell us it would be a little longer than normal.

That would not have been so bad, except they had slowed our airspeed to the point that we had to put some flaps down, and that increased the fuel flow in a big way. When that happened, I came back and told them our fuel was getting low, and this couldn't go on much further.

They said, "Roger, we will turn you back to the airport very soon."

We continued on and on. I finally grabbed the mic and said, "We are declaring an emergency and are making a right turn direct to runway two three left."

The controller came back all frazzled and said, "No. No, there's no need to declare emergency turn right; you're cleared visual approach to runway two three left."

I never retracted that declaration.

We made it fine. It would have been a major problem, however, if something had happened with any traffic in front of us that would have required us to make a go-around. Doing a go-around pours fuel to those engines like it's coming out of a fire hose. We would not have had enough fuel to go around, make the traffic pattern, and land. I was sure ticked over how ATC had hood-winked us on that deal but was grateful that Carter was back there to help our new flight engineer work through his part.

VI

In August 1995 it was time for the twenty-year high school reunion, and I was looking forward to seeing Rick Husband again. I'm sure you recall my sur-prise when I ran into him at the previous one. I didn't have a clue what his true aspirations were, but I figured that he had probably gotten on with an airline as I had or had decided to stay and make the Air Force a full career.

When we finally met and I learned what he was up to, the previous "Wow" would be an understatement on this one. He informed me that he had just been accepted in the space shuttle program and would be starting training soon. I was thrilled for him. How cool is that? My classmate was going to be a pilot and later a commander on the space shuttle. I felt truly blessed to know him. I gave him a brief synopsis of my career at American, and we went on to visit with our other classmates.

VIII

A little over six months after that reunion, Arlene decided it was time to al-low us to move to the DFW area. I was certainly glad to finally have that option. It would alleviate the stress I had experienced, and all the extra hours wasted in ten years of commuting to work.

The day to move arrived. I had rented a Ryder truck, and our son-in-law was going to help me load all of our belongings into the truck to make the run to Flower Mound. We were supposed to start early, and my son-in-law called to tell me the pipes in their house in Amarillo had frozen. He had to get their pipes thawed before he could come to Pampa to help me load.

I certainly understood that. Now I had to load everything that I could manage on my own, with a wind chill factor well below zero and snow on the ground. What fun that was. It was afternoon before he was able to get there, and we didn't leave Pampa until after 8 p.m. It was almost 2 a.m. when we pulled into the parking lot at the apartment complex in Flower Mound. We went in, lay down on the carpeted floor and went to sleep.

I had called Phil the day before to see if he could help us unload. He got there about 7 a.m., and we jumped up and got to it, took a lunch break, and finished around 3 p.m. At that point, Phil followed us to turn in the truck since I had done a one-way rental. Then he drove us to the DFW Airport.

I had my parents old 1970 Plymouth Fury in the employee parking lot. Since I was based at DFW, I was able to get an employee parking sticker there. I had used that car to get to Phil's house on the nights that I got stuck there unable to catch a flight home. Oh, the fun of commuting, but that was coming to an end. Praise the Lord.

When we got to the car it looked like it had been setting there ten years. A rainstorm had come through followed by a dust storm. You could barely see out the windshield, it was so dirty. We got in, and I decided I would just run the car through one of the drive-through car washes to solve that problem. By now it was getting close to 6 p.m.

There were a few cars ahead of us, and I thought I would call Arlene on my cell phone, no less, to tell her we were just about on our way home. I still found that to be incredible that I no longer had to drive around looking for a pay phone to make that call. Arlene answered and asked where we were. I proceeded to tell her we were about to hit the road, and I was washing the mud off the car so we could see where we're going.

Before I even completed my sentence, she tore into me in her normal fashion. She asked, "What have you been doing?"

I told her, "It was almost 2 a.m. when we got here, and we slept until Phil arrived."

I didn't get another word out before she announced that we didn't have to wait for Phil to get there and that we should be halfway home.

The call concluded, and I couldn't believe it. After all I had done the day before, loading most of the truck by myself in the bitter cold, driving over half the night, and unloading it, I was about to hit the road to drive over half the night again, and that's what I receive. All I could think was, "God, help me." When we got to Pampa well after midnight, my son-in-law took off for Amarillo, and I went in to be met with the same attitude that the phone call had concluded with.

We got up early to finish with the cleanup of the house that Arlene had been working on the day before. I somehow managed to get the old Plymouth back to Amarillo and myself back to Pampa. When it was all done, she and our daughter got in her Maxima, and I got in my Ford F-150 to head for Flower Mound.

IX

Once we got settled in the new apartment, we set out to buy a new house. After looking at a few we decided to build a new one and had it done in six months. What a relief that was. I was sure concerned over what the Bermuda grass was going to do to me since that's all there was to work with for all practical purposes.

After visiting a few churches in the area, we went to one that was very close to our home. Based on what I heard from the pastor in his sermons, I was pleased with it, but Arlene didn't like it. I just decided that's where I was going to attend. If she found something better, I would be willing to check it out, and we could go from there.

I was very glad to meet a couple who went there, Dave and Bonnie (deceased) Slack; they lived in our neighborhood. To top it off he was also a pilot for American. It wasn't long before we discovered another couple there, Blair and Judy Johnson, who lived fairly close, and he was an American pilot as well. Then, lo and behold, we met Dave and Anita Nelson, who also attended there, lived in Double Oak, and, guess what? He was also a pilot for American. They were all in a men's group that met every Friday morning for breakfast and were doing studies on biblical topics in various books. I was quite happy to get involved in that group.

We had not been in Double Oak that long when to our great surprise we learned my cousin, Myma Sue, and her husband, J.R., were living just three miles straight east of our location in Lewisville, Texas. They are the parents of Brad Wheeler. It was truly great getting to see them again because we hadn't made contact since Fred's funeral, and what a joy it was that we would remain close.

X

The first year went fairly well, but at some point in the second year our daughter was getting quite rebellious. She was going off the chart in her disrespect and rudeness. It was causing major problems, and Arlene would side with our daughter and defend her in all of it.

I was having a hard time with this. I had never come close to treating my parents in this fashion and was clueless to this type of behavior. At the time, I just assumed it was probably the same thing, age related, that caused my stepdaughter to move out and go to her dad's place.

I can't remember when exactly, but it was approximately toward the end of our second year since moving, that I decided to make a short trip to Germany to visit the family. I don't remember exactly why, but Arlene drove me to the airport to catch the flight. I had a great visit and felt refreshed by getting to see my relatives. When the day to go home arrived, I made multiple attempts at the Frankfurt Airport, trying to call Arlene to let her know that I was on the flight and when I would arrive. She never answered, but I left messages on the answering machine so I was sure she would be there.

I got on the flight and arrived at DFW. I walked out to the curb, looked for her, and she wasn't there. I stood there thirty minutes and started trying to call but no answer. After another half hour went by, I was really starting to worry. What could be going on? I was really worrying that something had happened to Arlene and my daughter.

I caught a cab and rode all the way home worried and wondering what I was going to find when I got there. She knew the day I would be coming home and when I would be calling her to confirm that I was on the flight. This could not be good, I thought.

When we arrived, I paid the taxi driver, grabbed my suitcase, and flew into the house, shaking as I unlocked and opened the door. I was coming through the side entry, as always, which goes through the utility room. When I stepped inside, I came to an immediate grinding halt. The washer and dryer were gone.

All kinds of things were going through my mind. I thought someone had come and was stealing everything when Arlene and my daughter walked in. I thought they might have tied them up and they might be here in the house, or they might have taken them with them, and who knows what?

As I proceeded my heart was racing. I stepped into the kitchen and everything looked fairly normal, but no, the dining room table was gone. As I continued, there were a lot of things still in place. When I got to our bedroom, the bed and some items there were gone.

When I went into the closet, the majority of Arlene's clothing was gone.

Now my head was truly spinning. As I continued, the office was fairly normal, but up the staircase and into my daughter's room, I saw her furniture was gone.

I went trembling down the stairs and plunked down in a chair. As I sat there shaking, it was all starting to come together. Arlene and my daughter had moved out.

The tears started to stream down my face. Why could I not please this woman, whom I truly loved with all my heart, I asked? As I sat there, I prayed and finally went to sleep. I woke up, and shortly thereafter the phone rang. I answered, and it was Arlene. She informed me that she and our daughter had moved to an apartment in Denton, Texas.

I wanted nothing more than for this marriage to work. We had already had counseling, and I was wide open to more of it. We tried a counselor in Grapevine, and I think it was then that we switched to Bill Hines, whom I had heard was a great marriage counselor from a biblical perspective. We had many sessions, and after six months Arlene agreed to move back.

I was so very hopeful that it could improve, but I was having a very hard time with handling the fact that the verbal emasculation and complaints were not going away. I never had anything that I thought was worthy of firing back at her, so as I told you previously, I would wind up being pushed to the foul language and name calling. Fortunately, at this point she no longer got in my face or chased me from room to room, and I no longer pushed her to end it.

Childish? Yes, I was just at a loss on how to deal with it. No matter how hard I tried to please, I could not do it. Sadly, I would not have been at such a loss if I had put my focus on Jesus Christ's sermon on the mount.

XI

It was probably less than a year after this that I began to hear an issue discussed, and I read some articles in the paper and news magazines on the subject of Y2K. Initially, I didn't give it much thought, but when it made its way into some of the discussion on the Christian radio programs, it started to pique my interest.

As the media ran with it, and we started to hear warnings from the government, I decided I needed to do some things to be somewhat prepared for my family if it got as bad as many were predicting. Arlene thought I was nuts. I thought that it was better to be prepared and wrong than unprepared and right in this regard. Regardless, she was quite irritated at my efforts. The fact that what I did was out of concern for them didn't amount to anything in her eyes.

While all of that was going on, my daughter was getting more and more rebellious and disrespectful. And as usual, anytime an issue developed, Arlene would side with her. It finally came to the point that I could not bear it any longer.

I proceeded to load my pickup with my belongings and headed for Amarillo. I had the old vacant house where I had lived at birth in my name, and that's where I would be until Arlene could finally show me some courtesy, respect, and honor for my role as a father to our child. I told her I had no intent to divorce, that I would continue to support them right where they were until she could honor those simple requests. I got in the F-150 and headed for Amarillo.

I pulled in at the old house on Hillside and proceeded to unload and make the place livable. It had been several years since it had been occupied, and it needed a good deal of work. For the next three months I went to work, flew back to Amarillo, worked on the house, and repeated the cycle.

I called Arlene quite often and talked. There was no remorse, and no intent to support my biblical position as a father and husband. I prayed every day for that to come to pass. I had certainly been less than perfect, but in eighteen years I worked, came home, stayed close to my family, devoted my time to God first, to them second, and me third with my few minuscule hobbies that I had tossed in the mix. In spite of it all, I had hope.

The month of November I was scheduled to fly with Ralph Miller as the first officer and Ans Wishing as the flight engineer. I enjoyed working with both of them. As the month progressed, I had some conversation with them about what was going on and how upsetting it was. Ans was a strong Christian, and I recall his emphasis that I needed to do everything I could to get things worked out and keep my family together. I agreed and hoped that could be so.

Then.

THE FINAL FLIGHT

I

November 22, 1999, and well, it's time to pick up where we left off after the first paragraph in the preface of this journey.

This was the second day of a three-day trip that Ralph, Ans, and I were doing. We had gotten to know each other fairly well. When it came to the flight attendants/cabin crew, sometimes we wouldn't even fly with the same group of them the entire day, so unfortunately, I can't remember their names and don't have access to the information any longer.

As always, I got the wakeup call one hour prior to pick-up that morning. I got up, showered, dressed, packed my bags, and went to the lobby. Once all the crew was there, we headed to the airport for another ordinary day. All of us jumped in and headed for the Tulsa International Airport. When we got there, Ralph and I headed to operations to print out the flight plan and look it over, while Ans headed out to the aircraft to do the first flight of the day preflight inspection.

The weather looked good with clear skies. It was to be a smooth, uneventful flight to DFW. As always, we checked the Notices to Airmen, which is information along the route of flight and at the airports that can affect the safe operation of the flight. Some examples would be an inoperative navigation facility, such as the very high frequency omnidirectional radio-VOR, a closed runway or taxiway at the departure or arrival airport, and other information that might affect the safety of the flight,

I wrote down the fuel we were to have loaded and subtracted the fuel burn that the flight plan showed; it looked like we would have at least 11,000 pounds of fuel left when we touched down at DFW. In case you're wondering, when you get into larger aircraft and turbine-powered general aviation aircraft, you calculate your fuel in pounds versus gallons. With jet fuel it comes out to 6.7

pounds per gallon of fuel. So, doing the math, we would be landing with at least 1,642 gallons of fuel.

That was the minimum I would accept on a day with good weather. You're probably thinking that sounds like a lot of fuel to demand just to land on a clear day. Well, you're right, but the Boeing 727 uses a lot of fuel, as I said. On take-off with 15° of flaps selected, those three Pratt & Whitney JT8D-15 engines would be burning a total of 27,000 pounds of fuel per hour. If you were on approach to land with thirty degrees of flaps selected and you had to do a go around for some reason, you would be burning even more than that.

To do well on fuel in the 727, you really had to get up to cruise altitude. Above 30,000 feet at cruise, the fuel flow would be down to 9,000 pounds per hour, a considerable difference. Ralph and I got things done in operations, and I completed it with my signature on the flight plan.

II

We headed out to the aircraft to do our part of the setup in the cockpit. We set up the airspeed bugs that we monitored and called out for takeoff: V1, Vr, and V2+10. We also set up our navigation radios and the course for the departure. While the passengers were boarding, we checked everything required before starting our engines. That was always done by challenge and response.

Ralph would read the item, and I would respond to ensure that everything was accomplished. While most of the responses applied to me, there were some items that Ralph and Ans would respond to aloud.

Now, please pretend that you are on an observation flight in the jump seat in the cockpit of the Boeing 727. You would be sitting right behind me, taking it all in.

The rudder pedals and seats came first. We would check that our seats were adjusted and locked and that the rudder pedals were properly adjusted for seat position.

The next things to evaluate were the flight instruments and switches. This pertained to quite a number of things. Ralph and I both checked our respective items to verify that each was correct. The first thing was our static source switches and our flight instruments, which had to be in the normal position.

Then our mach airspeed warning-mode switch had to be set; next the mach airspeed indicator needles had to show zero and the air speed bug set to the calculated V1 airspeed. The horizontal direction indicators were to have no gyro or computer flags showing with the pitch trim knob set at zero; the bank indicator had to be centered, and the mode selector set.

Radio altimeter switches were set in the on position. The barometric altimeter's had to be checked and set; engine pressure ratio bugs-EPR were set to the appropriate take-off power setting; the assigned altitude in our take-off clearance had to be set in the altitude alert; the field barometric pressure had to be set; and the RMI mode switches had to be set with no flags showing.

The course deviation indicators had to be set; radio altimeters and vertical speed indicators had to show zero; the clock had to be set to universal time coordinated; the standby horizon had to be checked; the third airspeed/Mach meter had to show zero; the air speed bug had to be set to the calculated V2 airspeed; the vertical gyro selector had to be set to normal; and the course deviation indicator had to be set to normal.

Whew! That was just flight instruments switches and bugs. We're not done yet.

Some of the next items were switches and lights on the overhead panel above the captain's and first officer's heads. Others are on the pedestal between the captain's and first officer's seat.

The anti-skid had to be off. This is quite similar to the antilock brake system that most cars have nowadays. Back in 1999 antilock brakes on cars were quite a new development, but they had been on big jet aircraft for decades.

The emergency exit lights had to be in the armed position. I'm sure you're familiar with this. It's those lights in the floorboard down the center aisle plus the lights over the emergency exits that the flight attendants brief you on prior to take-off. The *No Smoking* sign switch had to be on.

The anti-ice system switches had to be in the closed position. The valves these switches controlled took extremely hot air off of the engines and routed it out to the leading edge of the wings and to the nacelles of the engines to prevent ice buildup in flight. I'm sure you recall what icing conditions pertain to from that day in Oklahoma City.

The radar was set in standby. It was crucial for this to be off while on the ground. It was a powerful system, and your ground crew's getting zapped by this when they walked in front of the nose of the aircraft would not be good.

The omega navigation system had to have all of the data input. This is a system similar to today's GPS, and you would program your route of flight into the system. Nowadays, it's all automatically downloaded. How nice that would have been.

The transponder had to be in the standby position and set. This is the four-number code that ATC gives you that helps them identify the flight on their radar screen and shows them your altitude. If you fail to maintain the altitude assigned to you by ATC, the transponder will alert them.

The performance data computer had to be set. You had to put in weight data, temperature, and a number of other items, and it would calculate your EPR power settings for takeoff, cruise, and so on. The flaps had to be in the up position. You don't want them hanging down to catch something in the ramp area.

The throttles are closed at idle for engine start. The start levers are in the cutoff position. These levers send fuel to the engines and have to be off until the engine-start procedure.

The next check is the brakes and pressures. This is basically like the parking brakes on your car. They need to be parked for engine start, and the pressure gauge has to be in the green. The navigation radio frequency and course for the departure procedure have to be set. The circuit breakers are next. You want to make sure no circuit breakers are popped, and there are well over a hundred of these little things to look at and make sure.

Next item is the takeoff warning. This is a test you do of that system. It warns you if the flaps aren't in the correct position for takeoff and if a few other important things aren't correct. Then you check the oxygen pressure. You have to make sure the emergency oxygen supply is there.

From this point we proceed to the flight engineer's panel. The first item there is the fuel panel and how many pounds of fuel you have and how it is distributed in each tank. It's pretty obvious you can't pull over at the closest Exxon. The fuel quantity better be right, and it has to be loaded correctly. You don't want 10,000 pounds of fuel in the right wing and none in the left. That could ruin your whole day and everyone else's.

Then you check the hydraulic panel. You make sure the pumps are set correctly and the fluid quantity is right for each system. Engine oil quantity is next. This is another one like the fuel.

From there it's time to check the bleed air switches and then to the oxygen panel, the mask, the interphone that allows us to speak through the mask, and the goggles that we have to wear if there's smoke in the cockpit. Those have to be checked and adjusted to fit us individually.

The next item is turning the *Seat Belt* sign on. Please pardon my Texas drawl, but y'all know what this is all about. Then we do the logbook and flight forms, which include the flight plan and weight and balance paperwork. The logbook for the aircraft has to be on the plane. It documents all the maintenance and problems that the aircraft has had. If you don't have that and operate the aircraft without it on board, the FAA is going to be mighty unhappy. 'Nuff said.

Thus, we completed going over everything that needs to be looked at prior to starting the aircraft engines.

III

We had a delay that morning, and when it was resolved, our gate agent closed the door. I turned on the rotating beacon and verified the nav-lights were on. Ans verified that all the door warning lights were out, and the guide man cleared us to start. Ans turned off the air conditioning packs so that we would have the air needed to get those turbines spinning for the engine start.

I reached up and held the number one engine start switch in the ground position and checked that the start-valve open light came on. After N2 reached 20 percent, Ralph raised the start lever to idle which introduced fuel into the burner can. We monitored the turbine inlet temperature to make sure it didn't over-temp. If it did, we would have to return the start lever to cutoff.

As the engine continued to spool up, when the N2 reached 40 percent, Ralph called that, and I released the start switch and checked that the valve open light went out; Ralph and I checked all the engine instrumentation and the low oil pressure light to make sure it was out. We then went through the same procedure for engines two and three.

After they were all running, I advised the guide man that he was cleared to disconnect. He disconnected his headset and went out front. This was back when the airlines thought that it was most economical to start all of the engines and put them into reverse thrust to power back from the gate in place of using a motorized tug to push the aircraft back from the gate.

So that's what we did. It probably seems strange, but the guide man would give us the signal to move forward. After we used normal forward thrust to move a few feet, he would give us the signal to put it in reverse thrust. I put it into reverse and brought the N2 turbine rpm up to a maximum of 80 percent N2 to power back from the gate.

As we were powering back, the guide man gave us the signal to turn as needed. When we were back far enough, he gave the signal to go back to forward thrust. I brought the throttles back to forward thrust, and since everything was good, the guide man gave me a departure salute indicating to me that everything from his vantage point was good, and we could depart. I was required to announce that I had a salute, and then we called ground control for clearance to taxi.

I had no idea that would be the last time I would ever receive a salute as a captain at American Airlines.

IV

Ralph called ground control, and we received clearance to taxi to runway 18L. It was a fairly quick taxi at Tulsa, and we left all three engines running. At places where that was not the case, immediately after we started the taxi, we would shut down the number three engine to save fuel. In the process of doing that, Ans would have to control things on the electrical loads and the brake system. He would also have to manage things with the fuel system to make sure the fuel stayed balanced.

Ralph and I checked that our windows were closed and locked. As we taxied, we started checking everything that was required prior to takeoff. The first item was to make sure we all had our shoulder harnesses on; next was the fuel panel. Ans would make the call, and I would verify. Next, Ans announced that the fuel heaters were off, the pressurization was checked, and the auxiliary power unit was off. After that, Ralph called that the window heat was on, the anti-ice was as required, and the pitot heat was on and checked.

Ans called the take-off data, and I examined the required takeoff thrust setting, V speeds, departure speeds, flap settings, airplane configuration, and the load closeout data, which was the gross weight and confirmation that the center of gravity was correct, plus the stabilizer trim setting. I had to make sure they were compatible for the runway and conditions. When it was confirmed that everything was good, I announced that it was set for runway 18L, standard power and crosschecked. Ralph and Ans verbally confirmed set and crosschecked.

Next, Ans called flight instruments and bugs. Ralph and I once again verified that they were set and crosschecked. The next items were flaps and slats. I verbally verified that based on the takeoff power setting data that we received. It called for fifteen degrees of flaps; fifteen were selected, and we had a green light for the leading-edge devices. Ralph and Ans both verbally verified that.

The next item was to check the speed brakes warning horn. Then we verified that the stabilizer trim was set at what was required on the load closeout. Next the autopilot had to be off; the yaw dampers were checked; aileron and rudder trim were both set at zero, and the flight controls were checked. Ans checked the hydraulic panel. The takeoff PA was completed by yours truly. Then anti-skid was verified on; engine ignition was on; auto pack trip was normal; the transponder was on; and both DMEs were on.

We were cleared for takeoff runway 18L Tulsa, and as we took position on the runway the last two items to check before takeoff were the CSD cooler, which Ans switched to the ground off position, and the landing lights, which I made sure were on. Ans had to confirm that everything was checked and announce that the before takeoff checklist was complete.

V

I lined up the Boeing 727 with the centerline stripes and advanced the throttles to approximately 1.4 on the EPR gauge. After checking all the engine instruments to make sure everything looked good, I rapidly advanced the throttles to the standard takeoff power setting. While I did this, Ralph checked the aircraft compass system to see that it agreed with the runway heading, and he monitored the engine instruments to make sure we didn't over-temp on the turbine inlet temperature or have any other problem with the engines as we accelerated down the runway.

I held the throttles where I had them set, and Ralph put his hand behind the throttles to guard them. After the airspeed reached sixty knots, I switched from using the nose wheel steering control with my left hand to using the rudder pedals. Ralph made the verbal call at eighty knots indicated airspeed followed by the call at V1 rotate, which is where I pulled back on the yoke to raise the nose to the correct deck angle. Ralph called V2 and then V2+10. When the vertical speed showed a positive climb, I called positive rate gear up. At that time Ralph reached for the landing gear handle and raised the landing gear.

At this time, I held V2+10 on the airspeed with a maximum deck angle of twenty degrees until reaching an altitude of 800 feet AGL on the radar altimeter. I then lowered the nose to achieve a rate of climb close to 1000 feet per minute with a minimum of 500 feet per minute. The deck angle would be close to half of that required to maintain V2+10 on the airspeed. I retracted the flaps on the required airspeed schedule. As I accelerated to160 knots indicated airspeed, I called for the flaps to be retracted from fifteen to five degrees. Ralph carried that out. As I accelerated toward 190 knots indicated, I called for flaps two degrees and climb power.

At that point, I set the throttles at close to climb power and removed my hands from the throttles to put them both on the control yoke. As soon as I removed my hands from the throttles, Ans leaned forward to fine-tune them to climb power. As the trailing edge flaps reached two degrees, the leading-edge flap green light annunciator came on, and I called green light flaps up. Ralph complied once again. If our gross weight at takeoff were over 152,000 pounds, the speeds I just mentioned would have to be increased by ten knots. If the gross weight were over 176,000 pounds, the speeds would be increased by twenty knots.

I'm pretty sure we were over 152,000 pounds gross weight that morning, so once the aircraft was "clean," with gear and flaps up, and at or above 1500 feet AGL, I cycled the *No Smoking* sign off then back on, which gave the flight attendants an audible signal that they could leave their seats and start their duties.

At this time, Ans also turned the engine ignition switch off. I held 210 knots until we reached 2,500 feet AGL. At this time, I accelerated to 250 knots indicated airspeed and maintained a rate of climb close to 1,000 feet per minute, until reaching 10,000 feet above mean sea level-MSL on the altimeter.

Another item after clean-up was to switch on the performance data computer system to econ climb. It would give us our airspeeds and engine power settings. If it were inoperative, we would hold 250 knots up to 10,000 feet, as I said.

Since the sky was clear soon after we broke ground, all three of us were watching for other aircraft that could be out there, were not talking to ATC, and didn't have a transponder to help ATC spot them on radar. We would be very diligent in that until we got above 10,000 feet, but even above that altitude you had to be very watchful.

VI

In our initial climb, about the time we got the aircraft cleaned up, Tulsa Tower handed us off to Tulsa Departure Control and gave us the new frequency to contact them on. Ralph dialed in the new frequency on our comm 1 radio. He called Tulsa Departure, gave them our flight number, our heading, our current altitude, and the altitude we were assigned to climb to.

They replied, "Roger, radar contact."

Along with our American flight number, they then gave us a new altitude assignment and a heading to join our flight planned route.

As we continued our climb, we departed Tulsa Departure's airspace and entered the ARTCC's airspace, Kansas City Center in that area. After Tulsa handed us off to Kansas City, Ralph contacted them and gave them our current altitude and the altitude we were cleared to climb to. They responded with "Roger" and our flight number and cleared us to climb to our cruise altitude.

As we climbed, we used our PDCS to calculate our climb power settings on the EPR gauges and our climb airspeed. Passing through 10,000 feet on the climb, I did the cabin chime to alert the flight attendants that the "cockpit sterile period" had ended. They could communicate with us now if they needed to.

You see, the FAA imposed that rule in 1981 after they reviewed a number of accidents caused by flight crews who were distracted from their flying duties by engaging in non-essential conversations during critical parts of the flight. Basically, there can be no activity or talk once the aircraft leaves the gate until it reaches 10,000 feet in the climb that is not pertinent to the safe operation of the aircraft.

VII

Once we were above 10,000 feet, we held 300 knots up to 155,000 pounds until reaching mach crossover, or 310 knots above 155,000 pounds to the mach .78 crossover. At that point we held mach .78 on the mach meter until we leveled off at cruise altitude, and then we would accelerate to our cruise mach speed of .80 or .82 and then pull the throttles back to hold that. And just to throw you a little curve here, when we were in the climb, our power settings basically stayed the same. If we needed to speed up or slow down, we just raised the nose of the aircraft or lowered it.

Now that the sterile period was over, it was basically the typical water cooler talk. We talked about family, personal interests, news, hobbies, sports, even that horrendous subject of politics. On the subject of religion, sad to say—on my part at least— the discussion of faith was not near what it should have been. I wouldn't hesitate to share my faith in Jesus Christ, just not nearly enough.

During the remainder of the climb I flew the aircraft, Ralph did all the communication with ATC, and at 18,000 feet we both reset our altimeters to 29.92, which is the standard setting for all aircraft operating above 18,000 feet. Ans managed the fuel system, the hydraulic system, the pressurization, the heat and air in the cabin, and the company paperwork through the aircraft communications addressing and reporting system (ACARS). One of the items he had to do on the ACARS was the engine monitor log. He had to take readings off of all of the engine instrumentation and submit it through ACARS to our maintenance department. They used this information to track the health of the engines.

Due to the short length of this flight and the somewhat slow rate of climb of the Boeing 727, we weren't leveled off for long before starting the descent into DFW. Kansas City Center had handed us off to Fort Worth Center, which cleared us to descend and assigned us a new altitude. I initiated the descent and pulled the throttles back to idle. Typically, we would hold our cruise mach airspeed until reaching the 280-knot crossover; we would then hold 280 knots until 10,000 feet, then slow to the 250-knot speed limit.

We were coming in on the Bowie Arrival-Tulsa Transition. These arrival and departure procedures are given names relating to local area landmarks. Those of you who fly into Houston a lot and have a sweet tooth would be interested to know that you might very well be flying the Bluebell Arrival.

You see, you are flying right over Brenham, Texas, which is the home and headquarters of Blue Bell Ice Cream; therefore, one of the Houston Arrivals is the Bluebell. Back to where we were, the Bowie arrival comes in over Bowie, Texas, so that's where it gets its name.

As we did the descent, I was still doing the flying, Ralph was running the radios, and Ans was doing all the hard work. He checked that the pressurization was set and did his best to keep everyone comfortable with the heat and air. He kept the fuel load balanced and wrote up our landing data for us. He had to write out a card with our landing weight, our approach airspeed based on landing weight, the weather, and the altimeter settings.

As we passed through 18,000 feet, Ans called altimeters and barometric. Ralph and I complied, resetting the altimeters and the barometric set unit to the local barometric pressure and called, reset, and crosschecked. The next items for Ralph and me were the radio altimeters, which we turned on and tested and set. Ans turned on the gasper fan and checked that the pack cooling doors were open, and I turned on the landing lights which is always standard passing through 18,000 on the descent. Passing through 10,000 feet I did the chime for sterile cockpit again, and Ans had all of the hydraulic pumps on.

It was a beautiful clear day, and I remember glancing over at the Texas Motor Speedway where the NASCAR races are held. I remember looking at that as we passed by and wishing that I could make Captain Cecil Ewell's retirement party that I knew would be held there. I had a lot of respect for Cecil, as you are already aware.

I think the wind was out of the south that day, and after we were handed off to DFW Approach, they proceeded to vector us for a visual approach to Runway 18R at DFW. Ralph and I tuned our nav radios to the frequency for the ILS Runway 18R Approach, and as required we listened to the audio Morse-code identifier on that frequency to make sure it was correct.

VIII

Ans proceeded to do all of the before landing checks. There was one item that he had to call out, and Ralph and I both had to respond to audibly: altimeters, flight instruments, and bugs. The other was landing gear, which I alone would respond to when we got to that point. I would have to verify that we had three green lights indicating that all three of the wheels, the nose, and the two mains were down and locked and that there were no red lights.

Ans had to verify the rest of the items were done. The shoulder harness had to be on for all three of us, the *Seat Belt* sign had to be on, and the electrical panel had to be checked that frequency-voltage and loads were correct. He checked that anti-ice was as required and that the engine ignition was on. The fuel panel had to be checked that the quantity and distribution in each tank was right. All the fuel boost pumps had to be on, the cross-feed valve for tank 2 had to be closed, and the cross-feed valves for tanks one and three had to be open.

The fuel heater had to be off. The pressurization was checked that the cabin altitude and differential pressure were appropriate for landing. The speed brake handle had to be full forward; the *No Smoking* signs had to be on; and ACARS had to be in the data mode. The anti-skid had to be on and tested; the flaps and slats had to be 30/30 with the green light; the brake pressure was checked; and the autopilot had to be off.

Approach had vectored us to line us up on final, and during that time we had extended the flaps using the flap setting-airspeed protocol. When the aircraft was "clean" with no flaps the minimum speed was 190 knots; with two degrees flaps it was 175 knots; with five degrees a minimum was 160 knots; with fifteen degrees it was 150 knots; twenty-five degrees was 140 knots; and at thirty degrees we held V-ref, the approach speed that Ans had calculated for us.

Being on final at the initial approach altitude for the ILS 18R approach, I called gear down, and Ralph extended the gear.

Ans called, "Landing gear."

I replied, "Down three green, no red."

Ans said, "Before-landing checklist complete."

As we crossed the outer marker, we intercepted the glide slope and started our final descent to touchdown.

DFW Tower called shortly and cleared us to land Runway 18R, and we read back the clearance to confirm it. As the radar altimeter showed 500 feet AGL Ralph called it verbally when we passed 400; he called 400, then 300, 200, 100, 50, 40, 30, 20, 10. By touchdown, I had already brought the throttles back to idle. I immediately got on the wheel brakes which were applied by applying pressure at the top of each rudder pedal with my feet. I grabbed the speed brake handle with my right hand, lifted up, and pulled back to deploy them, and then reached forward and grabbed the thrust reversers for each engine and pulled them back to spool up the jet engines for max reverse thrust.

I steered the aircraft with the rudder pedals as long as the speed was sufficient. When we had slowed down, at close to 60 knots indicated, I disengaged the thrust reverse, grabbed the control wheel over to my left, and steered the aircraft with it to exit at the high-speed taxiway. After clearing the runway, I stowed the speed brakes, and turned off the anti-skid and landing lights. Tower transferred us to ground control; Ralph called ground and received our taxi clearance.

IX

As we taxied, I gave Ralph the command to retract the flaps; he also turned off the high intensity lights, reset the stabilizer trim to 0, and turned both DMEs, the radar, and the transponder to off. He also reset EPR bugs to manual and turned the window heat and pitot static system off. Ans reset the pressurization controller to 2,000 feet above field elevation, switched the venturi fan to ground venturi, opened the right number two engine bleed and closed the number three engine bleed, switched essential power to generator number one, switched the AC meter selector to external power, set the fuel panel to cross-feeds open, and turned one boost pump in each tank on.

He then advised me that I was clear to shut down engine three, which I did. Ans dialed up the ramp tower frequency on the comm 2 radio and got the update on our gate status. The gate was open, and they gave us our taxiway entry point. When we got to the entry point, ramp control cleared us to the gate. As I turned in, the guide men met us, and I followed the crew chief's guidance up to the jet bridge until he gave me the command to stop and park the brakes. Once I parked the brakes, I turned the seat belt sign off, and Ans set the electrical power. At that point I shut down all the engines. After those things were accomplished, Ralph proceeded to do the challenge part of the parking checklist, and I did the response to all the pilot items. Ans responded to the flight engineer items.

We completed all of the final things that had to be done on my final flight to park the aircraft. Everything was done, and I signed the logbook and entered any mechanical problems that needed to be addressed by maintenance prior that aircraft's next flight.

We had parked the Boeing 727 in the C Terminal close to Gate 22, according to the best of my recollection and what I have been told by friends. The next flight for me and my crew was to Nashville somewhere around the middle of Terminal A. Since we were late arriving and our next flight was departing out of a gate a good distance from our arrival gate, the company sent a crew van to pick us up and take us to the next aircraft to save some time.

As a passenger, when you leave the aircraft and walk out into the jet bridge, if you look straight ahead, you will see a door. That door opens to a staircase that goes down to the tarmac. It is used by crew members and ground crew to get from the tarmac up to the aircraft and vice versa.

The van was waiting for us, and I had already taken my flight bag and suitcase down to the tarmac. I looked up and saw that one of our flight attendants had set her suitcase and personal items out at the top of the stairs. She had left them there while she ran some paperwork in to the gate agent. Those stairs are made of metal that has teeth to it, giving traction if it's wet, but it's not a solid surface. It has holes in it. That's not really a problem unless you're wearing high heeled shoes where the heel can go into the hole.

So, I went to the top of the stairs to bring her bags down for her. I picked them up, turned to go back down the stairs, and the staircase snapped off from the jet bridge, dropping me twelve feet headfirst into the concrete.

Ans was standing down on the tarmac talking to one of the ground crew when he heard the sound of the metal breaking. He turned and looked just in time to see my head go into the concrete. He ran over to me, and I had blood pouring from my nose, mouth, and ears. I went into convulsions, and he got down and held me up to prevent me from drowning on my own blood.

Again, the next leg of our trip was to Nashville. It just so happened that Ans lived in a town just outside of Nashville and commuted to work from there. He was going to get to spend a night at home on our trip instead of at the layover hotel. Rather than say farewell and wave, as the ambulance took off to take me to Parkland Hospital, Ans jumped in the ambulance and accompanied me there. Ans was a true wingman.

It's hard to believe that a couple of hours after the ambulance sped out of the tarmac area with me in it, one of my other wingmen, VP of Flight Captain Cecil Ewell, taxied in on his final flight as well. He was about to turn sixty, which back then was the mandatory retirement age for an airline transport pilot. They had the fire trucks sitting on opposite sides of the taxiway where he would enter the tarmac to spray the water cannon across the taxiway over his aircraft as he taxied in to honor his career. What a contrast in how two pilots' careers at American Airlines ended on the same day.

While it can bring a bit of sadness to think back on never receiving that honor of my career with the water cannon, I immediately go back to what I've shared with many people who have asked me over the years if I miss flying or my career at American Airlines. Flying was my life. I absolutely loved it. But, as always, God gives me strength, peace, and joy in all things. Sometimes I find it surprising that I don't miss it, but then again, with God all things are possible, and it shouldn't surprise me at all.

OJI—TBI—ARDS—
WHAT A LIFE OF ACRONYMS

I

As I was on the way to the hospital, American Airlines notified Arlene that I had an accident at the airport, and I was on my way to Parkland Hospital in Dallas. When she arrived at the hospital, they had a large medical team working hard to keep me alive. Dr. Eugene George was the neurosurgeon in charge.

After they did everything they could to stabilize me, Dr. George came out to talk to Arlene and discuss the traumatic brain injury that I was dealing with. He basically informed her that if nothing was done, I would most likely be gone within twenty-four hours.

The second option was to make a round hole in my skull that could release the fluid and possibly allow the swelling of the brain to decrease. The third option was to do a double craniotomy which would be the removal of large portions of the skull, called bone flaps, on the upper right and left side of the skull. That would be a much more intense, possibly problematic surgery, but it had the best potential outcome for me. Arlene chose to do the double craniotomy.

That night at the hospital, my boss, Chief Pilot Captain Zane Lemon, and Chief Pilot Captain Dennis Eckenrod stayed into the wee hours of the morning with my family and friends. My dear cousin, Myma Sue, was there many days and nights, and Curtis and Amy and Curtis's sister Pamela as well. There are so many that I can't remember to name them all. To those who were there that night and many others over the upcoming months, I offer a huge thank you. It was really great to hear how Zane and Dennis had brought some humor and were able to get some smiles and laughter from the group over the next few nights.

I made it through the surgery, but within a fairly short time came down with acute respiratory distress syndrome. Along with that I also developed pneumonia. How serious is ARDS?

The American Lung Association says, "There are about 200,000 U.S. cases of ARDS each year. Most people who get ARDS are already in the hospital in critical condition from some other health complication or trauma. ARDS is a serious disease and even with the best medical care between 30–50 percent of those diagnosed with ARDS die of it.

Those surviving the disease will often have long hospital stays. One of the biggest problems with this disease is that many patients develop additional complications while they are in the ICU, such as pneumonia, collapsed lungs, other infections, severe muscle weakness, confusion, and kidney failure."

The ARDS required a tracheotomy and being on a ventilator. I had been in a drug-induced coma the entire time, and after three weeks they started to reduce the sedation and my eyes started to open. The first month everything was very problematic. It was the full course up and down. I drifted in and out of consciousness with my eyes open, but they didn't know if I were seeing. They didn't know if I were hearing, but finally I was able to respond to some commands. Liver function became a concern, and I was on the borderline of kidney failure.

They were able to remove the tube that went down my throat into my stomach, and I was put on a feeding tube that went directly into the stomach, but then a problem developed because of constant vomiting, so they had to stop that for a time. When they finally got me sitting up in a recliner, the position just drained me. After three weeks they put a cap on the trach, I was able to talk very softly, and they were able to remove the neck brace.

I knew that it was December 1999 and could count backward very slowly but would get confused and call Arlene by my daughters' name. Pockets of fluid were developing in the skull. I was still unable to pass the swallowing test and couldn't eat or drink, and I was having terrible headaches.

At the very end of the first month I was having trouble moving my right arm, and Arlene had noticed increased swelling in my right wrist. They x-rayed it and discovered that both bones were broken in the area of the right wrist. Boy, I'm glad I had been sedated. The physical therapist had been coming in and moving the wrist quite often. Ouch!

They planned to do surgery on the wrist the next week, but there were so many trauma patients requiring surgery and because of the holiday they were short staffed in the operating rooms. They decided to put the wrist surgery off and do it the same time they replaced my bone flaps.

II

After about five weeks, the swelling on the brain had gone down enough that Dr. George decided it was time to reattach the bone flaps to my skull. They took me into surgery for 7.5 hours and replaced them. At the same time the orthopedic surgeon came in and put pins in the wrist fractures. They are still there today.

The orthopedic surgeon said my arm was worse than she expected, but it went back into place well, and she was pleased. The nerve was not severed, but she said it could still be bruised, and it would take a few months to heal. The bone flaps went together well, and they did a CAT scan after the surgery. There were no blood clots, and everything appeared to fit well.

The next day I was really hurting and didn't want to move; my head hurt so badly. One eye was more dilated than the other. I was seeing double, and one eyelid wasn't opening as far as the other. The doctors weren't concerned and were planning to transfer me to Baylor Rehab Hospital, but about five days later things got worse.

I was throwing up repeatedly; I was hallucinating; my color was terrible; and my eyes got worse. They did a CAT scan and discovered fluid on the outside and inside of my skull. And I was dehydrated. They had to drain the fluid and get another IV going. I was looking better within a few hours, but I was returned to surgical ICU.

A few days later, the fluid had increased, and they were going to do surgery to put in a drain tube, but since I was doing well neurologically, they decided to wait. They did not want to operate because of the danger of infection. Unfortunately, of the four or five fluid samples that they removed, one had staph in it. They were hopeful that it had gotten contaminated after it was removed from my head.

They put me on the strongest antibiotic available and were watching for other signs of infection. They capped off the trach and expected to be able to remove it soon. A few more days went by, and they sent off more fluid samples; this time they all came back with staph in them. On top of that I was having double vision. Dr. George thought that was possibly related to the broken facial bones from the fall, so he called in a facial surgeon to evaluate that.

They also called in a gastroenterologist to find out why I was throwing up and getting absolutely no nutrition. Arlene talked to Dr. George for an hour, and he told her they did not want to do the surgery if anything else could work.

The next day things had reached the point that Dr. George met with another neurosurgeon, and they decided it had to be done. The infection was in the bone flaps. They would be removed and had to stay removed for an entire year to make sure the infection was gone. The bone flaps would deteriorate, so they would have to use them as a mold and create some synthetic bone flaps.

The next day, January 19, 2000, the surgery was done. They removed the bone flaps and sent them off as molds to create the synthetic replacements. Now the only thing between my brain and the outside world for the next year was my skin. They had to create a custom plastic helmet for me to wear anytime I was out of bed.

They got me started on a regimen of four to six weeks, through a picc line, of the most potent antibiotic out there. Three or four days after the surgery, they ran a tube down my throat to see what could be causing the nausea. They found no ulcers or any other problem, so the conclusion was that the problem was from the trauma to the brain and inner ear.

Within a couple of days, the double vision started to improve. It would come and go. The hearing problem was a result of the antibiotic and would eventually improve. Within a week I was doing much better and had received the helmet. It was absolutely miserable wearing that thing, though. It was extremely hot, and as hot-natured as I am normally, it was miserable. I was not looking forward to a year of that anytime I was out of bed.

III

About two months and a week into this, on January 31, 2000, I was finally transferred to Baylor Rehab Hospital where I would spend the next five weeks under the care of Dr. Mary Carlile. I got my first shower in over two months. Thank you, Lord. I'll bet everyone else was thanking Him too. Of course, that was the absolute least to be thankful to Him for considering what was to come.

Everyone was amazed at how well I was improving and the progress I was making at Baylor Rehab. They created an outcome map to chart my progress, and it was very good. The second week I improved nineteen points. I was eating well. They had me walking with a walker, and my voice was getting stronger. The third week I still improved ten points, which was still very good.

They removed the external fixator on my right arm, and the doctor was pleased with the way it looked. She said the nerve was not severed but was obviously injured since I couldn't straighten my fingers. She told us that it would take at least three to five months to a year to heal.

Since I couldn't straighten my fingers, they created a custom-made contraption. It went down my forearm to the palm of my right hand, and it had little pads for the ends of my fingers to lie in attached to rubber bands; that kept my fingers extended. This prevented the muscles from wasting away to where I could not use those fingers, and it allowed me to exercise them.

I was eating about 85 percent of my meals. When they stopped giving me the nausea medicine, I was waking up with a queasy stomach and was unable to eat breakfast. They did an EEG to see if my brain waves were normal or if there were any indication of seizure activity so that they could begin tapering off the seizure medication. I had not had any seizures through all of this. They finished the antibiotic and removed the picc line from my arm. The only thing that was left was the stomach tube. They wanted to make sure that I was eating and getting plenty of protein because my albumin was low.

After four weeks the therapists reported that I was reaching the goals they had set for me. I was walking alone; they had me climbing stairs and walking outside in the grass. I had very little endurance, though, and they were trying to increase that. It didn't take much for me to be exhausted. The nausea and headaches were not nearly as frequent as they were.

They removed the stomach tube, which meant I was finished with all the invasive things sticking out of me after three months. Yeah!

Now the plan was to send me home in about a week with no wheelchair and no walker. They would send therapists to my home to work with me for a couple of weeks, and then I would begin outpatient therapy.

And that's what happened. After five weeks at Baylor Rehab, it was time to tell them goodbye.

IV

Wednesday, March 8, 2000, I was home. What a surprise! Some of my dear pilot friends, my boss, Captain Zane Lemon, and some other precious people were hiding there to greet me as I walked in the door. I have a few tears welling up here, as I type and recall this. What a blessing that was. I stayed up until 10:30 p.m. that night.

The next day the three therapists—speech, occupational, and physical—came to the house. The physical therapist assessed the house for safety hazards and walked through it with me to look things over.

Once again, I was exhausted at the end of that day. They gave me exercises to do, and we tried to get all of my medications figured out. Other than being exhausted at the end of the day, I was doing quite well the first two weeks at home that the therapists were coming to work with me.

Then *kaboom!* After two weeks at home things started going downhill rapidly. I became much weaker and couldn't get around the house. Sadly, over the last four months all of the previous problems with Arlene had been completely gone from my mind. They were about to be refreshed.

I could not believe it when she proceeded to her usual mode of operation, making me out to be nothing but a lazy man. I had to be "up and at 'em" with no excuses. After what I had gone through the last three and a half months, to be hit with that was over the top. Unfortunately, I responded with curse words, and then proceeded to beat myself to a mental pulp for letting the pain of her disrespect and uncaring attitude prod me to responding the way I did.

Moving on, I could hardly eat, and after seeing three of my doctors, they couldn't find a reason for it. The middle of April, after three very difficult weeks of serious regression, I got admitted to the Centre for Neuro Skills, a post-acute rehabilitation center in Irving, Texas. I was admitted there and had a very difficult first week.

CNS was designed to get people with head injuries back into a normal lifestyle. Patients live in an apartment and do things as they would at home and go to the rehab part of the facility during the day to get therapy in place of going to work. I was in an apartment three miles from the rehab location. I was too weak to do anything on my own, but the hope was that I would progress to getting up in the morning, fixing my own breakfast and a sack lunch, showering, getting dressed, getting on a van, and going to therapy.

I was supposed to do therapy all day and go home in the late afternoon. I would have to fix my supper, clean the apartment, do my laundry, and then do leisure activities. We would also go on outings for some entertainment.

I would be given $65 a week to budget for groceries and would go to the grocery store to gather my weeks supply. I would be given $30 a week for activities and could choose what I would like to do. Saturday and Sunday would be leisure days.

I was at CNS for over a month and was unable to accomplish any of those things. I was going downhill rapidly. I was able to get in to see an endocrinologist and a urologist to get more evaluations done. The endocrinologist completed his testing and said that my thyroid was normal, but my testosterone level was low. That was the only thing that he found that was not within normal limits.

The urologist did kidney and bladder tests and said that the injury from the fall to my kidneys had healed nicely. The bladder tests were all normal. He believed that my problems were being caused by the head injury. It took some time, but I also finally got into a neurologist, and he ordered an EEG and an MRI.

After about six weeks at CNS I had declined to the point that I was unable to chew food and was having difficulty swallowing. One side of my throat and nose became swollen. They tested some drainage from my nose, and it tested positive for glucose, which meant that it could possibly be spinal fluid.

All of the information was sent to Dr. George, and he felt that I needed to be admitted to Parkland Hospital for extensive testing to see if they could determine what was causing me to decline. They were expecting a possible spinal fluid leak.

V

I went to Parkland for a couple of weeks, and all test results came back negative, so the doctors were really flummoxed trying to figure out what was going on. On June 13, 2000, I was transferred to Zale Lipshy Hospital. I would get more therapy there and have the same team of doctors that I did at Parkland.

They put a feeding tube back in my stomach since I couldn't chew or swallow. After I was there for over a week, Arlene met with Dr. George (neurosurgeon), Dr. Kowalski (physiatrist), and Dr. Dewey (neurologist). They still did not know what was causing me to regress. They thought that taking me off all medications might correct the problem, but it didn't.

They decided to start me on some different medications, one at a time, to see if they could find something to help. They thought that my injury was very diffuse, and that was why it did not show on the MRI. They thought that I may have had some late changes in the brain and some of the actual nerve cells had died. They told the family that I would stay at Zale Lipshy for several more weeks, but it actually turned into two more months

I don't remember much about the time at Zale Lipshy. The one thing that I do remember vividly was the second day there. The nurses came in to get me out of bed and sit me up. I remember begging, begging, begging them to let me stay in bed; I was so exhausted and felt so bad. They wouldn't, obviously for good reason, I had to sit up if I were ever going to recover.

They rolled me out in the hallway in the wheelchair and left me there for hours. It was brutal. At the end of the struggle to sit upright for those hours, I felt like I had done a triathlon. To this day I can't imagine why that was so hard and exhausting, but it was. As hard as it was, though, I knew God was going to sustain me through it just as He had many times at that point.

Sometime in that first month at Zale Lipshy the doctors changed one of the medications as a diagnostic tool. I started to improve almost immediately; the doctors weren't sure if the medication caused it. Anyway, I continued to improve. After about a month I finally passed the swallowing test and was able to start eating again, and they were able to remove the catheter. I was also doing very well cognitively. On August 18, 2000, I was released from Zale Lipshy and transferred back to CNS.

VI

Within a couple of weeks, I was walking alone again but had to have someone close due to dizziness. After about a month and a half, of the up-and-coming ten months back at CNS, I went back to see Dr. George, Doctor Kowalski, and Dr. Mezera, (orthopedic surgeon). They were all thrilled to see the change. Dr. Mezera told me to stop wearing any splints and to get busy and exercise my hand.

We set up an appointment with Dr. George four months out for a checkup. If everything were fine at that time, the surgery to replace the bone flaps would be scheduled immediately. An appointment was also set up with a dentist to assess the damage done to my teeth in the fall and by my grinding them when I was in the hospital.

Within a couple of weeks of the doctors and dentist appointment, my mom fell at home in Amarillo and broke her hip. She had surgery to replace the hip, which went well, but she was getting weaker and not recovering well. She was admitted into a nursing home as she was unable to walk. I was able to get approval from the doctors and a three-day pass from CNS to go to Amarillo and see her.

When I got off the flight and stepped outside of the terminal, I couldn't believe the snow on the ground that early. When I got to the nursing home, Mom wasn't doing well at all, and it was tough seeing her unable to fend for herself, as she had done since my dad passed away back in 1993. I wished I could stay there with her and really didn't want to have to leave and go back to my therapy.

What a string of troublesome events. Two weeks later, Arlene's mother passed away. She drove up to Spearman, Texas, where her mother had been in a nursing home, and stayed ten days. I wanted to go to the memorial service, so I flew up to Amarillo again. My son-in-law and stepdaughter picked me up and drove me to Spearman.

I was able to attend the service and see many of Arlene's family members; being able to reach out and be with them were good, but I recall how physically drained I was. It was also a bit unnerving, being out in public and getting some strange looks, wearing that unusual-looking helmet, especially with it making me so hot that the perspiration would just pour down my face.

A few weeks later, November 22, 2000, was the anniversary of my accident. That was one long year. And it was going to be another full year before I would feel fairly back to normal. After the first of the year, January 2001, I had the appointment with Dr. George. The site where my stomach feeding tube had been removed still had not healed. Three months earlier back in October, I had visited two general surgeons about that.

It was looking better back then, and they said to leave it alone. Now it had gotten worse, and Dr. George didn't want to do the surgery on my skull until that was completely healed, so he called in another general surgeon to look at it. This was disappointing to me, but they obviously had to make sure I didn't have infection present when they did the cranioplasty.

The new surgeon reopened the site and found a two-inch piece of thread from one of the stitches that had not come out. He removed it and some of the scar tissue. He had to go quite deep, so it was quite painful over the next few days.

I immediately went back to doing therapy from 9–4 during the day and just had to wait. It was going to be five to six weeks before the cranioplasty could happen. During this time, I got transferred to a transition apartment complex, the Grand Venetian, in Irving. By February 24, 2001, the stomach site had healed, and my cranioplasty was scheduled for March 9, 2001 at Zale Lipshy Hospital.

I went in on March 9 at 7:30 a.m., and it was a real joy to have my boss, Captain Zane Lemon, there to wish me the best. When the procedure was complete, Dr. George came out to talk to my family at 11:15 a.m. He was pleased with the surgery. He placed an artificial bone flap in my head to replace the one that was removed back in January 2000, and he had started me on an antibiotic before the surgery to combat any infection. They got me up that afternoon and walked me a short distance. I did very well.

Dr. George told everyone that they would watch me very closely over the next two weeks for any complications. He said after two weeks the likelihood of problems becomes less each day after that. He also had me up a lot over the weekend and was very pleased with my progress. I did so well that they actually released me from the hospital four days from the time the surgery was done.

They moved me back to the original apartment at CNS, not the transition apartment, so that they could monitor me closely. I continued to improve with no sign of infection. For some reason I developed insomnia and couldn't sleep. So, we had to make an appointment with a neurologist to figure that out.

The next two months were something else. On April 21, 2001, Arlene's father experienced a massive stroke and passed away. She had to go back up to the far northern part of the Texas Panhandle to take care of all of that. I also made it up there for his funeral service, which was a very sad day. I really liked him and had always enjoyed the time I had spent with him.

In May I had many doctors' appointments, and there was a great deal of stuff taking place to get me lined out to finally go home. I was still dealing with the lack of sleep. They sent me to a place to have my sleep evaluated and wound up getting me a CPAP machine to see if that helped. I was not at all fond of that thing and just could not get used to it.

I quit using it after a few months when I tried several nights without it and finally felt like I was sleeping most of the night without it. We had vestibular testing done. My balance was OK, but my brain didn't process the information correctly, so I felt dizzy a lot of the time. I was also having an issue with eyesight from the processing problem.

VII

If all that I just shared weren't enough, here I am fighting insomnia, a feeling of dizziness, eyesight changing, family funerals, and I'm informed by Arlene that I have to put on a suit and tie to go talk to some lawyers. What? Well, I'm going to have to backtrack a little here.

I was oblivious to all of this as it happened, but I learned that several months into this ordeal, after the very first time that I regressed severely and had to go to CNS and Zale Lipshy Hospital, Arlene was informed that as soon as the sick leave that I had accumulated ran out, I would be put on long-term disability.

That meant that our total income at that time would be from long-term disability insurance, which would not kick in for several months and would be a huge cut in pay. So, there we were, faced with also having to put our house on the market along with everything else.

Arlene was advised by friends to contact the APA and get them involved, so she did. I found it stunning when I learned that our APA President, Rich Lavoy, just washed his hands of doing anything to help me and basically indicated nothing could be done. My friends were not satisfied with that and told her to contact our APA Base Representative, Captain Larry Foster.

From what I've been told, he was not happy with what he learned and set out to make things right. He set up a meeting with Arlene and the new Vice President of Flight Captain Bob Kudwa. When they arrived for the meeting, what a coincidence, Captain Kudwa's wife just happened to be there. He made an attempt to usher Arlene out to visit with his wife while "the boys" discussed things. While I've heard that Arlene was quite nervous over this meeting, she didn't fall for that and stayed to hear it all and give her input.

The management team whom were against us were Captain Kudwa, Captain George Foster and Paul Barry. Those whom were there to support us were Captain Larry Foster, Captain Dave Slack, and Captain Randy Popiel. It truly blessed me when Dave shared that in that meeting, even though he was on the management team, my boss Captain Zane Lemon nodded in agreement with almost everything that Larry said should be done for me.

I was told Captain Kudwa listened to everyone and proceeded to reveal how he had a head injury previously and basically indicated that if I gave it some effort, I would recover fine and be back "on the line" in due time.

He then went on to tell everyone that he would have to give it some thought, and he would let them know his decision soon. Time passed, and word came down from Captain Kudwa that there was nothing American Airlines would do. Once again, Captain Foster, the base representative, was not pleased with that. He told Arlene he would continue to pursue it.

There was one other thing of interest. When I was still at Zale Lipshy Hospital, I vaguely remember some visitors. It was Captain Cecil Ewell and another gentleman. He came to Zale to visit me and had with him Bob Baker, who was the executive vice president of American Airlines at that time.

It was not a good day for me. I remember feeling honored to have them come to see me, but it was a struggle to communicate and stay awake while they were there. It was quite interesting coming to Zale for future appointments with Dr. Kowalske to see Mr. Baker's name on a plaque in the hospital. He was on the board of directors at Zale.

Shortly after Mr. Baker and Captain Ewell visited me, word came down that the company would allow me to be paid what I would have earned had I continued to fly for two years. After that, the remaining sick leave would run out, and it would be long-term disability for me. They also required that I come into the airport and do some type of office work two or three days a week, once I got well enough that CNS would approve it.

After the two years, it would be finished. That would keep us above water until the long-term disability pay kicked in and allow some time for other possible recourse. Captain Foster wasn't at all satisfied with that, but he told Arlene that was probably the best that was going to happen.

VIII

A number of people had told Arlene over the previous months that she needed to file suit. She knew that in the past, I was very displeased with lawyers and those they represent in frivolous product liability lawsuits. I'm sure I don't need to go into a bunch of examples. Arlene wasn't keen on lawsuits either, but it became apparent there was no other recourse.

I had been doing my job in a normal, and as I was led to believe, safe fashion. Unfortunately, there was a problem. Our Texas politicians had bowed to the corporate lobbyists and made it the law that if your employer participates in workers-comp insurance, you cannot sue your employer no matter how negligent or at-fault they are.

The airport could not be sued either. The only recourse pertained to the design and manufacture of that staircase. It turned out that the company that built it knew there was a problem, and Arlene was told they even had an employee at DFW evaluating things to come up with a solution.

Along with that, American Airlines knew there was a problem as well and were held to no accountability for what had happened to me in my service to them. And it goes without saying, the day this happened to me, every jet bridge staircase at every airport in this country was inspected to see how big the problem was and to find a solution to it.

Arlene interviewed several attorneys and chose Mark Werbner of Dallas to represent us. Now, here I am a patient at CNS, having to go suit and tie to be interrogated by attorneys while I was dealing with all these physical and cognitive problems. In learning that, you might be wondering why in the world that would happen.

As they say, "Show me the money!"

The lawyers for the company that was being sued had to do everything they could to dig up dirt on me and make a jury have no empathy for me. They learned that Arlene and I were separated at the time of the accident, and they dug back seven or eight years and found the record of me filing for divorce and all that entailed. They thought that it would be beneficial to their cause in making me look bad, so I had to go in and answer their questions under oath.

Considering what I had gone through and was still going through, this might sound pretty loathsome, and it is. The fact is, however, we are all sinners. Were it not for the grace of God and His forgiveness through the sacrifice of His Son, Jesus Christ, we would all be facing a serious consequence for the many wrongs that we have all committed. While that was irritating to me at the time, it didn't take me long to come to that realization, have compassion for the parties, pray that they repent and come to Jesus for His forgiveness, and forgive them on my end as He requires.

IX

On May 24, 2001, the Allied Pilots Association gave a luncheon for me at the Marriott Hotel North of DFW Airport with well over a hundred in attendance. They invited many of the management pilots including Captain Cecil Ewell-Retired, Captain Bob Kudwa, Captain John Hale, and many others whom I can't recall.

The medical personnel, including the ambulance crew that took me to Parkland, were honored and given small glass globes with a gold-plated Boeing 727 inside for all that they did for me. The four main doctors who cared for me, Dr. George, Dr. Apple, Dr. Kowalske and Dr. Carlisle, attended and spoke.

God had truly blessed me with the best medical team and rehab therapists that one could hope for along with my fellow pilots and friends who did everything they could to help me and my family through this. And Arlene had truly poured out her time and effort to seek the best possible outcome for me. It was such a special day. I could barely talk when they asked me to come up. I was so thankful to God for His divine intervention, gave Him the honor and glory, and I thanked everyone who had done so much for me.

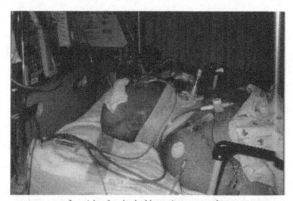

Jay, right after the double craniotomy procedure

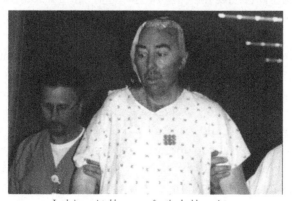

Jay being assisted by nurses after the double craniotomy

RECOVERY AND ANOTHER DAY IN INFAMY

I

As I mentioned, I was going to the DFW Airport two or three days a week to work, once CNS approved it. That continued for at least five or six months after leaving CNS. Even after I got home, I was having some major ups and downs.

It was a bit unpleasant that first day at home as I walked into our garage and spotted my flight bag sitting there on the floor. When I asked Arlene, what was in that plastic bag lying beside it she informed me that it was my captain's uniform that I was wearing that day.

I was curious why it hadn't been cleaned and hung up. It should not have surprised me, but I was a bit stunned to learn why. Arlene informed me that it was soaked in my blood, and the paramedics had actually cut the jacket right up the middle seam in back to remove it from me in the ambulance. Into the trash that went.

I was also struggling remembering where things were at the airport. Here's an airport that I knew like the back of my hand, and I was afraid I was going to get lost and not find my way down into the bowels of that place where the flight department offices were.

In all of that though I had quite a memorable experience there in the office. They had me doing something on the computer pertaining to delay codes that were submitted by the captains on their flights. I was sitting there working on that and one of our pilots walked by and saw me through the window. He came in, shook my hand, and asked me if I remembered him.

I recognized him but couldn't recall his name, and I knew we had flown together. After I shared that with him, he introduced himself. He went on to inform me that we had flown a trip that laid over in Tampa. As he continued, it was brought up that the three of us had gone to dinner and were walking back to the hotel. When he said that, it was all coming back to me.

As we were walking down the sidewalk, a fellow on the other side of the street proceeded across the street toward us. When he reached us, he requested money. As he spoke, I glanced across the street and saw another restaurant. I told him I didn't have any money to offer but asked if he was hungry. He looked at me and said that he was. I asked my friends to wait while I ran over there and came right back.

When we got in the restaurant, I told him to get whatever he wanted. He ordered one thing and asked me if he could have another item. I told him that would be fine and then he asked for another. I was happy to do it for him. He thanked me, I paid the bill and took off to join the guys back across the street. We just continued back to the hotel and that was that.

After my pilot friend completed his rendition of that, I told him that I remembered it quite well. He went on to tell me that my doing that had really stirred his heart and that he had thought about it several times. As he continued, he informed me that when he learned of my on the job injury and followed the updates on my status that he was moved even more by it.

My response was to tell him how I knew our Lord would want us to help in that way, but not to hand out money for more alcohol or drugs, which appeared to probably be where the money would go had we done that. I was quite glad that he came in to visit. It wouldn't be long until I would be in a new location where my fellow pilots would be at a distance and unable to come in and talk with me.

II

For something new they transferred me up to the ramp tower, where American Airlines employees communicate with all the flights, inbound and outbound, giving them clearance to and from the gates. I really didn't have a clue what I was doing up there on the computer, but it was good therapy, at least.

I would also get to look out on the tarmac from the tower and listen to everything that was going on. Occasionally I even got to chime in on the radio and say hi to some of the pilots I had flown with, whose names I recognized on the data associated with the flights. My name was well known with many of the pilots at American Airlines, and I got a lot of uplifting words when I would call in on the radio and say hello.

One day that I remember up there quite well, however, was another day in infamy. In the ramp tower off to the side they had a television that was always tuned to one of the news channels. I had arrived at 7:30 a.m., and I went to observe all the activity in the tower as I looked down to the tarmac. As I went from station to station there in the tower, I decided to walk over to that television to see what was going on that morning.

I had only been there a couple of minutes when something awful appeared on the screen. A Boeing jet was flying into one of the towers of the World Trade Center. Shortly after that, as the first incident was being reported, another Boeing jet appeared and slammed into one of the other towers.

As I stood and watched, that image of the lives of my fellow crew members, pilots, flight attendants, and our customers on American Airlines Flight 11 and United Airlines Flight 175 being ended in that heinous fashion was devastating. My dear, new friends in the tower got me to come sit with them as they worked.

They were some wonderful people in continuing the complicated task they had, knowing what just happened. On top of that, unbeknownst to me, they called and got hold of the fellow who was driving me everywhere and told him to come get me and take me home.

They didn't want me to have to stay there and witness the stress that was sure to come as the day progressed. That was truly traumatic to me at that point in my recovery, but once again the Lord gave me peace.

My driver's license had expired, so a few more months after 9/11, when I finally got to the point that they thought I could drive safely, I needed to be evaluated and have some lessons. So, we had to find someone who could do that. It's humorous now, but here I was, a guy who had previously pushed the throttles up on the Boeing 727-200B to extract 45,000 pounds of thrust from the three Pratt & Whitney JT8D-15 turbojet engines, climbed to over 30,000 feet, and cruised at over 500 mph, and my knees were knocking as I got in the car to drive to downtown Dallas during rush hour. Come to think of it, my knees still knock, a bit, getting in that mess during rush hour.

After all of that I got my driver's license renewed. Arlene had sold my Ford F-150 while I had been in the rehab facility, so we had to go get a new vehicle for my use. I wound up getting a 2002 Dodge Ram Pickup. I was now able to get back fairly close to normal. I still had some struggles to deal with, but I was truly blessed to be where I was.

It had truly been an ordeal for Arlene as well, with the loss of both parents, having to go and help my mom, and bringing back my things that I had taken to Amarillo. My cousin Pamela helped her with that.

One of the final things I remember in the two years of my life that I just shared with you was sitting down and reading emails and cards that had been sent over that period. My cousin, Curtis Hail, whom you've already heard about many times, was one of the founders of a church planting mission group called Global Mission Fellowship. They had been doing mission work in Russia, Eastern Europe, South America, and many other places.

I got to read how he had people all over the world praying for me. God certainly honored those prayers and poured out one miracle after another. In fact, I had received the nickname "miracle man" from several friends who witnessed me in the hospital and others who knew the details.

There is another thing that sticks with me, though. I had several acquaintances say to me after I got back into a fairly normal routine something along the line of, "I'm glad it wasn't me. I don't think I could have the faith you do if that had happened to me." Back when those comments were made, I was still struggling a fair amount with communication, but I certainly should have done better than I did.

I wish I had shared this question. How can I complain when Jesus, the Son of God, came here, lived a perfect sinless life in order to be hated, despised, beaten beyond recognition, crowned with thorns, and nailed to a cross, to pay the price for my sin? There are times when I fail to immediately ask myself that question when things aren't going the way I would prefer, but it's my heartfelt desire to correct that.

In this, I've shared a pretty intense time in my life. I hope you can see, as I do, God's grace, mercy, and answered prayer. The fact that I can be here with the cognitive ability to share my life story is all to His glory.

I also give thanks that in the legal proceedings the Lord provided, and we were given an offer that allowed us to retain our house and carry on. It is truly a joy to give Him the glory in all of it and share the good news of God's mercy, grace, and love in Jesus Christ. To wrap this chapter up, I had always had a desire to participate in some of the ministry-related trips that Curtis was involved in, but I could never match any of those with my scheduled vacations.

Well, guess what? That was a possibility now.

THE CALL—DR. STRAUB IS AMAZED—
GLORY TO GOD IN GAZA

I

Just a little over six months after my release at CNS, Curtis came out to see me at home and brought Tom Doyle with him. Tom had been a pastor for many years and had decided he wanted to switch his ministry to international church planting.

At that time, Curtis had taken over a part of the ministry that had separated from his original organization and gone on its own, and Tom was coming on board there. The new ministry was based on a visual tool, the Evangecube, created by some associates in Curtis's ministry.

They came in, sat down, and proceeded to inform me that Tom was going to initiate the organization's ministry in the Middle East and would like me to consider joining Tom on the first trip. They indicated that they thought the story of God's grace, all of the miracles He had poured on me over the last two years, and my faith could be uplifting and beneficial. They asked if I would like to join in.

I asked Tom where he planned to go. He shared that our first stop would be in Israel and that part of our time there would be spent with a minister in Gaza City. From Israel we would proceed on to Amman, Jordan. From there we would catch a flight to the United Arab Emirates.

I had never thought that I would have an opportunity to go and walk where my Lord and Savior had walked, and the thought that my testimony could be beneficial would have never entered my mind.

I told them I would give it some thought and let them know. For several days I just kept rolling it around in my head and praying. I was thinking, "Me?" I had always thought about sharing Christ on trips with Curtis, but the idea of talking about me and my life experiences had not seemed very relevant to me.

The more I thought about it, however, the more it became clear that what I had just experienced, how I had never given up on God through all of it, and how He had intervened was something that was good to share. I called Tom and told him to count me in.

II

Right after that was set in motion, I got to thinking that the family in Germany had no idea what had happened to me. I always had to initiate the communication, so I decided I should probably try to get in touch with them.

I contacted Rainer, and he asked me how I was doing. I told him I was doing well, and I went on to share what had happened along with a lot of the pertinent details. I'm sure you recall that Rainer is a medical doctor. In his response he indicated that he was more than a bit surprised that I was alive after what I had experienced.

Just days after that initial contact with Rainer, he got back with me to say he was coming to the United States very soon for a medical conference, and he wanted to come to Dallas to see us.

That was great news. After looking at the dates he gave me, I emailed him and said that would work. We would be home and were looking forward to his arrival. I also contacted our cousins, Bill Crawford and his sister Barbara Wilbanks, to see if they would like to come down from Amarillo and meet Rainer. It was great that Bill and his wife Connie were able to make it; unfortunately, Barbara couldn't get off work.

When we picked him up at DFW Airport, it was a real joy to see him again. We asked what he would like to see while he was in Dallas, and he immediately told us he wanted to go to Dealey Plaza and see the Sixth Floor Museum. We had never been there, so that was a good choice. We could all see where that sad day in our nation's history took place. It brought back all those memories of the day I've already shared with you when President Kennedy was assassinated.

From there it was off for a good Tex-Mex meal and then on to Billy Bob's in Fort Worth, so Rainer could get his picture taken on the mechanical bull with a cowboy hat on and his left hand up high in the air. We all had a great time with the visit, and Bill was really glad that he and Connie were able to come and meet Rainer and spend some time with him.

We were all wishing he could stay longer, but at least we got to see each other again. In some of our conversation pertaining to my accident over the two days, Rainer indicated that he really was amazed that I was alive, much less doing as well as I was. This was another confirmation to me of God's hand in my life being sustained.

III

August 2002 arrived, and it was time to depart for the Middle East. I was going to have to fly to Chicago and meet up with the rest of the team. It would just be four of us: Tom, Peter Pintus, and Allen Redall (who is now deceased), from Colorado Springs, where Tom was living at the time, and me. This might seem a bit odd, but I was still a bit behind the power curve at this point. After all my years of going through Chicago O'Hare Airport hundreds of times, I was nervous about not finding my way there. I was relieved when I got to the gate and not long after spotted Tom walking up.

I was also quite surprised at having more security to go through at the gate to get on the flight to Tel Aviv, but it certainly made sense. I was so excited on the flight that I couldn't even get to sleep. I finally dozed off for a very short cat nap shortly before we landed.

We got off the aircraft, went through customs, and met up with our driver, Munir. He was there to load our stuff in the mini-van and transport us everywhere we had planned to go in Israel. When that was accomplished, the four of us piled in and took off.

First stop was Jerusalem. We would be staying at the Christ Church Guest House for part of our stay in Israel. Every day we did sightseeing along with the ministry. Tom had actually gone through all of the training and testing to be a licensed tour guide in Israel, which was way cool.

While we stayed in Jerusalem, we walked through all of the Old City of Jerusalem divided into the Jewish Quarter, Christian Quarter, Muslim Quarter, and Armenian Quarter.

We met a gentleman who ran a shop in the Christian Quarter and was related to the man who had acquired the Dead Sea Scrolls from the Bedouin shepherd boy who originally found them. Everywhere we went, I was absolutely astounded at what I was seeing and the people I was meeting.

One of the evenings in Jerusalem, we met up with David Dolan, a news reporter based in Jerusalem covering events of interest in Israel. I was familiar with him; don't forget, I'm the newshound. I had read a number of his articles and heard him when he reported for CBS Radio and a number of Christian media outlets. He had authored three books pertaining to Israel and the biblical significance of the times we live in. I couldn't wait to read them.

When we had walked through all of the quarters in the Old City, it seemed practically desolate, and the shopkeepers would just swarm the four of us. Tom had advised us ahead of time to stick with him. As we went into Bethlehem it seemed almost desolate as well. Something finally started to sink in. We were there in the middle of the Second Palestinian Intifada, and Israel's tourism had been decimated by the bus bombings and everything else.

Munir had seemed almost apologetic at loading us in the mini-van that first day, and I didn't quite understand it. He had been accustomed to loading up Sar-El Tours' customers in nice big tour buses. I didn't have a clue as to how much it had changed in such a short time.

After we went through the Church of the Nativity there in Bethlehem, a Christian businessman took us out to show us an area where they thought that Jesus had actually been born. It was interesting and made much more sense than that he was born in the middle of town where Constantine's mother Helena had the previously- mentioned church commissioned as His place of birth.

To wrap up our stay in Jerusalem we went to the Garden Tomb area to see where many actually think our Lord was buried, along with seeing the Garden of Gethsemane and the Mount of Olives. It was such an emotional experience. To know that was where our Lord had gone and prayed and sweated blood in knowing what awaited Him on the cross, to see where He was most likely buried, and to see where He proclaimed that He will return at His second coming was very stirring. That night, with our walk from Christ Church to the Wailing Wall, our stay in Jerusalem had come to its conclusion and would be forever ingrained on my heart.

IV

The next day we journeyed up to Nazareth, and once again we met people who appeared absolutely elated to see us. It was unbelievable to feel like we were almost the only people there, and we basically were except for some Israeli citizens just there on a weekend get-away.

While we were in Nazareth, we went to see a recreation of what it was like back when our Lord grew up in this town. That was quite the treat to have people dressed in the clothing of that day and doing the type of work that was prevalent then. We also saw the cliff that was most likely where the residents of Nazareth tried to cast Jesus to His death. It's indescribable to see the Bible come to life as you drive from one place to the next.

From Nazareth it was on to Gaza City. At that time the population of the Gaza Strip was around 1,500,000, and the estimate of the number of Christians there was just under 3,000, with the remainder being Muslim. It was fairly tedious getting into Gaza. We had to clear Israeli security to get in, and we had to present our passports and answer a lot of questions.

Once we were allowed in, it was a long walk to reach the people from the church who were picking us up. They were so glad to have us there to join them. The first place we went to was to The Teacher's Bookshop, a Christian bookstore established by the Palestinian Bible Society. There we met Rami Ayyad, who managed it and carried out a wonderful Christian outreach there.

All four of us had each brought a large suitcase full of the Evangecubes that I previously mentioned. We gave a number of them to our hosts there, and Tom did a training session to explain how to use it in presenting the gospel message.

This was the first place that Tom had me share my testimony. I had never enjoyed public speaking, but somehow, I had some comfort in doing it even though I was a bit worried that I was going to forget what I planned to share with them.

When that day ended, we were taken to an apartment of some of the church members. It was where a couple lived who actually had passports and could come and go. They had gone to Egypt to visit family and let us stay in their home while we were there. It was a long day, and I basically fell in the bed and went right to sleep.

The next morning, I woke up and thought I heard conversation in the kitchen area. I got dressed and joined them. I sat down, and they asked me how I had slept. I told them that I had slept fairly well. They all had a bit of a grin on their faces, and Tom said, "You sure did."

I asked them, "Did you not sleep well?"

Their response indicated that was not the case, and when I asked why not, I got one more question: "You didn't hear anything last night?"

I told them I hadn't heard anything.

At that point they informed me that an Israeli helicopter had fired a missile into a building just down the road from our location in the middle of the night. They had already gotten the scoop on some of the details. It was a bunch of radical Hamas members who were taken out by that missile. Whew, I was kind of glad that I did sleep through that.

The next thing was to attend the service at the Baptist Church where I was to share my testimony again. The regular pastor was not there that Sunday, so I met their associate pastor prior to the service. Now, as I look back on it, they were very patient with me. It was fairly long just saying it in English, especially with the fact that I'm not a fast talker, but having to speak a sentence or two and then have it translated into Arabic more than doubled the time.

I had another issue that my guys at the back of the church got a big laugh out of. Somewhere in the mix of things I tossed in some of the Texan verbiage and said, "I was fixin' to." I can't remember now what the remainder of that sentence was. What I do remember was the translator's eyes getting really big and his looking at me funny as he tried to figure out how to translate what I had just said. When I finally realized the problem, I'll bet my face turned ten shades of red in my embarrassment. It's funny now, but I'm sure you can feel my pain at the time.

I have to say, though, it was more a blessing to me getting to meet my Christian brothers and sisters there than anything I had to offer them. To see them walk the walk and live their lives devoted to Jesus Christ and share His love with those who would receive it humbled me beyond measure. It really pained me to depart the next day, but I was sure I would return and be blessed with more time with them.

It was way more tedious coming out than going in. Our bags were searched extensively, and more questions were asked. It's perfectly understandable, though, with the hatred of the Jewish people that dwells in that area. Munir picked us up and transported us to the border to cross into Jordan. It was great getting to know him, and I felt like I had made a new friend.

V

When we went through the Jordanian entry, they opened our bags and saw all of the Evangecubes and started questioning us. They took Tom off to question him individually. Tom has a great sense of humor, and soon we heard the guy questioning him break out laughing, Tom came out of the office, and the four of us were in Jordan. What a relief that was.

I wish I could say that about the cab ride from the border to Amman. I thought that guy was going to send us over the edge of a cliff numerous times with his crazy driving.

What a joy it was to get there and meet Pastor Jamal at the West Amman Baptist Church and the brothers and sisters who worked with him in that ministry. He and his staff are truly great servants to their community. I shared my testimony once again in that church, and we passed out Evangecubes. Tom did the training again. We were driven to another town a couple hours from Amman. There we were taken to a church that was filled with refugees from Iraq, where once again the cubes and training were given to the people. It was late when we got back to Amman. It was going to be a short night.

VI

Rise and shine. We got up and took off to the Jordan Evangelical Theological Seminary. It was a real treat getting a tour of the school and getting to visit with one of the professors. He filled us in on the ministry, how it began equipping believers to minister to people in over twenty Arab speaking countries. That is truly a wonderful ministry that God is using immensely with Dr. Imad Shehadeh's vision and commitment to ministry.

When we left there, it was back to West Amman Baptist, where I shared my testimony once again. We were there several hours with Tom doing some training again. Pete and Allen were very active—just as they had been every day. I was truly impressed with the love and service that Jamal and his staff were committed to there in Amman. They were true disciples of Jesus and are carrying out the great commission in a great way.

Now we were off to the Amman airport to catch a flight to Abu Dhabi, UAE. That was quite the flight. Well over half of the three and a half hours of that flight, I had a boy in the row behind me kicking the back of my seat while his parents did absolutely nothing about it. That was trying my patience, and I was so glad to finally arrive.

When I stepped off the plane to walk across the tarmac to the terminal; however, I was about ready to go back and resume the kick-my-seat status. For Heaven's sake, it was midnight, the temperature was over 100°, and the humidity was just shy of 100 percent. By the time I got into the terminal, my clothing felt like I had been dunked in a tank or something.

When we made it to customs and they started to go through our bags, the inspector pulled out one of the Evangecubes, took it out of the box, and proceeded to examine it. The four of us were standing there expecting to be taken aside and put on the next flight out. They asked Tom why we had them, and he said that they were gifts to the people at the church that we would be visiting, which they were. The customs agent put it back in the bag and let us proceed. I'm sure you can imagine how thankful we were at that.

We were met by one of the members of the Filipino Church that took us to stay with them at their apartment. It was a short night but a real joy getting to meet more of them. The next day was truly a blessing getting to hear about their faith and their lives as they worked in the UAE.

We went to their church service where we met more of them and gave them our gifts. Once again Tom showed them how to use them in sharing the good news about our Lord. The Evangecube is a seven-picture cube that opens to show pictures that can be used to give the major points in a Gospel presentation.

Right after the Filipino service we stayed for another conducted by an Indian Church. The Christians there had to share one building where each group was allowed to have their service. It was really enlightening to witness the different forms of worship and the way the sermons were delivered to the congregations. We just had that one day of working with those two groups.

The next day had just a small amount of sightseeing. We drove a car up to Dubai and saw the world's only seven-star hotel, the Burj Al Arab. It was an amazing design that looked like a gigantic sailing ship. We wanted to step in and take a look but learned we couldn't even walk in the door with the clothing we were wearing.

That was a quick day. We went back to Abu Dhabi and then to the airport for the flight home. I was very glad to get some sleep on the flight this time. I couldn't wait to share about the trip when I got home. I had renewed my involvement with the men's study group that I had attended prior to my accident and told them about the trip.

I really couldn't find the words to convey our need to lift our brothers and sisters that I had met in prayer and how they had inspired me in my walk. I truly wished that my friends in the group could meet them and be blessed as I had.

I also enjoyed sharing the trip with my friends in the flight office at DFW and up in the ramp tower. The time that had been required of me to go to the airport and work was about up. There was no other job awaiting me. When I had some conversation pertaining to that possibility with Arlene, she informed me that she had already been told the only jobs that might be available would pay less than my disability pay, and if I went back to work for American in one of those positions, my disability pay would be gone.

It was clear that my career had come to an end. Those days of being in the climb in the 727, breaking out of the clouds at 500 miles per hour, flying between some towering cumulus clouds on both sides of us and the beauty of it all were gone. But it was apparent that God had something else in store. For that I was filled with joy, couldn't wait, and was truly grateful. I was ready for the next chapter. The Lord in His mercy had prepared my heart and my mind for it.

THIS NEW HOUSE—NO! NOT RICK!

I

Back when Tom and Curtis came to our home for that previously mentioned visit—actually, a little before that—Arlene had set out to find some land to purchase and build a new house. She told me that her financial planner friend had advised her to put more of our assets in our home, so that was her focus.

She had taken me with her as she searched for the land, and I was fine with that, but I was not that keen on the amount of land and the size of the house. To me it was too much, but Arlene insisted that the financial planner said it would be a good thing.

Since I wasn't going to be doing the yard work, it was going to be a fairly big expense hiring it done, which I wasn't too keen on either. Unfortunately, my days of doing the yard work were over.

In fact, just prior to this, I had developed a skin problem on my scalp. When I went to the dermatologist, he did a full exam and said there were a couple of moles on my back that he needed to biopsy.

He did that, and a few days later the office called and informed me that the biopsy had come back positive for melanoma. They informed me that the doctor wanted me to come in and have that surgically removed as soon as possible.

I went back, and he did it in his office. He had told me on my first visit to be sure to use sunscreen and avoid the sun as much as possible. This time he told me to definitely stay out of the sun and to use sunscreen, even if I were just going to be in the car driving.

What a blessing it was to discover that when I did. That doctor retired, and the lady who took over his practice, Dr. Adams, discovered more of them over the next few years adding up to a total of six. If I hadn't caught those when I did, it could very easily have ended my life. Once again, I'm so thankful for our Lord's mercy, grace, and divine intervention.

II

As Arlene stayed focused on her new house project, in just a little over three months I joined Tom again for another trip. This time our group had increased from four on the first one to around twelve, and the trip was to Israel, Gaza, Jordan, and Egypt. I would once again share my story of God's grace, mercy, and miracles in my life in a number of places. The first two days were a bit of site seeing in Jerusalem again, but from there it was on to Gaza.

This time I met the actual pastor of the church there, Hanna Massad, with whom I have a strong friendship and fellowship to this day. What a blessing it was getting to know him. On this trip we stayed with another Christian brother who was living in Gaza but had also lived in the United States.

On one of the nights we were in his apartment and having a great conversation with him, since he spoke good English. Someone knocked on his door. When he answered, there stood a young man who was very well dressed. You could tell by his attire that he was not a typical resident of Gaza.

They stood there and talked in Arabic for a good time. At the end of their conversation our host introduced us; we shook hands and the young man departed. Our host sat us down and proceeded to tell us what that was all about.

This young man had come to faith in Jesus Christ about a year before. In Islam, it is way more than a no-no to leave that faith and become a Christian. This young man's father was quite well off financially, and his son was coming up in his father's business.

When the father initially learned that his son had come to faith in Jesus, he basically just denied it and tried to ignore it. That night, when the young man came to our host's door, however, his father had set out to have him killed for putting his faith in Jesus. The young man was seeking a place to hide basically and asking for some advice from our host.

When our host finished sharing this, it was heart wrenching, and we all got down and prayed for this young man and his family. I wish I could share the outcome of this, but unfortunately, I have not heard any news.

While in Israel we also stopped in the two Circassian villages and shared about our Lord. It was quite interesting to learn about how these people were refugees who settled in Israel in the late 1870s. They had been Christians for over a thousand years but were Islamized by the Ottoman Turks and Crimean

Tatars. We actually went door-to-door and were welcomed, and I shared my testimony in a couple of the homes.

We had split up into two groups. While everyone had been welcoming to our group, the second group had not been quite as well received. The people in one of the homes they visited reported them to the mayor of the town, and we were asked to depart, which we did. We were just thankful that we had been able to share the good news of our forgiveness in Jesus in the homes that did welcome us.

Before leaving Israel, we met up once again with Nizar Touma, pastor of the Nazarene Church in Nazareth. We met with him briefly on my first trip, but this time Nizar got to show us some of his ministry in action with the precious little children they were teaching in their day school there at the church. What a joy that was!

Once again, we made it to Jordan and met with our wonderful brothers and sisters at the West Amman Baptist Church. It gave me great joy to meet up with Jamal and everyone else again. One final place we stopped was the Roman Theatre in Amman. It was built back in the second century when Amman was actually named Philadelphia. It's a 6,000-seat theatre that is still used to this day. We received a special treat in being given a tour by one of the locals there who shared a great deal of its history with us.

I hated to leave, but the next day it was off to Cairo, another place I could have never imagined being while doing what we were doing. When we arrived, we were met by a Cairo police officer. Now that was quite unexpected. Tom said we would be accompanied by this officer everywhere we went. He would be in our minibus with us, and there would be a police car following behind us with its lights flashing.

We were told that this was for our safety as US tourists. Gee, I was not sure that the flashing light on the police car behind us everywhere we went didn't make us a target. And it was a shock to learn that being US citizens would require that. The officer was friendly, and it was a pleasure getting to talk to him some on our travels in Egypt.

Getting to go to the Coptic Christian Church in Cairo was fantastic. I wished that I could understand the language. Even so, I could sense the strong devotion and faith in Jesus Christ that they radiated. Another absolutely incredible experience there was going to Cave Church. As stunning as this place is, the story behind it is even more so.

Back in 1974, Farahat Ibrahim was being called to minister to the Coptic

Christians who lived and worked in Garbage City on the outskirts of Cairo. I'm sure you're questioning this name. Yes, this is the garbage dump for Cairo.

Mr. Ibrahim created a church in a cave that now seats 20,000. It's the largest Christian Church in the Middle East. It was incredible to see all of the carvings in the rock at the entrance and inside the cave. One that is still etched in my mind is at the entrance and is a quote from the Bible, "If they keep quiet the stones will cry out."

While we were there, it was amazing going to the Egyptian Museum in Cairo and getting to see the Sphinx and some of the pyramids. Another treat was taking a little dinner boat ride down the Nile River. There we got to see a dance that originated in Egypt, the belly dance. My rib cage got sore just watching that.

The next exhibition was a whirling dervish. Now, I hate to expose my ignorance, but I had heard that term as a child. I thought it was just a funny term for a child who couldn't sit still or something. To learn that it's a Muslim mystic dance was quite the deal, and to watch this guy spin around in circles for minutes made me feel dizzy just watching it.

Once again, it was a wonderful trip, and I felt that it blessed me far more than I could have blessed anyone with my testimony. The ministers whom I met and my brothers and sisters in the Christian faith were such a pleasure to meet and get to know.

III

The day after I got home, I made a drive over to the new house that was in the construction phase to see how it was going. Arlene was the general contractor and had just hired a retired contractor on retainer. She paid a set fee for him to assist her and help get some good subcontractors whom he had used.

It was about mid-morning. When I got back to our house and walked in the door, the phone was ringing. I answered, and it was Ellie, my dear friend Michael's wife. She asked me if I had heard. She sounded very emotional, and I asked her, "Heard what?"

She said, "About Rick."

"Rick who?"

"Rick Husband."

"What about him?"

Her voice started to tremble a bit, and she went on to explain that Rick was on a shuttle mission, and that just minutes ago, it exploded on re-entry just south of Dallas. *Oh, my God*, I thought to myself, as I tilted my head back and gazed upward. It felt like my heart was in my throat. I said I had just returned from a trip to Israel the day before, and I didn't even know he was up there on a mission. She told me that she just wanted to let me know, and we told each other goodbye.

I just went into the living room, basically dropped into my chair, and turned on the TV. As I sat there and watched the news reporting this tragic event, I felt devastated, and just like a few other times in the past, shed some tears. I couldn't believe this. I just kept telling myself, "No this can't be."

After some time, Arlene arrived back at the house and walked in the living room. When she could see the streaks down my face, she asked, "What's going on?"

I told her what had happened. She sat down and watched the news for a bit but had other things to do with to the new house and went about her business.

I just sat there all day as the news continued and asked the Lord over and over, "Why did you save me all those times and let this happen to Rick?"

As the day progressed, however, his strong faith in Jesus Christ became apparent in the news. I could see that his faith was going to be made even more apparent as time went on and that God would be glorified even more by Rick's faith in the Son of God, Jesus Christ. That gave me a true peace in all of it.

I went to Rick's memorial service in Amarillo and only recognized a couple of people there, but it was a big crowd, and there was no way I was able to see everyone who attended. It was wonderful hearing Steve Green singing "God of Wonders." When Rick's wife Evelyn co-wrote and had his biography, *High Calling* published, I couldn't wait to read it. Yes, God was truly glorified in Rick's life and death.

IV

About a month after we moved to the new house in April 2004, it was off to Israel again for me, and what a wonderful trip that was. The first blessing was in Tel Aviv getting to meet Avi Mizrachi, a Messianic Jew who, with his wife, Chaya, led the Adonai Roi Congregation and ministered to the Jewish people there.

Avi was also the executive director of the Dugit Messianic Outreach Centre. For those who don't know, Messianic Jews believe the New Testament in that Jesus (or Yeshua, the Hebrew spelling of the name) is truly the Son of God and all of the other doctrinal elements of the New Testament. They are born again believers in our Lord.

I got to share my testimony with their congregation, and our group was able to partake in the Passover Seder there at their church. It was absolutely wonderful getting to be a part of that. It was also wonderful hearing how Avi came to faith in Jesus after he got out of the Israeli Air Force and came to the United States. He wound up getting trained in Dallas, Texas at the Christ for the Nations Institute.

While we were there a number of us walked the streets in Tel Aviv, sharing our stories and using the Evangecube to present the good news once again. Avi had briefed us well on what to expect. As usual, some of the recipients were cordial, and a few were far from cordial. Avi and Chaya have a wonderful ministry, and if you care to learn more about it, you can check it out at Dugit.org.

On this trip we also made our way to Bethlehem, which was a bit of a challenge. It was April 2004, and the Intifada was still in gear. At first it looked like the Israeli security was not going to let us into Bethlehem for our safety. Things were tense. We did make it in, though, and we were so glad we did.

Once we got through security, we continued on to Beit Jala, a little town adjacent to Bethlehem. In Beit Jala is a Christian ministry named Beit Al Liqa', founded by Johnny and Marlene Shahwan. It's an absolute testimony to their faithfulness and desire to show everyone the love of God, to bring hope to the hopeless, and to, as they say, "provide an oasis of peace to meet the living God."

They started their ministry in 1996, and in 2000 purchased some land. Four years later in the midst of a war-torn city stood this four-story outreach sitting on a hill. They provide daycare to the children of this area, have a guest house for visitors to stay in, and provide summer camps and monthly events. Their love is so overflowing that the Muslim parents in town bring their children to day care there.

Their love for the people in town is truly amazing. While Bethlehem and Beit Jala at one time had a majority of Christian residents, at this time 80 percent of the Christians had left because of persecution and lack of jobs. I was truly blessed to have Johnny come to our home and visit and share about this ministry a little more than a year after I met them in Beit Jala.

V

We ended with a journey south to Gaza. I can't put into words what a blessing it is knowing Pastor Hanna, his immediate family, and his church family there. I wish everyone could know him and his love for our Lord and everyone he comes in contact with. They live their lives day-to-day giving Jesus the glory and sharing His love. There were a number of different ministries going on that trip: women's, men's, and grade schools'. We all hated to leave; it was so centered on our Lord.

It was way more difficult getting in this time, and getting out was incredible. The previous two times weren't easy, but this time we had a much longer walk to get to the building that we had to go through. I don't remember the exact number on this trip; it was around fifteen or sixteen. When we got to the building, it was one at a time. It took us over two hours to get everyone through, and it was just us.

When our turn came, we had to walk in and lay our suitcases on a long table. There was no one in sight. Then unexpectedly a bunch of high-powered spotlights came on so brightly we really couldn't see anything. Someone would speak to us over a loudspeaker, and we had to answer their questions while our luggage was out of sight, being gone through, and completely examined.

When that was complete, we were ordered to step into this thing, put our feet where the footprints were, and hold our hands above our heads. Oh, and we had to remove everything from our pockets. This sounds familiar today. It's the x-ray machine that we're all aware of today in the airports, but this was before those existed in our airports. That was unnerving then. We concluded that trip, and it was back across the Atlantic to get home.

A HEART TO HELP
AND A BROTHER MARTYRED

I

About six months later our first grandchild arrived. In February she came on the scene in the same hospital that my daughter had, and what a joy that was. My stepdaughter and son-in-law had been hoping for this blessing for quite a while. We were all waiting in anticipation. It's hard to say, but I think our son-in-law was the most excited of all. I could tell he was elated.

II

A short time after our granddaughter's wonderful arrival, I set out on a mission to help people get where they needed to go for medical assistance. With all that our Lord had blessed me with in that arena, I really had a heart to help others. I was aware of an organization called Angel Flight that coordinated transportation for patients who had no ability to get to hospitals where they needed to go.

I learned that a fellow American Airlines pilot had started a similar organization, and after talking with him, I started doing some research. Since I couldn't fly an aircraft on my own anymore because of not having the required medical certificate because of the brain injury, I had to find out if I could get insurance and actually fly the aircraft myself with another pilot on board who would actually be the pilot in command.

I learned that I could do that, but there would be some pretty major restrictions. Each pilot had to be checked out in the airplane and signed off by a flight instructor. They had to be named on the policy, and I could only have four pilots listed.

There was one other option. I could have anyone who was a certified flight instructor and qualified in the plane who was not listed on the policy fly with me. I quickly came up with four friends and a couple of CFIs who were willing. I thought that would work, so I went on a search for an aircraft.

I really wasn't all that keen on a single-engine aircraft after the engine failure caused my landing on Highway 98 in Semmes, Alabama. And I definitely didn't want a potential repeat of something like that with a patient going to get medical treatment on board. With that in mind, I was looking for an older twin-engine aircraft that was halfway affordable for me.

After a fair amount of searching, I found a 1972 Cessna 310Q with a RAM Conversion. It was owned by a retired neurosurgeon in El Paso, Texas. I went and looked at it and was pretty impressed with the avionics and all the other options that it had.

The RAM Conversion gave it 300 hp turbocharged engines; it had a Garmin 530 GPS, two forms of weather detection: a Stormscope lightning detector and Nexrad radar capabilities with the Garmin. Along with a number of other items, it had de-ice and anti-ice equipment.

I had a pre-purchase inspection done by an airframe and power plant mechanic there in El Paso. I definitely wanted them to take a very close look at the de-ice boots, and I'm sure you recall why I was very motivated to do that. Everything looked good, and I purchased it. The doctor flew it to Denton, Texas for me and caught a Southwest Airlines flight back to El Paso.

The American Airlines pilot, whom I mentioned, offered to let me keep it in his hangar at no charge since I was donating the use of it through his ministry-organization. That was truly a blessing to me. At least that would be one fixed expense that I wouldn't have. I immediately set out to get the friends checked out in the plane that would be on my insurance.

One of them was a guy you know well by now, Captain Phil Atkinson. There's another you also know quite well, the gentleman who had blessed me and made a terrible wrong right and then, once again, did what he could to come to the rescue after he had retired, former V. P. Of Flight, Captain Cecil Ewell. The other two pilots on the insurance were a former neighbor and friend, Captain Mark Middleton of Southwest Airlines and a long-time friend from the men's Bible study, Captain Dave Nelson.

It truly blessed me getting to help people in this way. One of the first trips was up to Salina, Kansas to take a patient down to Houston to the MD Anderson Cancer Hospital. There was another trip that I was unable to go on because of another commitment. It was taking supplies to a town in Mississippi after Hurricane Katrina.

Cecil and Doug Dunbar of KVTT News, who's also a licensed pilot, flew that trip along with a couple of other pilots and aircraft that were involved in the organization. What a thrill that was to see Cecil and Doug flying in formation in my plane on KVTT News at the conclusion of that trip.

During the time I had the 310, I only did two personal trips in it, but they were real treats. The first one was when Rainer Straub came for a visit again. Phil and I took him up to Amarillo to see where I grew up and to Umbarger to see where our mutual relative, my grandfather, John Straub, had settled in the Texas Panhandle after he and one brother emigrated from Germany.

From there we drove Rainer to the Palo Duro Canyon to let him see the beauty there. After all that it was back to Amarillo to meet up with Bill and have a good meal and fellowship. This time Bill's sister Barbara Ann was able to meet Rainer, and it was truly a great time. While it truly was a joy to be at the controls again, I hated to have to jump back in the Cessna and fly back so quickly.

The next day we had a great party with many friends and relatives who came to meet Rainer. Everyone truly enjoyed meeting him, and he had a great time as well. I think the highlight of the evening was when he yodeled for us. That was over the top, and everyone loved it. My cousin Myma Sue, who is since deceased, mentioned that many times and said how much she enjoyed getting to meet him.

The next day we got in my Dodge Ram and headed off to San Antonio. Rainer was participating in another big medical research conference there. We had some great conversation along the way, and when I dropped him off at his hotel, the time together had been way too short. I was really wishing that there weren't so many miles (or kilometers) between us. We exchanged hugs, and I told him *auf wiedersehen*.

The other personal trip was when Phil, Dave Nelson, and Michael Mabrey went to Oshkosh, Wisconsin with me for the annual air show of all air shows. It's put on by the Experimental Aircraft Association, and what an experience it was!

It's amazing how the show comes off. According to the EAA website, the July 2918's show's eleven days saw approximately 601,000 attendees with 19,588 aircraft operations, which computes to 134 takeoffs/landings per hour. That's amazing.

When we were there, it was day after day of fantastic demonstrations of airmanship. We got to see the top aerobatic performers and teams in the world along with everything imaginable that's aviation related. We actually got a sneak peek, world debut, of the upcoming Honda Business Jet.

The time I had the Cessna was a great experience, and it was absolutely wonderful getting to help people. But after about a year, about four months passed where hardly any trips came up, and for the few that did, none of the pilots on my insurance was available to go. I sat down and started running the numbers and came to the conclusion that it was costing way more than it was accomplishing. I decided that I should probably sell the plane and find a more productive way to use that money in ministry.

The last trip I did in the Cessna 310 was with Cecil. Of all places, we went up to my hometown, Amarillo, and picked up a young girl to take to Houston. She was being treated for melanoma. Hers hadn't been caught as soon as those that I experienced, so it was far more critical for her. I pray that was a total success for her.

III

I'm going to backtrack a little. Not long after my very first trip to Israel in August of 2002, I was feeling burdened by something President George W. Bush was quite active in. When I had returned from my second trip to Israel a few months later, I felt I needed to express my concern.

I sat down and handwrote a cordial letter to President Bush expressing my scripture-based concern over his and our nation's involvement in pressuring Israel to hand over land in their nation that would then be controlled by another group of people who had vowed to annihilate the Jewish State from the face of the earth.

I also shared a bit of my recent experience of God's miraculous healing and that the Holy Spirit had burdened me to express my concern over this. Sad to say, I never received even the standard form letter reply on this subject from President Bush's office.

Israel bowed to that pressure, evicted their citizens from Gaza, and handed over the land that God had deeded to the Jewish people to be controlled by their sworn enemies. I knew it was a huge mistake for them and for Americans because of our President's being at the helm of that error. In all of that, I'm still quite surprised that I didn't catch something that appears to be an immediate fulfillment of my concern.

It was almost two years later when I met William Koenig at a Messianic Jewish Synagogue in Dallas. He was there speaking on issues pertaining to our nation's dealings with Israel, and he had just published a book, *Eye to Eye*.

I was completely stunned at something I learned. As Israel proceeded to hand over Gaza and evict their citizens from that land, under pressure from our president and others, Tropical Depression Ten began to form off the west coast of Africa.

A little over two weeks later, that tropical depression had morphed into Hurricane Katrina and hit our nation with devastating ferocity. Mr. Koenig proceeded to inform us that the percentage of our US citizens who were made homeless by the "act of God," as the insurance companies called it, was equivalent to the percentage of Israeli citizens made homeless under the pressure of President Bush.

It appears that he should have heeded the concern that many of us presented him with. I'm sure that many would not agree with Mr. Koenig's and my view on this, and there have been many debates on this subject, I'm sure. All I can say is that my view on this is something that comes from my decades of study of scriptures and God's covenants with the Jewish people. With all of the miracles that our Lord has poured out to sustain me, it's my conviction that the Holy Spirit has put this on my heart.

IV

Getting back to where I left off, I remember that not long after getting out of the ministry I had done with my aircraft ownership, I made another ministry-related trip to Jordan. I hadn't been on one of these for right at two years. If you recall, I shared about how the ministry that Curtis was in originally had divided into different groups and that he had taken charge of the Evangecube group. At this time, they had basically gone back together, and it was named E3 Partners. E3 stands for "Equipping God's people to Evangelize His world by Establishing healthy, multiplying, transformative churches everywhere."

Tom and Curtis were both on this trip along with another gentleman, Jason Elam, former kicker for the Denver Broncos, the winner of two Super Bowl rings, and tied for a number of years with having kicked the longest field goal in NFL history.

He wanted to devote a good deal of his life to ministry once he was retired from professional football, and it was truly a joy getting to know him and seeing his strong faith in Jesus Christ along with his desire to fulfill the great commission that our Lord commands of us.

On this trip they were training pastors and lay people from all over the Middle East, and I would be sharing God's work in my life once again. I guess I was questioning my part in all of it, probably because I felt that what I had been doing the last two years hadn't really accomplished that much and had cost a lot of money. As always, though, you never know what God is doing in the background that you are completely unaware of.

As I stood there listening to someone speak, I was running those questions through my mind wondering if I were accomplishing anything by being there. Then all of a sudden, one of the gentlemen from Iraq in the group walked up, gave me a bear hug, and introduced himself. He then asked if I remembered him.

I was embarrassed to tell him that I didn't. That was no problem for him.

As he put his hand on my shoulder, he said, "Well, I remember you!" He went on to tell me that when I had been in Jordan three years prior, my testimony was what convinced him that he needed to go to seminary and commit his life to full-time ministry as a pastor. What a blessing it was to hear that.

I said, "You never know." You just have to be available.

Along with the ministry training we did, we had a great opportunity to go to Jerash, the ruins of one of the former cities of the Decapolis and see a reenactment of some Roman Legions marching to war along with the chariots and everything one can imagine.

We also made it to Petra. What a thrill it was to walk through that narrow passageway with canyon walls on both sides and then have the old treasury that you see in all pictures of Petra come into view. The only thing I didn't appreciate from our visit at Petra was the camel ride. Whoa, I'll never do that again. The uncomfortable seat, the smell, and that beast continuing to turn its head back and slobber on me was way bad. What a great trip it was, though.

A few months after that trip, it was off to Istanbul, Turkey. And a few months after that, it was back to Israel and Gaza. In Gaza I was blessed with meeting Andrew van der Bijl, otherwise known as Brother Andrew, aka, "God's smuggler."

It was truly a joy to meet him and learn of his work for God in smuggling Bibles into places all over the world where Bibles are forbidden. I was truly blessed to meet this brother and learn of his strong faith and his missionary zeal.

V

Shortly after I returned from that trip to Gaza, Tom called me and said that someone from Trans World Radio had heard about my testimony that I had shared again in Gaza and wanted to interview me. He said they were a Christian Radio Network that broadcasted all over the Middle East and asked if he could share my phone number with them. I said I was more than happy to do that.

The next day I got the call. They asked me to just share with them over the phone what I had shared in Gaza. They said it would be translated into Arabic and broadcast over their entire network. I was truly humbled by that and glad to give God the glory in any way possible.

That year, 2006, turned out to be very busy, and I met quite a number of wonderful brothers and sisters in Christ. As always, they ministered to and encouraged me immensely. That concluded a great year.

Sometime in November of the next year, 2007, I received news that absolutely devastated me. Tom Doyle told me that our Christian Brother, Rami Ayyad, whom we met on my first trip to Gaza, had been kidnapped and murdered by Muslim extremists. He had been running The Teacher's Book Shop, the only Christian bookstore in the Gaza Strip.

I could barely restrain the tears and talk with Tom as he shared this. The fact that Rami and his wife were expecting their third child when this took place made it even harder to bear. I later learned that the bookstore had been hit with pipe bombs the previous year to intimidate Rami to close the store. He stood strong in his faith, however, and continued to show Christ's love to the people who came there after he restored the place to operation. What a blessing it was to have met and known this dear Christian brother.

What a great sadness it was to also learn that Pastor Hanna and his family had been threatened as well in the midst of this, and he had to get his family out of Gaza to protect them. I praise God and give him thanks that they were able to move to another location in Jordan and continue their outreach and ministry to those in need of God's love and compassion.

In 2008 it was another wonderful trip to Israel, but what I just shared was burning in my heart. And I was thinking of the potential stress my brothers and sisters were feeling there in Gaza.

A piece of writing comes to mind by a young man in Africa who was forced to either renounce Christ or face death. He refused to renounce Christ and was killed. Here's what he wrote, which people found after his murder.

> I am part of the "Fellowship of the Unashamed." The die has been cast. I have stepped over the line. The decision has been made. I am a disciple of Jesus Christ. I won't look back, let up, slow down, back away, or be still. My past is redeemed, my present makes sense, my future secure. I am finished and done with low living, sight walking, smooth knees, colorless dreams, tamed vision, worldly talking, cheap giving, and dwarfed goals. I no longer need pre-eminence, prosperity, position, promotions, plaudits, or popularity. My face is set, my gait is fast, my goal is Heaven, my road is narrow, my way is rough, my companions few, my Guide reliable, my mission clear. I cannon be bought, compromised, deterred, lured away, turned back, diluted, or delayed. I will not flinch in the face of sacrifice, hesitate in the presence of adversity, negotiate at the table of the enemy, ponder at the pool of popularity, or meander in the maze of mediocrity. I am a disciple of Christ Jesus. I must go 'til He comes, give until I drop, and preach until all know. And when my time is up, He will have no problem recognizing me. My colors will be clear. How about you? Will you live the surrendered life of a faithful steward and join the fellowship of the unashamed? Will you go 'til He comes and preach until all know? Will you live this week in such a way that your colors will be clear?

Tom Doyle was leading us once again. Curtis and his dear wife, Amy, Del Tackett of Focus on the Family and the Truth Project, plus Jason Elam and four more Denver Broncos joined in. There were also a number of folks from E3 and others whom I didn't know as well. I just watched those in our group who hadn't been there before feeling the awe of walking where Jesus walked, healed, taught, was crucified, and rose again. There's really no way to describe it.

As we spent the last night there in Jerusalem, I was just thinking about what a wonder and joy it will be when Jesus Christ returns, establishes His Millennial Kingdom, and rules from that great city.

BOEING TO BOX TRUCK
AND A TEN-YEAR CELEBRATION

I

Moving into 2009, my new church got me involved very quickly in a ministry that I truly enjoyed. One of our members, Mikie Doyle, was very active in a food ministry, and she was contacted by Feed the Hungry to see if our church would consider something.

It turned out that a major charitable organization in the DFW area had quit taking donations of fresh vegetables from a local produce wholesaler, who was looking for someone to pick that up. It was going to require us to rent a box truck weekly that was at least twenty feet long and would need to be refrigerated in the summer for sure. We would just go and get the truck completely loaded with fresh produce and give it away to needy people.

They knew I had some time available on Tuesdays and asked if I would consider going early on Tuesday mornings to rent a Penske Truck, drive to the wholesaler, get the truck loaded, and then bring it to the church parking lot. It would sit there until the afternoon when other church members could help unload it, and we would give the food away to anyone who came to be blessed by it.

It was truly incredible. We put the word out the best we could to let people know that we were going to have a lot of produce to give away. The first time we did this they loaded fourteen pallets of boxed produce over six feet high on that truck. As they closed the door to send me on my way, I wondered how in the world we were going to give all of that food away.

Around 4 p.m. Pastor Ray and a good percentage of our members showed up to help unload. A lot of the people who were receiving the food also helped in the unloading process. We created a human chain to pass those huge boxes of produce from the truck to the sidewalk where we lined it all up to be given out. At the end of it all we had hundreds of empty cardboard boxes that had to be broken down and taken to the dumpster, which they completely filled. It's too bad that recycling all that cardboard was not an option.

After around six months of doing it this way I found a used forklift for us and a pallet jack. It was incredible in how it improved things. I could unload that truck in about twenty minutes. We also found a used White Freightliner not long after that to purchase that had a refrigeration unit on it.

That was cool adding some new equipment to my credentials: from captain on the 727 to left seat in the White Freightliner and running the forklift. We did that food ministry, which helped feed over a hundred families, for a little over seven years, and it was very rare that I missed a Tuesday. This was not bad for a church based in a small strip mall facility that had around fifty members.

II

There were no ministry-related trips in 2009, but there was a very special day for me that year. November 22, 2009 was the ten-year anniversary of my nearly life-ending injury at American Airlines. I went to flight ops at DFW and put up a poster inviting fellow pilots and employees to come to my home and join me in celebrating God's mercy, grace, and miracles that He blessed me with over the two-year recovery period. To those families and friends who joined me in that, I say thank you, along with a very special thanks to Ans and Julie Wishing, who came all the way from Nashville.

I've already shared how Ans came running when he saw my head go into the concrete, and I can't tell about him holding me up to prevent my drowning in my own blood there without getting emotional. It was a wonderful celebration, and I thank those who came to join me in that. It was great getting to visit with Ans and Julie late into the evening, and I was very grateful that they spent the night with us. I wished we had had more time to spend with them and everyone else.

III

Less than a month later, it was a flight to Santa Barbara to see my daughter be graduated from Brooks Institute of Photography. I was so happy for her in that accomplishment. That was no cakewalk. I still remember cringing when I heard about one of her photo shoots where she was up close to a black panther that had no restraints on it. Yikes! It was a real joy to see her earn that bachelor's degree, which is something I had never achieved. Our son-in-law, my stepdaughter, and granddaughter came as well. That was very uplifting for her.

With all of them there we couldn't resist making a trek down to Disneyland. That was a great time. The last time we had been there was when my stepdaughter was around ten years old. I'm surprised she and Arlene didn't remind me of an experience I had on that trip. As we were walking along and I was minding my own business, some fine bird pooped on my forehead. They both got a great laugh at that back then—me, not so much. Of course, I find it very humorous now.

IV

It was back to Israel and Gaza in August of 2010, which I was really looking forward to, not having made it to Gaza on that trip to Israel in 2008 after Rami was murdered. Things had gotten extremely difficult getting into Gaza by this time, however. We had to fill out paperwork to send to Israel weeks ahead of time. When we got on the plane to head to Tel Aviv, our group was approved to enter Gaza.

We ran into Brother Andrew in Bethlehem again. That was truly a surprise and a pleasure to get to see him and visit with him this time. I had seen him on that previous trip when we were in Gaza, but there was never an opportunity to meet him or talk with him.

While we were there, he shared about how he and his wife had been detained fairly recently as they were leaving Saudi Arabia. He told us that he and his wife were truly getting concerned. They could tell that the Holy Spirit had intervened, and the authorities' demeanor completely changed, and released them to board the flight out. Praise God.

Once again it was great getting to see Johnny and all of his group at Beit Al Liqa' while we were in and around Bethlehem. What an inspiration they are in how they pour out Christ's love to all the people there. That area around Bethlehem was a Christian majority ten years prior and now is less than 10 percent Christian, so they are truly showing their love.

Once we arrived at the security point to go into Gaza, we were hit with some very disheartening news. They weren't going to let us all in. Now the really strange part of it was that they were going to let three of our group in, and one of the three was me. I was fine with that, but the problem is that the three of us were unable to carry out the ministry-related things that had been planned. Those who had planned all of the events were stuck on the other side patiently waiting for the problem to get resolved

The three of us just went in, and our brothers and sisters who had been waiting for us took us to dinner. We were able to visit with them and pray with them. A bit later in the following day, the remaining twelve of our group began to be allowed in sporadically, but the delay totally messed up a lot of the women's ministry things that were planned along with other events.

It was still great to get to spend time there, however, and see the church and the Christian School that was still honoring and serving our Lord in the wake of the tragedy of losing Rami and Pastor Hanna having to leave. Even though things didn't go as planned, it was truly a heartwarming joy to get to be there and fellowship with these people who love our Lord and live their lives to be His true disciples.

After we departed Gaza at close to noon, I started feeling really bad and before very long was having flu-like symptoms. We made a couple of stops en route to Tel Aviv to get on the flight for home. I was feeling so bad that I didn't even get off the bus at those stops, even with one of them being for lunch.

I had made a big mistake in choosing to make that trip on a standby seat basis. It wouldn't have been such a problem were it not for my illness. I couldn't get a seat on any of the flights that evening and wound up spending the entire night in the terminal. I finally got one around mid-morning.

V

Praise God, a month later I was ready to go again and set off to India. Several months prior to that, Babu, a Christian Brother from India with whom I had gotten acquainted in the food ministry at church, had heard a portion of my testimony. He asked me to share all of it with him, and after I did, he was really moved by it. He immediately told me that I had to come to India and share it.

I was really moved at how emphatic he was that I had to come to India and share it there. After a few weeks of Babu's telling me every time he saw me that

I needed to come to India with him and speak, I decided that I would do it. So, as I said, I was headed to India. It was non-stop from Chicago to New Delhi, and then from there it was all the way to Thiruvananthapuram at the southern tip of India.

When I got off the plane, there were Babu and some of his Christian brothers to meet me. They took me to his property and showed me around. I was amazed at how Babu spends a great deal of his time there doing ministry and the rest back home in Texas ministering as well. He has the building in India set up as a school and his residence while he and his family are there.

At the school they do biblical training for men, and for women they have a sewing class where they train women to earn a living in that as well as biblical study. After showing me around, they took me back to town where I would be staying. It was a very nice room where I was quite comfortable, and there was a restaurant there that served good food. I was really glad that I had become very fond of Indian food. The first time I had tried it was back when I was flying to London as first officer on the 767.

Babu just had me stay at the hotel until close to the evening service time because the rain was pretty intense. The first evening was a celebration of the students' accomplishments. Babu's wife, Gracie, was handing out diplomas to the ladies who were graduating from the sewing school, and they were blessing them with a sewing machine as a gift to help them earn a living with their new knowledge.

After that, Babu asked me to hand out diplomas to the men who were graduating from their class of biblical study. That was absolutely wonderful getting to see the women blessed in that and to see the men who were digging deeply into the knowledge of God's word.

When that part was complete, Babu had me share my testimony, and then he preached along with another pastor who was there for the multi-day event. I couldn't understand the Hindu, but I could see their hearts were on fire with the Gospel, and the majority of the people hearing it were obviously having a revival of their hearts. It was a great three days getting to be there to experience and participate in this graduation and revival.

On the fourth day it was a flight back to New Delhi, and Babu's brother Isaac picked me up at the airport. He took me to a hotel and had everything planned out for me to make a trip the next day to see the Taj Mahal.

The two days of sightseeing that Isaac had planned out for me ended with his dropping me off at the airport to catch my flight home. He had been such a blessing in adding so much to this wonderful trip. Getting to witness Babu minister to all of those people and to learn that my testimony had drawn one of the Muslim women to come to faith in Jesus were such treasures.

VI

Four months into the next year, 2011, brought a new addition. My step-daughter and son-in-law blessed us with our second granddaughter. That was another blessing from God, and I was so thankful that she was 100 percent healthy. It almost appeared that Arlene and my daughter were going to move to Amarillo, and I couldn't blame them for that. Those grand-babies are so precious. On my end, I was just wishing that Arlene could see some value in me as well. That just wasn't going to happen.

Somewhere around this time frame she was doing her usual berating of me, and I just said, "Why don't you just file for divorce?" It was clear she couldn't stand me. Since I had returned home from the hospitals and rehab facility, she wouldn't give me the time of day. There had been no intimacy. She wouldn't even go out to eat with me unless it were in a group setting.

It was coming up on ten years of this type of treatment after returning home from the hospitals and rehab. She had basically degraded everything I had done: my ministry trips, the food ministry, and everything in between.

On my end, there was one thing that I tried to put first, God, and I put them next. I truly loved my family, but to her the only way to demonstrate that was to be a slave to them and do everything they said, their way.

Back when my daughter was about to graduate, Arlene and I had gone out to Santa Barbara the month before the graduation, and I had gone shopping with her at an art sale in one of the city parks.

As we walked along, I reached over to hold her hand as we walked. We went along like that for maybe twenty yards, and she jerked her hand away from mine. I was stunned. There wasn't any conflict taking place. She couldn't even tolerate my holding her hand.

Not long after my return from India, I told her we needed to get some counseling. She agreed to it somewhat reluctantly, so I got in touch with Bill Hines again, and we proceeded to meet with him. As always, Bill was precise and biblical in his approach to solving our problems.

He laid out where I needed to change, and I did not disagree. He also did the same pertaining to Arlene. As the upcoming months passed, I was trying and truly wanted to do it right. On her side, I didn't see any desire for that.

VII

Finally, in September of 2011 Arlene came up to me and asked if I would be available to join her at home to meet with a fellow we knew from my former church. She told me he wanted to talk with us about a financial investment. She specified the day and time, and I told her that I was fine with that.

That day and time arrived, and I was just sitting in the living room reading something on my laptop. The doorbell rang, and I heard Arlene say that she would get it. I stayed in the chair and continued to read expecting them to walk into the room shortly. When I sensed someone coming up behind me and walking into the room, I turned to see them. I was going to stand up and shake his hand, but it wasn't who I was expecting.

I recognized the fellow, and he was another individual from the former church that I had attended. He said hello and walked across the room to take a seat. Arlene came in behind him, stood over to my left, and didn't sit down. As she stood there, she had a very serious expression. When I glanced over at the other fellow, he had a very serious look as well. With this not being the person whom I was expecting to meet, I was wondering what had happened.

As I sat there looking puzzled Arlene proceeded to speak. In very short order she informed me that she had filed for divorce. As my lower jaw hit the floor, I sat there and waited to hear her elaborate. From what I recall, she had basically not said anything else, and the doorbell rang again.

She told me to keep my seat and that she would answer the door. As I sat there with the other fellow sitting across the room saying absolutely nothing, Arlene returned with another lady following her.

This new visitor called out my name with a question in her tone.

I said, "Yes."

She extended her hand with some papers for me to take. After she served me the papers, she departed. Arlene then ordered me to gather what personal items I needed and get out. At that point I glanced over at the individual across the room, and he said nothing. He just sat there watching me.

I was stunned and was starting to shake a bit. I told her that I needed some time alone to think through what I would need and where to go. She informed me that they would be waiting right there for me to depart. I got up and went upstairs to the media room where I had in the past spent most of my spare time reading, playing my guitar some, and watching the news on TV.

I sat down in my recliner and started to pray. Where was I going to go? I no longer owned the house where I was born and had lived the first four years of my life. I had sold it just a few years prior. As I sat there, I recalled that Phil had a house up in Tioga that he and Jan just used as a weekend getaway occasionally.

I called him and told him what had just happened and asked if it might be possible for me to stay at that house until I found something else. He said, "Sure," and that he would meet me there with a key. I told him I would let him know when I was headed that way.

I had to sit in my chair a bit longer to regain some strength. I finally got up and headed downstairs to gather up some clothes, my shaving kit, and my laptop. After I got the car loaded, I went in and told them I was leaving.

I got in the car and headed to Tioga. Phil was there when I arrived, and he let me in and showed me around the house. After he had me educated on everything pertaining to the house, we sat down and had a fairly long talk. He was very concerned for me and empathetic. He told me that Jan was as well. It was a great comfort to have their concern and support. They were very kind to give me a good part of their time over the next few days coming to see them and lifting me up in this ordeal.

As I sat there that first night, I was just devastated. As I've said before I loved Arlene with all of my heart and wanted nothing more than to please her and have her respect. I spent that entire night just running it back and forth: what could I do to make this right? There were all sorts of things going through my mind. What to do?

Just two weeks prior to this, I had done something completely stupid in hopes of gaining back some companionship. I was just grasping at straws. To explain, prior to my accident, I had blond hair. Somehow the injury changed that to something between brown and black.

Arlene had made several comments since I got hurt about her dislike of my hair not being blond any longer, so I went out and signed up to get that physical attribute fixed. How dumb was that? It wasn't cheap, and they couldn't even make it blond.

The next day I called her and asked if I could come and get some more of my things, which she allowed. I made a few trips over that first week.

As some days passed, I would communicate occasionally, and I asked or begged some mutual friends to tell her I was willing to go anywhere in the country and stay as long as necessary to get the absolute best counseling possible to restore our marriage.

I even thought it would be good to get Pastor Nelson to counsel us. He had driven down to Lewisville, Texas and taught a men's Bible study that had met for probably close to twenty years. I had attended it every week since shortly after I got my driver's license renewed after my injury. He had developed some health issues and decided to transfer that class to some of his associates, but I continued there after he left and am still there now.

I thought this pastor was one of the best teachers, next to John MacArthur and a few others, whom I had ever heard. We didn't really know each other that well personally, but he knew who I was because some of my fellow American Airlines pilots attended his church, along with the fact that I had made the news around DFW for almost two years. I called to tell him what was taking place and asked if he could possibly talk to Arlene and maybe get her to let him counsel us or help convince her to go to anyone else in the country who could help us. He told me he would contact her.

After a couple of days, a mutual friend of Arlene's and mine informed me that she had told him the pastor had called her. She gave the friend a quote of what the pastor had said to her. When this friend went on and shared the quote with me, I didn't believe it and said, "There's no way he would have said that." The mutual friend told me he couldn't believe it at first either but went on to say that she was emphatic that was exactly what the pastor had said.

As I thought about it, I decided that was a derogatory statement that he would never make. I thought it made both of us look bad, so I decided I needed to inform him about it. I managed to get him on the phone and told him that Arlene was running around quoting him. I went on to say I was concerned for his sake. Before I said another word, he proceeded to recite verbatim what I had been told he had said. I'm going to be kind and not repeat it here, but believe me, it is etched in my brain.

I just about fell over. I couldn't believe what I was hearing from a brother in Christ who had not even spoken to me on the subject of my life experience with her. I thanked him for his time and said goodbye. That was so painful and devastating that I was feeling sick at my stomach and actually thought I was going to throw up. I could not imagine that a pastor would make such an insulting, ungodly, unchristlike statement based on a one-sided conversation.

Pastor Nelson's ministry and his work for the Lord will be blessed with great reward on Judgment Day. While my life as a disciple of Jesus Christ will pale in comparison, I find nothing in the Gospel or Epistles that would justify his treating me in that fashion.

I had actually started attending the men's Bible study that he had continued to teach at his home church after he had backed out of the one in Lewisville. He has around 300 guys who show up to hear him teach there every week. I continued to attend a few of those classes after the verbal ambush he laid on me, but I decided I needed to forgive and move on. It was a bit too painful.

Arlene had told me, on day one basically, to get an attorney, which I finally did after several weeks. Nevertheless, I continued to pray and hope for a restoration. I even called a lady in Georgia who had written a great book on marriage and did marriage counseling to get us the best counseling possible. Arlene would have none of it.

I finally started the process of dealing with all of it. I had been alone for over ten years. As I already stated, Arlene wouldn't give me any of her time after I returned home from the injury, and I had felt very lonely for a long time. In spite of all that, I had absolutely no desire to find anyone else. I was strong in my commitment to our wedding vows. And as I already shared, the only time I had ever done anything divorce related with Arlene was in a stupid attempt to get her to end her disrespect and verbal emasculation.

After about two months the Lord calmed me and gave me peace. It finally sank in that reconciliation wasn't going to happen. No matter how much I loved, cared, and provided for this woman, she would never respect me or love me. I had tried to earn that as she demanded, and it was an impossible task. It was time to move on.

As the meetings with the attorney took place, I was stunned, once again. She was demanding half of everything. Texas is a community property state, but she was demanding half of what was supposed to be my monthly income for the rest of my life, the monthly annuity payment that was received for my on the job injury that ended my career. Texas was not even an alimony state, and that could be classified as alimony on steroids. I couldn't believe this.

My attorney was adamant that I should not bow to that, and I decided I was not going to. As this dragged on for months I was really feeling at the low point of my life. It's hard to believe now, but I was feeling more down and defeated than at any point of that traumatic brain injury ordeal.

That's where Satan wants you, and boy did he make hay of it.

Jay and Brother Andrew in Bethlehem

FRYING PAN INTO THE FIRE—
A BIBLICAL EYE OPENER

A little less than six months into the divorce proceeding, I had just finished unloading the vegetables from the truck, and a lady that I had known for a few years was there. She didn't attend my church regularly, but I had always enjoyed visiting with her. Since it was very clear that my thirty years with Arlene were finished, I asked her if she would like to join me for dinner, and she accepted. She was very strong in her faith, and I enjoyed having our meal together.

We spent a good deal of time together over the next two months having dinner and going to a few movies and church events. I really liked and cared for her and had a strong desire to go deeper in a relationship, but she told me that she just couldn't commit to a relationship. She shared some of the pain she had experienced and that her focus was on her walk with the Lord. I certainly couldn't fault her for that.

So, getting back to Satan's being on the prowl, I was at church, and another lady who was single, "Melissa," visited with a mutual friend. We were introduced, and I invited her to a dinner that the singles group in our church was having that week. She accepted the invitation. When that dinner took place, she didn't make it. I was a bit disappointed, but that's how it goes.

The Sunday after that, Melissa showed up at church again. There was a group of us who usually went to lunch after church, and I invited her to join us, and she accepted. She sat by me at lunch, and in the conversation she apologized for missing the singles dinner. I told her that was not a problem.

She went on to share that she had forgotten she had a previous commitment to go to a Christian home group meeting that night. As she went on talking about that meeting and the location where it took place, I was shocked. It had taken place at my house, or I guess I should say, the house I was half-owner of.

When I asked her whose house it was, she couldn't remember the name. When I asked if it was Arlene's house, her eyes got big, and she said it was. I went on to ask her if she remembered my last name from when I introduced myself that first time, and she said she didn't. When I told her my last name was Straub, she about fell over.

Our time at lunch seemed to go very well. When the group was about to disperse, I asked for her phone number, and she shared it with me. I called her a couple of days later and asked if she would care to go and have coffee. She said yes, so we met and spent a good deal of time talking on various subjects.

I got the impression that she was strong in the Christian faith, so I was interested in getting to know her better. We dated, spent the majority of our spare time together, and after just a couple of months started discussing marriage.

I had let the loneliness of the last ten-plus years and the need for love and some affection get to me. It floors me the level of foolishness and stupidity that I let it take me to. She told me that she truly loved me, and it went way too far. She was staying with me into the early morning hours.

After that had continued for a couple of months, I finally came to my senses and told her we needed to confess our error to God and stop that until we were married, if that were what we wanted. I knew it was a major wrong. Good grief, no matter how many years I had been basically alone and left out, how could I forget what this same sin had brought on me for thirty years? How in the world could I be that stupid?

I thought she would be totally understanding and in agreement since she had put great emphasis on her love of God and how she revered His word and what it reveals to us about His ways in the Bible. When I shared my concern and what we needed to do, she basically blew up.

When I tried to reason and tell her that I was committed to her and wanted to marry her when all the mess was finalized, it didn't really matter to her. Wow, I should have been able to read the writing on the wall with this, but when she finally settled down, I convinced myself that everything was OK.

A few months later Arlene had changed attorneys and hired a bulldog. She was determined to get that half of what was supposed to be my salary for the rest of my life. That was absurd. Her new attorney called me in for a deposition. She sat me down and she proceeded to grill me about our marriage history and of course asked every possible negative question where the answer put me in a very negative light.

After all of that the attorney asked another question. I don't know why, but I was shocked. I should have known how low Arlene would go. She had ordered me to not come near my former home, which I had honored, except for the day that my attorney and I went to gather the remainder of my personal belongings. But she or one of her allies had clearly been over to my place and documented the time that Melissa's car was parked at the place I was living. So, her attorney obviously asked that personal question, and I answered truthfully.

After a few more months I told my attorney to set up a mediator to end this mess. That was a long day, but this mediator convinced me that if it went to court there was a strong possibility that a jury would award her 50 percent of that portion of the settlement from my injury that was my monthly income. I could hardly believe that, but I had had enough.

If it went to court, the legal fees that were already ridiculous would be over the top, and that's another thing the mediator used to twist my arm. At the end of the day I said do it, give her 50 percent of the whole thing, as this was more than I could bear. I was completely stressed.

As I walked out of there, I was ready to forgive and move on. I felt a peace that I had not felt in almost thirty years but was I ever-clueless as to what awaited me.

When that mess with my now ex-wife was completely finalized, I set out with Melissa to find a new house to make a new home for us. As things proceeded toward our wedding day, however, there were many problems developing that should have led me to end the relationship immediately. The problem was that I cared for her and just couldn't bring myself to do it. We actually went to counseling, and Melissa presented it as all my problem.

The last time we went she got up and flew out of the room when the counselor presented a potential need for a change on her part. Gee! Where was my common sense? Gone for the time being, apparently.

We got married, and she exploded that very night over my not following her directions in the exit to take getting back to the hotel after our wonderful dinner that we had. Good grief! That was just the beginning. We went on our honeymoon, and after two days it turned into a repeat of the wedding night. It was unbelievable.

After we got home, the credit card bill was immediately much higher with things on it that we never discussed. At month five, however, when I opened it, I felt like I was going to keel over from a heart attack: $30,000. Yes, you read that right. I removed her from the credit card account, but I was making every effort to work through it and for us to recover from this. I took us on a weekend trip to work through it, which turned out just like the honeymoon trip, a complete disaster. I could not believe what was taking place.

Two months later we were preparing to move. I went to the mailbox, opened the new credit card statement and another $30,000 bill was staring me in the face. I sat down and started going over the charges. It was all the same places that her previous charges had been made to.

I called the credit card company and told them I did not make those charges. I told them the only thing I could surmise was that Melissa had gotten my new credit card number off my card when I was asleep. They told me they would get back with me after they looked into it.

When they called back, they informed me that all of the charges that I had not made myself were removed from my bill, and they asked me to return any of the items to the retailers if I could locate them. My head was reeling over this. When I approached Melissa about it, she denied the whole thing.

The day to move came, and at the conclusion of the day she was on a tear again. I put up with it for about three more weeks. The way it was going I was going to probably be dead from something stress related or be bankrupt within two years at the rate things had gone. I decided I had to end it and went to my attorney to file for divorce. After three months it was done. What a relief, but it was certainly going to take some time to recover.

Thankfully I still got to drive the truck and do the food ministry on Tuesdays. I also got active in another men's Bible study that met in my neighborhood. It wasn't long before that group decided it had grown to the point that it needed to split into two groups, and they asked for a volunteer to host the new group when it split. I was happy to do it, so I volunteered my home. If I weren't reading the Bible or catching up on some news, I spent a lot of time just sitting staring at the walls.

After three months of it, I finally decided that was enough of the "woe is me." It was time to go out and get some exercise at the gym. I even got into volleyball a bit. I hadn't done that since high school and actually enjoyed it.

I knew that I really needed to get with it in the physical fitness end of things and was being faithful to get there and exercise, but there was something gnawing at me. Over those last three months of mostly reading the Bible and catching the news, a book that I had seen advertised almost ten years before kept coming to mind.

I finally purchased that book and two more written by the same author, Joel Richardson, whom I have come to know personally since then and count as a dear friend and brother in Christ.

Reading those books, digging into the Bible even more, and reading several more books by some authors who had come to the same conclusion was quite the eye opener. I had wondered for a long time; where was the biblical evidence that without question the Roman Empire would be reborn, and the antichrist would come from there? When I read those books, I was convinced that the biblical evidence was quite strong that the son of perdition would arise out of a rebirth of the Islamic Caliphate. And I feel that a part of all of the miracles that God has poured out to sustain my life up to now have been to give me some fortitude to encourage people to examine His word, and be spiritually prepared to stand firm in the faith.

A BLESSING FROM ABOVE

I spent the better part of the next year reading those books and others. I was also praying, staying active in the food ministry, and spending time at the gym. I was focused on that alone. Sometime in October, my friend Pete Belding, who attended the men's Bible study that met at my home, could sense the loneliness in my life.

He started telling me about a lady who was attending the dance class that he and his wife were in. He said I should come meet her. I had been so broken and so hurt that I could not open my heart for anyone to hurt me again. I was polite and thanked him, but I had absolutely no interest. I thought of the years I had been married and was never loved. I had been deeply wounded, and my mind had accepted the fact that I would live alone and die alone.

As the next few months went along, Pete would mention this lady to me on occasion. I continued to be polite but had absolutely no desire to risk another debacle or potential decades of disrespect and complaints. My mind questioned the fact of true love that the Bible speaks of. I wondered, does this really exist?

Around the middle of January 2015, Pete gave me the lady's business card as he was about to head out the door on Saturday morning. He indicated that he had worked extremely hard to extract that from her. I nodded with a smile and thanked him for his hard work on my behalf.

The realization of never being truly loved was such a deep hurt. I had spent my entire adult life desiring to be truly loved, respected, and happily married. I tossed the card on the counter and went about my day. A few days later, early in the morning, I was gathering up some junk mail and other things that had accumulated in the same spot to send them to file thirteen.

When I looked at the card, I noticed that she was a realtor in Ardmore, Oklahoma. It really surprised me that she was driving all the way to Denton,

Texas to take dance lessons. As I was about to toss the card, I noticed her website address. I thought I would take a look at it out of curiosity with perhaps just a glimmer of hope.

When I sat down and pulled it up on my computer, I found the page that had her brief bio. As I read that, it made mention of her church membership and involvement in several Christian ministries. I thought that was quite positive. You don't see that many business websites where the owner's faith and walk with Jesus are mentioned. After seeing that, I sat there and thought long and hard about meeting her at the dance class as Pete had suggested, and I began to pray. "Lord is this you? Am I to meet this lady?"

That evening, as I sat alone watching the news, the house was dark and quiet. I was searching for true answers. I had been cut to the core when the person claimed her Christian walk, how she honored God's view of marriage, and on and on. The problem was that in that case there was absolutely no evidence of it other than words. As I thought and prayed, I finally felt led to give Letha Khaladj a call to see if I could join her at the dance class.

I called and introduced myself. I went on to share that Pete had spoken very highly of her for quite a while, as a matter of fact, and that he had shared her business card with me. I pressed on to say that I heard about the dance lessons she was going to at our clubhouse and asked if I could join her. She was very kind and said she would enjoy that and that Pete had shared many kind words on my behalf as well. I told her I would see her then and would enjoy meeting her. She indicated that she would be looking forward to it as well.

After the call I decided to send her the link to my website so she could know a little more about me. She responded and thanked me for sharing that. The next day came, and it was time to meet her. When I walked in, she was already there, and she was beautiful. I didn't know that she came early for a private lesson with the instructor, Henry Evans, before the group lesson that Pete and his wife Mary Jo attended. While I've never been much of a dancer, it was a true pleasure to join Letha in that.

When the dance lesson was completed, I wanted to get to know her more. She had a great smile, and you could tell that she loved life. So, I asked her if she would care to drive into Denton and get some coffee at Starbucks. She immediately responded with a yes. She's not a coffee connoisseur but said she would enjoy some tea and fellowship with me and getting to know one another. So, we did that.

We had a great conversation, and the time went by so quickly. We focused our discussion on the Lord and our life experiences, both good and bad. I have no idea how it happened, but I just gave her a rapid-fire tour of my past including the serious major wrongs on my part. I was totally transparent. Letha was as well.

We had been talking quite a while, and she got a text message from a friend about a trip to Destin, Florida that they were going on the next day. In that, I learned that she had to leave Ardmore at 6 a.m. the next morning to drive to Love Field in Dallas. It was now 9 p.m., and she still had over an hour to drive home from where I lived.

I felt bad about how late it was with all that was on her plate early the next day. We went back to the clubhouse, and I shared what a joy it was meeting her, and I told her I hoped she had a great trip with her girlfriends. She said that she really enjoyed meeting me too.

We communicated by text a little while she was on her trip, and she sent me a great picture of her at the beach. She had a beautiful smile, and it made my heart glad. The day she was flying home, I noticed the weather was a bit nasty where she was. So, I called her and told her what to expect with her flight home. Once she landed, I called her again, and I called her every day thereafter.

My mind was racing with truly wanting to know more about Letha. With the Super Bowl coming up, I was hosting a party at my home with some people from my church coming, so I invited her. She came and was a great help. We had a wonderful time together that day.

I think back on this with truly fond memories of her. I began to call her twice a day, and as soon as the sun would come up, I would text and tell her good morning. I decided to ask her for a date every weekend.

I was spending all the time I could with her, making a daytrip to see the bluebonnets down at the Texas Hill Country, going out to some movies, going to see the US Navy Blue Angels, sharing great dinners gazing into her eyes, and anything else I could think of just to be with her.

I decided to get her a hotel room for her to stay in one or two nights on the weekend, so we could spend more time together and attend church on Sunday. She even came down way early on a Tuesday to join me on my food ministry journey. She rode with me in the White Freightliner to pick up the load of produce, unload it, and distribute it to the needy people that afternoon.

I was truly amazed that this sweet lady wanted to drive all those miles and take time out of her day and business to spend time with me and join in the things I was doing.

I saw in Letha a true princess. I sensed a warm, loving heart in her that was directed at me. It was truly genuine, not a facade like my previous experiences. I was really starting to feel that I could give my love and devotion to her without feeling at risk.

It was a real treat on the trips that I made up to Ardmore getting to meet her family. Her son Gary Don, his family, and her grand-daughter Harlee were the first. She came from a large family, having two older brothers and two younger sisters. It was truly a wonderful family.

I'll just share two highlights, starting with the humorous one from her oldest brother, Bruce. Letha had basically not dated since her divorce a few years prior, and Bruce was quite protective of her.

When she told him she was going to meet me right before our first date, he told her not to get in a car with me and asked her all kinds of questions about me that she obviously couldn't answer. Basically, all he had was my name and the fact that I was a former pilot for American Airlines.

Well unbeknownst to her, he took that and had a relative of his who was a private investigator check me out. She was aghast when she shared that with me. I couldn't help but grin at her embarrassment, and I couldn't blame him either. I was absolutely fine with it.

The other highlight pertaining to her family was learning about their American Indian background. Her grandmother on her dad's side was 100 percent Choctaw Indian. It was wonderful learning about that and everything else she shared pertaining to her family. Another apparent fact was their close family bond. They shared genuine love for one another, and all five siblings had remained close.

I began to see and realize who she was. The things that mattered most to her were eternal things of life. I saw a strength in her and a calmness I had never witnessed before. As we dated, I realized that she was the pearl that many look for and yet never find. We shared deeply of all of the brokenness of our lives and how both of us were so very fragile. We both were broken vessels.

I knew this was a gift from God and an answered prayer. In my dark and lonely days I had barely been able to lift my eyes and ask our Lord to forgive me and have favor on me and bring me a wife who could truly love me, be one in spirit and mind, and have our lives be of one accord. I realized our Lord desired to show me His plan for marriage, a spiritual marriage.

As I began to feel a true love for Letha, I was humbled that the Lord had chosen to bless us with one another in the last chapter of our lives. She is a true romantic, loves flowers and holding hands, and has a tender heart. I prayed that as our relationship deepened that one day, I would marry her and that we would encourage one another and hold one another when we were no longer able to stand.

It wasn't all that long until I was totally convinced that Letha was truly a wonderful lady who definitely put Jesus Christ first. And I felt sure that she would love, honor, and respect me in the manner that God designed for marriage. I proposed to her, and she responded, "I will a hundred times; yes, I will!"

I truly couldn't wait to begin our life together, hand-in-hand, and put all of the pain of the past behind me. This was truly my prayer to love one another, pursue Christ, heal from all of life's hurts and disappointments, and look to our Lord to guide the way.

When we discussed a date, time, and location, it was my thought that the one-year anniversary of when we met would be great. Letha agreed, so we would be married right where we did our first dance, on the same date and hour. I was really excited about it, and so was she.

A new chapter was about to begin. With this coming in the near future there were some things to consider. Would I sell my home and move to Ardmore, or would she sell her house and move to my location? To complicate things, Letha owned a real estate brokerage firm and was working full-time. It blew me away that it was her desire to follow me, be with me, and love me, no matter where I was.

I had never witnessed anything even close to this in my entire lifetime. I had read the description of a woman in Proverbs 31 a number of times. Based on my personal experience, I would have found that an impossibility, were it not for the fact that it was in the Bible. I could see it in her, however.

After talking about it, we decided it would be best to put her house on the market fairly soon. As you will recall, I had already been getting a nice hotel room for her for a minimum of four nights a month.

With all of that, I found a short-term rental here in my neighborhood. With her house closing within two months of being listed, it was even better that we had that for her to move to.

There were a number of people who were surprised that we did that, but our desire was to do it God's way. We didn't want to tempt ourselves or come across that it was OK to live together outside of marriage. It isn't. I had already failed at that and had a miserable marriage.

When that day arrived, what a joy it was to see the doors open and Letha come walking down the aisle in her beautiful wedding dress with the wedding march playing. As she proceeded the tears of joy just started to trickle down my face. When she got to me and we were both facing Pastor Ray Harper, the duet, "From This Moment On," by Shania Twain and Bryan White was played.

It was so wonderful joining this precious lady in taking those blessed vows of marriage. And I can't forget to tell you how appreciative we were having my longtime friend, Michael Mabrey, as my best man, Jody Douglas as Letha's maid of honor, and our two friends who were instrumental in our meeting one another, Pete Belding and Nancy Toppan, standing there with us.

The pastor's words in the ceremony were the best I've ever heard. They spoke deeply to my heart in a mighty way as God joined us together as one. Afterward, the celebration was truly a treasure to us both with the dinner and the dance following.

Our first dance was to the song "Amazed," by Lonestar, and that night I myself was truly amazed at the grace given to us by our heavenly Father. What a holy moment it was. When it all concluded, Letha's friends Jody and Kristin had instigated quite the decor on our automobile to announce our nuptials to everyone on the road. That still puts a smile on our faces when we reminisce about it.

I had asked Letha where she would like to go on our honeymoon. She asked me to surprise her. I chose one of the most beautiful places I had ever been, a beautiful location with a lake frozen over, ice carvings, and taking a sleigh ride through the trees around the lake was over the top in beauty and romance.

Sitting with her in the lounge and sipping on a hot chocolate while looking out at the lake is a moment forever imprinted on my mind. As we drove through the mountains on the day prior to our departure, we were wishing so much that we could stay. I didn't want this moment to end.

Jay and his bride, Letha, on their wedding day

WOUNDED AND FORGOTTEN

As you proceed into this final chapter, one might find it sad or troubling. It can certainly be that but let me put your focus on a word that you will find in the final paragraph: joy! That is still and will remain a key word in my life.

I had been working on writing this book for about six months when I was made aware of something that I had sensed very soon after my recovery; however, I was almost incredulous with the intensity of what I was about to learn and experience at this time.

We are told throughout scripture that there will be a multitude of trials in our lives, but taking on the reality of being wounded and forgotten and being told by upper management at American Airlines, to my face with Letha sitting by my side, that they had no place for me cut me to the core and ran deep. Here's how that came down.

Over two years ago, I started to hear how Chairman and CEO of American Airlines Doug Parker had given the pilots a fairly substantial pay raise, basically with no union negotiations involved. He just did it. That was really good to hear, and I found it encouraging. I had never seen anything like that since 1986 when I came on board at American.

While that was great news for the active pilots, as time went along, and I continued to hear about this, I decided it was time to politely ask for something to be done for the pilots on long-term disability. My LTD pay has not gone up one penny in the sixteen years that I've been on it, and from the LTD group I'm in it hadn't gone up in over twenty years.

So, I wrote Mr. Parker a courteous email sharing that I had heard how he had blessed the current active pilots with a raise. Knowing that he was not employed at American when things happened to me, I gave him a very brief description of my career's end and job injury. I asked that he please consider a pay raise to those of us on LTD.

I waited a month, and there was no reply. I resent the email and still no reply. I decided to contact Captain Dan Carey, president of the APA, the union that I had paid my dues to while on the payroll at American. He called me within a few days. When I shared what had happened pertaining to my email to the CEO, he started off by expressing empathy over what had happened to me with my injury.

At this point he informed me that he agreed that LTD pay needed to be increased. He said he was going to give that a great deal of attention and indicated that he thought my involvement would be beneficial in getting something done. I told him that I would be more than happy to get involved. At the conclusion of the conversation he informed me that he would have someone get in touch with me. I thanked him and told him I would be looking forward to hearing from them.

It didn't happen.

After once again waiting more than a month, hearing nothing, and having attempted communication ignored, I set out to see what could be done on my own. I got in touch with a friend, Captain Steve Farrah, who had told me over a year prior that he had introduced a resolution at one of the APA meetings pertaining to the inadequacy of the LTD pay and benefits at American, and he had named it after me. In our conversation he gave me the name of another pilot to get in touch with on the subject.

I called that gentleman and—what a shock! He informed me that a group of pilots on LTD would be meeting at a steakhouse in Arlington, Texas the very next day. He was planning on flying to DFW to attend. I went to the meeting, which was in early March, and met and shook hands with almost everyone there.

As I introduced myself, many of them almost did a double-take when they heard my name. Most were well aware of my experience. As the meeting progressed, I was left almost speechless at what I was learning about American Airlines' treatment of, and actions against, many of the pilots on LTD. I was equally startled to learn that there were over 900 of our pilots on LTD. That truly puts in perspective how critical health and passing the FAA Medical Exam is to those who get people safely from point A to point B.

The APA had wanted to send someone to that meeting at the steakhouse, but they were denied access, for good reason. I learned that the APA had basically dumped our group. The meeting was to be attended only by pilots currently on LTD, or who had been, who wanted to improve things. What a shock to learn later on that someone who attended only matched part of that criteria and was an APA sleuth. That's pretty pathetic.

Getting close to the end of the meeting I was asked to come up and share my experience for those who might not know what had happened to me, which I did. Everyone was very kind, and I got the impression that those who had attended this meeting were ready to get active and right some horrendous wrongs.

When Letha got home that evening, it was clear to her that I was troubled, and when she asked what had happened at the meeting, I was at a loss for words again. I was able to share a few snippets of what I could remember, and she was appalled.

Over the next few days I was contacted by a few of the attendees. One of them was First Officer Lawrence Meadows. He was very empathetic toward my status and CEO Doug Parker's refusal to give me the time of day. He was also a bit dismayed at how Captain Dan Carey had indicated support and a desire to get me involved, but just dropped it.

It wasn't long before Lawrence revealed some things to me that were appalling. He asked me if I were ever offered a reasonable accommodation by management. I didn't have a clue what he was even talking about, and he informed me that the Americans with Disabilities Act (ADA) required that I should have been offered that.

He went on to inform me that several management pilots and a few that weren't in management were given jobs in the flight department at full pilot pay and benefits until retirement because they had medical problems that prevented their passing the FAA Medical Exam and a few other issues. I couldn't believe what I was hearing.

Lawrence went on to share a copy of a lawsuit that he filed. I am just going to share some of the high points that you can read more about in Appendix A and that affect Lawrence and many others mentioned at the end of the filing. You may find the legalese and some of the terms used in this a bit hard to understand, but if you read over it, you will definitely get the gist of what has taken place. It should certainly reveal the reprehensible actions that the pilots on LTD at American Airlines have been dealt by their union and the company. Anyone who wants to read the entirety of it can get a copy of it on their own because it's a public document filed with the court.

After I got active in these issues some of my story and information wound up in the hands of Captain Kimble Neel. Does that name ring a bell? Yes, that's the gentleman who gave me my very first flying lesson back when I was twelve years old.

I had heard that Kimble had gone to work for America West Airlines back when I was still an active pilot at American, which meant that he had retired as a pilot for American Airlines, since America West had merged with US Air, which wound up merging with American Airlines.

I was quite surprised and happy to receive an email from him. In it, he shared that he had just learned what had happened to me in my service to American and how sorry he was. He said he would love to talk with me and shared his phone number.

When I called him, I gave him the whole scoop, and he informed me that he knew Doug Parker personally, having been on the Pilot's Negotiating Committee at America West when Parker was in management there. He said he wanted to email Mr. Parker and Robert Isom, president at American, to share his thoughts. I told him I would be thankful and more than happy for him to do that. When he did, he shared it with me and told me I could share it here with you.

> Mr. Parker,
>
> Recently, I had the opportunity to visit with Captain Jay Straub. Jay was a student of mine more than 40 years ago. He rode his bike to the airport to take flying lessons.
>
> Until a couple of days ago, I was unaware of Jay's situation. The incident in 1999 ended his career and very nearly ended his life. In my opinion, American Airlines and the leadership of the Allied Pilots Association handled this disgracefully.
>
> A gesture on the part of American to improve Jay's and other similarly situated pilots' long-term disability would indeed go a long way to enhance good will among the entire pilot group. My opinion.
>
> Respectfully,
> Kimble J. Neel
> Captain American Airlines (retired)

What a surprise that Kimble received no response.

Moving forward, in all of the discussion that followed that meeting at the steakhouse, those who had appointed themselves leaders of the group were basically going to just hand it over to the APA and try to have some influence. Based on everything I had learned and just experienced with the APA president, that wasn't going to accomplish a thing.

Lawrence and I decided to do what we could on our own to hopefully get some attention to the issue. There was one thing for sure: we were definitely going to be at the next APA Board of Directors meeting—either inside or outside. You see, the APA had designated those of us on LTD as inactive members, and the constitution and bylaws specified that inactive members could not attend board meetings.

To be effective you certainly have to have participants and some media coverage. I thought the media would be no problem. The news media in the DFW area covered my injury for almost two years. A few years after that, a reporter heard me call in on a radio program to voice my concern on a brain injury event that was making the news nationwide.

On that call I didn't give my name or anything to share my identity, but that reporter knew it had to be me. He called me to verify it and see if he could come out to interview me, which I agreed to. I contacted him about the LTD issue and our upcoming efforts to address it, but I received no response.

I thought Doug Dunbar at the CBS Affiliate would jump at it. If you recall, I shared how he and Cecil Ewell flew my Cessna 310 to Mississippi to help Hurricane Katrina victims. I emailed him and told him a small portion of what I had learned pertaining to LTD and how hundreds of us were being dealt with by our union and the company. I asked him if he or another reporter from his station could come and cover our protest. He said he needed to know the issues. I responded and got no reply. I thought it must have gotten lost, so I resent it. No response came.

This was unbelievable. I tried one more of the reporters who came to report on me in the hospitals. She responded, but there was no help in getting the television news media to cover this. As I thought back on it, from what I could recall, in all of the news coverage that had been saved for me to see when I finally recovered, there was nothing in it revealing any complicity on the part of American Airlines to what had been dealt me.

It was becoming way clear how American Airlines' advertising dollars give them free rein in squelching anything that would shine a light on their disgraceful actions.

It was laughable when three months later I was sent an article, "American

Earns Top Score in 2018 Disability Equality Index and Named Best Place to Work for Disability Inclusion." This score of 100 came from the American Association of People with Disabilities (AAPD). When I went to the AAPD website and scrolled down to the bottom of the page, it had a list of sponsors. Guess who is one of many sponsors? Ah yes, none other than American Airlines. They got the top score indeed, the best score money can buy.

When the day finally arrived for the APA board meetings to start, Lawrence and I plus my dear and lovely wife Letha and a number of other LTD pilots were there and ready. When Captain Dan Carey, the APA president pulled in, we weren't sure what his response would be, but he came over and shook my hand and had his picture taken with me.

As the board members trickled in, we met them with coffee and donuts and visited with them. Lawrence knew Captain Carey pretty well and told him that he should allow me to share my concerns with the board. I was really quite surprised that Captain Carey ceded the time of his opening remarks to me.

He introduced me, and all of the board members gave me a standing ovation as I approached the podium. At the completion of my speech they gave me another standing O as I went back to my seat. In my speech I shared my experience and my request for the union to take a stand for all of the LTD pilots and for me. You can see my speech at the site that Lawrence created (disabledairlinepilotsfoundation.com).

Letha and I were there every day that week that the meetings took place. On the final day, a reporter, Conor Shine, and a photographer from *The Dallas Morning News* whom had been contacted by a fellow LTD pilot, arrived and spent well over an hour interviewing me. Conor covered airline-related news, so I was thankful that he found it newsworthy and came to do some true journalism.

As I shared the events of the accident, I was speechless once again as I shared the part of my dear friend Ans Wishing holding me up to prevent me from drowning on my own blood. If you watch the video on the site linked in the preceding paragraph, you will get a glimpse of it as well. It's rare that I share that and don't get choked up over Ans' doing that for me.

The article was supposed to come out the next week, but the in-flight tragedy with Southwest Airlines, where the catastrophic engine failure took place, the passenger sitting by the window was killed, and the female captain executed the emergency procedures as prescribed with no further loss of life, took place.

Obviously, that put our news piece on the back burner for a while. It did come out a few weeks later on the front page of the business section, and the picture of me they printed was when I was emotional in sharing about Ans and his intervention.

We came to the multiple days of board meetings again in May to represent our cause. Considering I got those two standing ovations, it's rather pathetic that we barely had half of those men and women be willing to do the right thing for those of us on LTD.

As they say, "Show me the money." Since we are no longer officially on the American Airlines payroll, they can't take our monthly dues money any longer, so there you have it. I already shared how worthless all that dues money I had paid was for me when the company tried to deprive me of my contractual captain's bid.

The June board meetings came, and I was almost there by myself. Lawrence was unable to attend those, but Lawrence and I along with our wives went to New York City to attend the annual American Airlines shareholders meeting. Being shareholders, we were there along with a number of other American Airlines employees to express our concerns to American management over various issues.

After CEO Doug Parker gave his report, they took questions from the shareholders. After a couple of those present asked their questions, I raised my hand and took the mic. In Appendix B you can read a copy of exactly what I said to Mr. Parker, except that I left out the second paragraph to shorten the time a bit.

I received applause from many of the attendees. I'm not sure about the American Airlines board because my focus was on Mr. Parker. He initiated his response by informing me that he never received the emails I sent, or he would have responded. He then went on to tell me he was sorry for what I had experienced. He continued in sharing that he had expected V.P Elise Eberwein to have been there that morning, which she wasn't, and that he would forward my request and my information to her.

After we had been home for about a week and having received no communication from Ms. Eberwein, I sent her an email with my plea and gave her a copy of my plea to Mr. Parker. I waited a week and after no reply resent the email. After waiting another week, I printed a copy, and Letha and I took it to the American Airlines headquarters to hand deliver it to Ms. Eberwein or her assistant.

After giving them my ID and why I was there, I was told by the security personnel I couldn't go in. I would have to go to the back of the building where the mail was received. They informed me that someone would be waiting for me. Letha and I drove to the back, but there was no one to be seen. I pulled up where it appeared that large mail or shipping trucks might be backing in and got out.

I found a door with a phone mounted on the wall next to it. I picked up the phone, and when it was answered, I shared who I was and why I was there. The person arrived at the door and informed me that they would make sure Ms. Eberwein received the envelope. Unbelievably I, a former captain for this institution who went through what I went through in my service to this company, was routed to the back of the building to an exterior door to ensure communication with these people.

I waited and never received a reply after that. So, I sent the letter certified mail but still received no written reply to this day. Immediately after sending that, I learned of a meeting that the company refers to as "Crew News." It was fast approaching. That's when Doug Parker goes to meet with company pilots to communicate with them, and it would be at the American Airlines Flight Academy.

I went to it, and when Mr. Parker concluded his comments and was taking questions, I got the mic again. I repeated to him what I had said to him at the annual Shareholder's meeting. I told him how I had tried multiple times to communicate with Ms. Eberwein, the person he had said he would refer this to, with no response.

He said, "Well she's standing right behind you."

I turned, and Ms. Eberwein walked over to shake my hand with a rather sour look on her face.

The next thing you know, a lady on the other side of the room had retrieved a mic and introduced herself. It was Neisha Strambler-Butler, vice president—benefits. She informed me that she had received my communication and that she had been on vacation, and that's why I hadn't been contacted. That might have sounded good to the other American Airlines pilots at the event who were mostly new captain upgrades, but if they knew the time that had transpired since I spoke to Mr. Parker at that meeting in New York, I'm sure they would have known that it was all bluster.

Ms. Strambler-Butler went on to say that she would like to visit with me at the end of this meeting. I said that I would be pleased to visit with her. At the conclusion, some of my fellow pilots stopped by to give me their best, and Ms.

Strambler-Butler made her way to me, followed by Ms. Lucretia Guia, vice president labor relations—deputy general counsel. Ms. Butler was all smiles just as she had been when she grabbed the mic. When she spoke, she gave me her card and asked me to call and set up an appointment. I thanked her and informed her that I certainly would.

That appointment was set up, and Letha and I went to AA headquarters to meet with them. Ms. Strambler-Butler and Ms. Guia came in and introduced themselves to Letha. After we sat down Ms. Strambler-Butler said they had reviewed my case, and she asked me to basically share again what my request was. I just repeated that I was requesting for them to do the honorable thing and make me whole in what I lost thanks to American Airlines' negligence.

At that point Ms. Guia mentioned that I had received some compensation in a settlement with another company. I informed her that I couldn't discuss that due to the non-disclosure, and she said they had all of the information.

How do you like that? I'm not allowed to share that information, but they get access to all of it, no problem.

I informed Ms. Guia that the settlement was irrelevant and went on to share with her that I had learned how a number of other pilots were given those jobs that I have already talked about. She responded that those were management pilots, and I informed her and Ms. Strambler-Butler that they were not all management pilots, and some were even pilots who had been involved in aircraft accidents; go figure. Had Ms. Guia done a little more homework, she would have seen on my resume that when I was hired, I was an honors graduate with a degree that included a certificate in aviation management.

I went on to share the other disgraceful experience I had been dealt by this company. I got to the part where I had to put my dad in the ground before he ever got to see that fourth stripe on my uniform, which he had asked me about time after time. I noticed Ms. Guia reach up and wipe the corner of one eye, but there was no verbal response.

At this point, Letha entered the conversation and expressed her concern over my being put in the retiree medical Insurance pool with a maximum of $300,000 coverage since the age of approximately forty-three, when I went on LTD. Isn't it interesting that I'm classified as retired in that regard, but am not officially retired? That does not compute.

They informed us that they had checked, and most of my $300,000 was still available. Yes, thanks to God and no thanks to them. And also, thanks to the fact that I had paid for a large portion of my medical expenses out of pocket since the end of 2002, I did have something left. Just one little blip of a medical issue, and that would be gone in a heartbeat.

One can clearly see how right versus wrong is irrelevant to American Airlines management. Ms. Strambler-Butler stayed firm that there was no wrong in their not giving me a job as they had the pilots I previously mentioned and went on to inform me that there was no position available for me at American Airlines. The entire thing boiled down to this: On top of the gross negligence, near death, almost two years of pain and suffering, ending my career that I cherished, I learned it had been topped off with nothing but discrimination against me. When I stated the discrimination, it was vehemently denied. That was pretty much the end of the conversation. We thanked them for their time and asked for a follow-up as we left the office

Several weeks later Ms. Guia emailed me that they would like to get with me for the follow-up. I asked when she would like for us to come and meet with her, and she said a phone call would be sufficient.

We set up the appointment, and the day before it was supposed to take place, she emailed to inform me that she had a family emergency and couldn't make the appointment. I responded and told her I would pray for her on that and would wait to hear back from her. After a few days, she emailed back with a day and time for the call. I responded, asking if I were to call her or vice versa, and didn't get a reply.

When the day and time arrived, I went ahead and called her office number and informed her assistant who I was and why I was calling. The lady that answered informed me that Ms. Guia wasn't in the office yet, but she would pass it on. I thanked her, and my phone rang immediately after I disconnected from that call. It was Ms. Guia calling from her cell phone.

She proceeded to inform me that my efforts had their attention, and they would be giving some focus to the current pilots at American who are on LTD. I thanked her for that, and then she moved on to say they had presented my personal request to those above, and that it stood where it did the last time we spoke.

At that point, I was just thinking how God tells us in the Bible that He metes out justice for His people, and it's all in His hands. I thanked her for the call, and I told her goodbye. She responded in kind. I sat for a moment and prayed that those hearts of stone could be drawn to repentance and come to faith in Jesus, our Redeemer.

I take absolutely no pleasure in making the following statements; as a matter of fact, as I write this, I hold a great sadness for the other parties. The management at American Airlines at the time of my tragic on the job injury, with their gross negligence, had my blood on their hands. They just mouthed kind words and rinsed it off.

If I were a betting man, I'd bet that, had I been a captain at Southwest Airlines, CEO Herb Kelleher would have been at Parkland with my family. I know of one of his employees who had a minor physical problem, and learning of it, Mr. Kelleher purchased something out of his pocket as a gift to help them.

Moving on to the current group, I must repeat that when I read CEO Doug Parker's statement about regaining trust from American employees in *Fortune* magazine, and he told me personally at the shareholders meeting that he was sorry for what happened and would refer my plea to Elise Eberwein, I had hope.

Unfortunately, with everything they did after that meeting in New York, Doug Parker, Elise Eberwein, Lucretia Guia, and Neisha Strambler-Butler washed their hands of me and negated my faithful service to their company.

They and their previous cohorts have done their deeds with impunity, and their actions are, as Captain Neel said, a disgrace. This applies as well to Captain Dan Carey, the legal team, and half of the base representatives at APA for their shameful refusal to give me the representation that I had paid my hard-earned union dues for, along with the hundreds of other pilots on LTD under their watch.

A week or two after that final conversation with Ms. Guia, I got a call from a gentleman whom I do business with, a strong Christian who knows of my former position as a captain at American Airlines. He had tickets to the Snowball Express fundraising dinner that he would be unable to attend and said he would love for Letha and me to take them if we could. I was truly humbled, amazed, and thankful for his offering those to us, when I later learned from another party the thousands of dollars that those two tickets cost.

The Snowball Express is a Gary Sinise Foundation program to aid the families of disabled and fallen veterans and first responders. American Airlines donates the use of their hangar, sets up the huge event, provides air travel for the military families to this event and others, and does many other wonderful things to aid these military veterans and families.

It was truly a joy to be there and see what was being done for these marvelous veterans and family members. It was truly heart wrenching, however, when

President of American Robert Isom spoke. I listened to his emotional words for those who were being honored that night; I got a knot in my throat.

I was just wondering what the thousands in attendance at this event would think if they could see a flashback of my being held on the tarmac at DFW in my captain's uniform going into convulsions with blood pouring out of my nose and mouth, and from there fast-forwarding through my two years of recovery, and climaxing with a witness of my experience at the hands of the current American Airlines management and how they treated me when I made my plea to be made whole in what had been done to me.

Pertaining to the people I just mentioned, past and present, at American Airlines and the Allied Pilots Association, it's as I said. I made my plea and presented the facts of my loss and abuse multiple times, as I should have. However, as stated, they had washed their hands of me, and I have given it over to God.

While I've known how critical it is to forgive, it has really been etched on my heart and mind with what I've been sharing in this chapter. It's coming up on twenty years now that there's something I see every morning when I get up and look in the mirror. You'll have to Google a diagram of the skull to know what I'm talking about.

On both sides of my head, just above the Zygomatic bone, in the area of the Sphenoid, the Temporal bone and a small portion of the Frontal and Parietal bone, there's a major change to how I looked the first forty-one years of my life.

In that area all of the fatty tissue and flesh that was there is gone, and it looks a bit caved in from how it was before. That's obviously a result of the surgeries that were required to save my life. Moving up from there, on the left side of my frontal bone and parietal bone, there's a large indent that doesn't look normal. The indentation is not quite as noticeable on the right side.

What's this all about? Every morning when I look in that mirror there's one thing that comes to mind. Forgive! That is what our Lord, who made that unfathomable sacrifice for us, requires. He tells us to forgive all wrongs. That is so critical. He tells us that if we will not forgive, we will not be forgiven. I also pray that the wrongs I committed and that I have shared here, and any that I have not, can be forgiven by the parties involved for their benefit.

While I and all disciples of Jesus Christ must forgive the debt in the wrongs we've been dealt, that is not the end of the story. The real issue is the other part in receiving God's forgiveness, and there is only one way to receive that.

The way that is done is to confess our wrongs and sins, and from there to move on to repentance, and from there to put our trust in Jesus Christ's sacrifice for our sin and follow Him. That is my hope for all those whom God has put in my path.

As I said, this may appear to be a sad ending. Absolutely not! It's nothing more than the most current event in this part of my journey. You see, Jesus told us to take up our cross and follow Him. He also asked what it will profit a person if they gain the whole world but forfeit their soul.

The thing of utmost importance is that I take joy daily in the Lord's healing my wounds, the physical and all the other types that I've shared. The immense joy of the blessings that I've received in my life, and the wonderful, kind, and loving people, whom God has blessed me with in this life cannot be taken from me. For that I am thankful beyond measure.

I'm so appreciative of the love that my sweet and precious wife, Letha, has shown me. She truly lifts me up when I'm feeling down and gives me encouragement to continue to run the race.

Most of all, I'm thankful for God's word that are filled with encouragement and truth to lift us up.

> Therefore, since we are surrounded by such a great cloud of witnesses, let us throw off everything that hinders and the sin that so easily entangles, and let us run with perseverance the race marked out for us.[2] Let us fix our eyes on Jesus, the author and perfecter of our faith, who for the joy set before him endured the cross, scorning its shame, and sat down at the right hand of the throne of God.[3] Consider him who endured such opposition from sinful men, so that you will not grow weary and lose heart. (Hebrews 12: 1–3)

I pray that in my life, and as I shared my story, you can see the sweetness, joy, and peace of God's mercy, grace, and power through Jesus Christ. Without that, I would have been dead long before all the miracles He poured out in Dallas, Texas, and I would be a bitter man on many fronts, especially with what I have learned since March 2018. By the grace of God, however, I do as it says in the previous paragraph. I throw off everything that hinders, the sin that so easily entangles, and I fix my eyes on Jesus.

I pray that those who have read this and don't know Him can come to Him, find hope in the midst of your trials, and have the joy that I have. For those who do know Him, I pray that this will encourage you to keep your eyes on Him, stand firm in the faith, fight the good fight, and have the peace that passes all understanding as we are told in His word.

EPILOGUE

Two weeks after I finished writing the final chapter of this book, Letha and I made another trip to Israel with Tom and JoAnn Doyle. Throughout that trip as we drove through that special little sliver of land, Israel, and the city of Jerusalem, where God tells us He has put His name, I thought deeply on my life.

My fall to grace has opened my eyes to how fragile life really is. It can change in a moment. We are just vapor. My life has come with a number of trials, disappointments, miracles, and blessings, and God has held me in His hand through it all. I have to choose to see the best in all things and be grateful that I am alive and can walk, talk, and function as a human being rather than dwell on the loss.

We are all going to be sifted one day. I was able to stand for one reason only, Jesus Christ, and that offer of His grace is there for anyone who will repent and give their lives to Him.

As all of that swirled in my mind, I recalled that Tom had said he wanted me to share my testimony with some Jewish survivors of the Holocaust in Sederot, which is very close to the Gaza Strip.

Once again, I had to remind myself that I am in His hands. I was feeling more than a bit nervous. I wondered how in the world my testimony could bless these people who had endured what they experienced under the Nazis and most of the world that had rejected them and basically handed them over to that atrocity.

Just a few weeks prior to our arrival, these precious people had to run, or at least walk as fast as they could, to the bomb shelters as hundreds of rockets poured into their area from Gaza, courtesy of Hamas.

My time came, and Tom introduced me. I went up and proceeded to give them a brief synopsis of how my career in aviation came to be. From there I went straight to how it ended on the tarmac at the DFW Airport. I concluded with how I would have missed out on the blessing of getting to meet with them had it not been for the divine intervention of their messiah, Yeshua Ha-Mashiach, Jesus Christ, and I thanked them for allowing me to share.

As I proceeded to the back of the room, where Letha and I were seated, I could sense that this had touched them. Many reached out and shook my hand, and one of the men stood up to shake my hand and give me a hug. I learned that a few of those who had attended had already come to Jesus in saving faith, and I pray that what I shared can be a catalyst to draw more of them to their messiah.

Maranatha come Lord Jesus!

APPENDIX A

IN THE UNITED STATES DISTRICT COURT FLORIDA SOUTHERN DISTRICT, LAWRENCE M. MEADOWS, Plaintiff, v. ALLIED PILOTS ASSOCIA-TION, a Texas Labor Association, and PAM TORELL, An individual, and DOES 1-10, Defendants. FIRST AMENDED COMPLAINT, Case No: 1:17-cv-22589-JLK, JURY TRAIL DEMANDED

On December 26, 2007, AA's Corporate Medical Director, without cause or notice, abruptly terminated Plaintiff's then existing disability benefits under the old pension funded *"Program"*; and unilaterally placed him in an approved Unpaid Sick Leave of Absence *"USLOA"* status.

Plaintiff timely filed an Administrative Appeal to American Airlines Pension Benefits Administration Committee ("PBAC"), who reviewed and denied his disability claim through third party disability claims evaluator, Western Medical Evaluators ("WME") on June 8, 2008.

Supplement-F of the pilot's Collective Bargaining Agreement, required that all disability claim disputes be referred to a *"Clinical-source"*; but AA and APA violated this clause of the CBA, because WME was nothing more than an administrative medical billing service.

WME was not a *"Clinical-source"* as required under the CBA, but instead was a tiny 6 employee medical billing service that was rife with fraud and procedural irregularities; WME's corporate medical director medical license had been revoked by the Texas Medical Board, it's office manager was a convicted felon, and its principals fabricated and forged doctors' evaluation reports.

After two years of waiting, and APA's failure to resolve his disability dispute, Plaintiff timely filed an individual ERISA disability lawsuit against American Airlines in US District Court, of the Florida Southern District ("FLSD") at his own expense.

On March 23, 2011, the Plaintiff was allowed to conduct special court ordered depositions of AA's Corporate Medical Director, Chief Nurse, and HR Senior Budget Analyst. Based on those depositions, and AA's last minute, untimely production of documents; the Plaintiff, discovered the existence of the secret *"Pilot Disability Nurse Case Management Cost Savings"* reports; which were used by American Airline's Medical Department to fraudulently deny and/or terminate rightful pilot disability benefits based on *"cost savings"* alone. These reports showed that 421 pilots were receiving disability benefits; and that during December 2007 Plaintiff was one of 84 pilots being tracked and targeted for cost savings, all of whom had their benefits terminated.

The very next day On March 24, 2011, before all the evidence was in the record, FLSD Court abruptly entered Final Summary Judgment order in favor of AA.

Shortly thereafter, Plaintiff was shocked to discover that AA's third party disability claims reviewer, WME, used in furtherance of AA's *"Pilot Disability Nurse Case Management Cost Savings"* scheme, was shut down for felony medical claim fraud.

Eventually WME was shuttered, its principals were charged with felony medical claim fraud, sentenced to confinement, and forced to pay fines and restitution to its victims.

Not until mid-2011, did Plaintiff discover documents which show AA terminated WME's contract on August 8, 2008, within one day of its principals being indicted for felony medical claim fraud. APA knew this, but never disclosed to Meadows, or other similar situated disabled pilots; thereby prejudicing their ability to successfully litigate their claims.

AA or APA never subsequently offered Plaintiff a proper

claim re-review by the WME's legitimate institutional replacement reviewer, the Mayo Clinic.

In mutually selecting WME, a medical billing service, both AA and APA willfully violated the CBA, by failing to provide its disabled pilots a full and fair review of their disability claims by a *"Clinical-source"* as required under Supplement-F.

American Airlines and APA also breached their fiduciary to duty by failing to exercise proper due diligence, when mutually selecting WME, which was in fact a procedurally flawed and fraudulent disability claims reviewer.

In April 2011, Plaintiff timely filed a Notice of Appeal with the 11th Cir., and a Rule 59 with the FLSD based the newfound evidence, but the FLSD denied said motion, due to lack of jurisdiction.

Just a couple of days after Plaintiff exposed that American Airlines was a conflicted fiduciary; which was attempting to aide with the gross underfunding of its pension plans, by implementing the secret *"Pilot Disability Nurse Case Management Cost Savings"* scheme, facilitated through a fraudulent claims reviewer. AA retaliated, and attempted to punish Plaintiff by falsifying meet and confer certifications in order to file untimely and unmeritorious costs and attorney's fees motions totaling $52,680.20 for 3 depositions.

Subsequently, Plaintiff filed a Rule 11 motion; and the FLSD Court struck AA's pleadings, and denied its cost and attorney's fee motions as moot.

In June 2011, based on his ERISA disability suit denial, and American Airlines steadfast refusal to acknowledge his disabling condition; Plaintiff, mailed a certified request to AA Corporate Medical Director, requesting Fitness for Duty Exam and issue a Return to Work ("RTW") clearance, as provided by Sec. 20 of the CBA. But the Corporate Medical director never responded, ignoring said request.

Plaintiff Engaged in Protected SOX-WB Activity

Based on American Airlines pilot disability cost savings scheme, implemented through the use of WME, Plaintiff reasonably believed AA was intentionally underfunding pilot's rightful disability pension funding obligations, which thereby artificially inflated its corporate earnings reported on their financial statements. Which for publicly traded company, gives rise to securities fraud under the Sarbanes-Oxley ("SOX") Act.

APPENDIX B

Mr. Parker, ladies and gentlemen of the board, as a shareholder, I appreciate this opportunity to share the tragic ending of my career as a captain at American Airlines with you and present you with a plea.

To start off I'll give you a very brief synopsis of my career. Another American Airlines captain who retired around two years ago, Kimble Neel, whom I think you know personally, Mr. Parker, gave me my first flying lesson when I was twelve years old. I got my first major flying job at the age of nineteen, flew corporate aircraft for eight years, and then was hired by American Airlines. In my thirteenth year at American, due to company negligence, my career ended, and were it not for the prayers of many of my Christian brothers and sisters around the world and the wonderful medical team that God blessed me with, my life would have ended as well.

November 22, 1999, I had parked the 727 in the middle of Terminal C at DFW. The company sent a crew van to take me and my crew to our next gate. I had taken my flight bag and my suitcase to the ramp and looked up to see one of the flight attendants set her bags out at the top of the jet bridge stairs. She had to take some paperwork to the gate agent, so, knowing how treacherous it could be for a flight attendant, wearing high heels, coming down those steps that have holes in them, I went to the top of the staircase to bring them down for her. When I picked her bags up the staircase snapped off and dropped me twelve feet headfirst to the tarmac.

My flight engineer, Ans Wishing, heard the metal snap and turned to witness my head go into the concrete. He went running to me to evaluate my situation and as he knelt there beside me, I proceeded to go into convulsions and had blood pouring out of my nose and mouth. He was a true wingman. In fear that I would drown my own blood he held me up slightly, there, until the ambulance arrived.

I had a severe traumatic brain injury and the doctors at Parkland Hospital informed my ex-wife that I would be gone very soon if they did nothing. Of the three options she was given, she chose the double craniotomy procedure. They removed two large portions of my skull that they call bone flaps, one on each side. I survived the procedure and within days came down with acute respiratory distress syndrome which is very often fatal on its own.

I then came down with pneumonia. Within three weeks the swelling and fluid on my brain had gone down well enough that they were going to put my bone flaps back in. When they did the MRI and CAT scan on my brain, they also x-rayed my wrist do to swelling that had been noticed and discovered that it was shattered. It was a good thing I had been in a drug-induced coma, since the physical therapist had been twisting that wrist around for several days. For the last eighteen plus years, wrist movement is very limited and is not very comfortable.

Within a short period of time problems started arising, and they did blood tests. After a number of tests, it was confirmed that I had staph infection in my brain. The neurosurgeon was hoping for anything other than having to remove my bone flaps again. Unfortunately, there was no choice. He had to do that, and he had to leave them removed for a year to make sure the staph was gone. I spent sixteen and a half of an eighteen-month period in three hospitals and a traumatic brain injury rehab facility.

As I lay in Zale Lipshy Hospital with my ex-wife facing the necessity to put our home up for sale, retired VP of Flight Cecil Ewell took company President Bob Baker to witness me in my trauma. Mr. Baker agreed to pay me for two years, after that, run out my sick leave, and then it was LTD pay.

At the age of forty-three, my medical insurance was reduced to $300,000 for the next twenty-two years of my life. I have developed several medical problems from the accident, one being that several years after my return home, I learned that due to the pain and trauma of that time in hospitals and rehab,

I had ground down all of my teeth to the point that they all needed to be capped. That cost me over $40,000 out of pocket, and prior to the accident, I had only had two cavities my entire life. To save time I won't delve into the rest of the medical issues that I still deal with from the accident.

I had no Jetnet access until a year ago when Elise Eberwein finally fixed that for me. I had pleaded for help on that multiple times in the past.

My LTD pay hasn't gone up a penny in the seventeen years that I've been on it. After I sent you a couple of very polite, cordial, and informative letters, Mr. Parker, that you never responded to, I started some investigation into LTD and learned some things that absolutely stunned me.

I am going to let others who are far more knowledgeable than me address the intricacies of the things that have been dealt to hundreds of our disabled pilots, that need to be corrected. On my side of the fence, I just learned three months ago that I was now classified as an MDD pilot, my seniority had been eliminated and I am a pre-bankruptcy LTD pilot that has in many ways been tossed in the trash heap.

I learned that over the years, since my accident, a number of pilots came down with medical issues that caused them to lose their medical certificate, just as I did, except that my loss of medical certificate was due to an on the job injury in my service to this company.

These pilots whom I just mentioned were given special assignment jobs in the flight department and were paid full flight pay in those jobs, until they retired, or were able to go back to flight status. Company rules said that the jobs they were doing were supposed to be carried out by active pilots. That rule was waived for them, but I was never contacted with an offer to do this and had no idea that was an option, which it apparently wasn't for me. As a matter of fact, I have not been contacted by anyone at AA since the day I went on LTD except for one of the chief pilots at DFW, that made a recommendation to me pertaining to retirement, a number of years ago.

As I was thinking about this meeting today, I recalled an article in Fortune Magazine last February that was focused on you, Mr. Parker, and the issues of trust and leadership that were getting your attention. In the article you acknowledged problems with trust, pertaining to customers and employees.

Here is a direct quote from you, "It's one thing to build trust with a group, but it's completely different to regain trust when you've lost it." "We just have to do trustworthy things over and over and over again every day." I commend you for what you said, and it gives me hope. I hope that you will do the honorable thing and make me whole in what has been dealt me in the loss of my career due to negligence by past leadership at American Airlines.

I ask to be paid what I would have earned, had my career not ended due to this on the job injury, just as those who were given special assignment jobs were minus what I have already been paid in LTD pay. I ask for the medical insurance that I would have as an active pilot and do to the pain and trauma that I was dealt for almost two years I would ask for A1 or Air Pass travel for me and my wife for the rest of our lives.

As a shareholder I thank you, Mr. Parker, for this opportunity to share this and once again ask that you do the honorable thing for me and my fellow pilots on long-term Disability to regain trust in American Airlines and you as CEO.

ABOUT THE AUTHOR

Unbeknownst to either of them, at the age of 12, Jay Straub was put on a path by his best friend that would lead him to fulfill the wildest dream he could have ever imagined. Fourteen years later, Jay would be a pilot, becoming a captain, for what is today the largest airline in the world. That path started with his first flying lesson at the age of 12, followed by his first flying job at the age of 18, which progressed to flying for several corporations and culminated with being hired at American Airlines at the age of 26.

In that career, Jay experienced two inflight emergencies that he gives God the credit for in his survival, followed by the grand crescendo, an on the job injury that ended Jay's career and would have ended his life were it not for the power and grace of God. In the almost two decades since that event, Jay has spent a good deal of his life traveling to parts of the world speaking and giving the glory to his Lord, his Redeemer, Jesus Christ. He and his wife Letha both take joy in that. Jay can be reached at Jay@JayStraub.com

Made in the
USA
Monee, IL